BEYOND THE ENLIGHTENMENT

BEYOND THE ENLIGHTENMENT

LIVES AND THOUGHTS OF SOCIAL THEORISTS

ROGER A. SALERNO

Westport, Connecticut
London

Library of Congress Cataloging-in-Publication Data

Salerno, Roger A.
Beyond the Enlightenment : lives and thoughts of social theorists / Roger A. Salerno.
p. cm.
Includes bibliographical references and index.
ISBN 0–275–97724–2 (alk. paper)—ISBN 0–275–97725–0 (pbk. : alk. paper)
1. Sociologists—Biography. 2. Sociology—History. 3. Sociology—Philosophy. I. Title.
HM478.S35 2004
301'.092'2—dc22 2004044376

British Library Cataloguing in Publication Data is available.

Library of Congress Catalog Card Number: 2004044376
ISBN: 0–275–97724–2
0–275–97725–0 (pbk.)

First published in 2004

Praeger Publishers, 88 Post Road West, Westport, CT 06881
An imprint of Greenwood Publishing Group, Inc.
www.praeger.com

Printed in the United States of America

The paper used in this book complies with the Permanent Paper Standard issued by the National Information Standards Organization (Z39.48–1984).

10 9 8 7 6 5 4 3 2 1

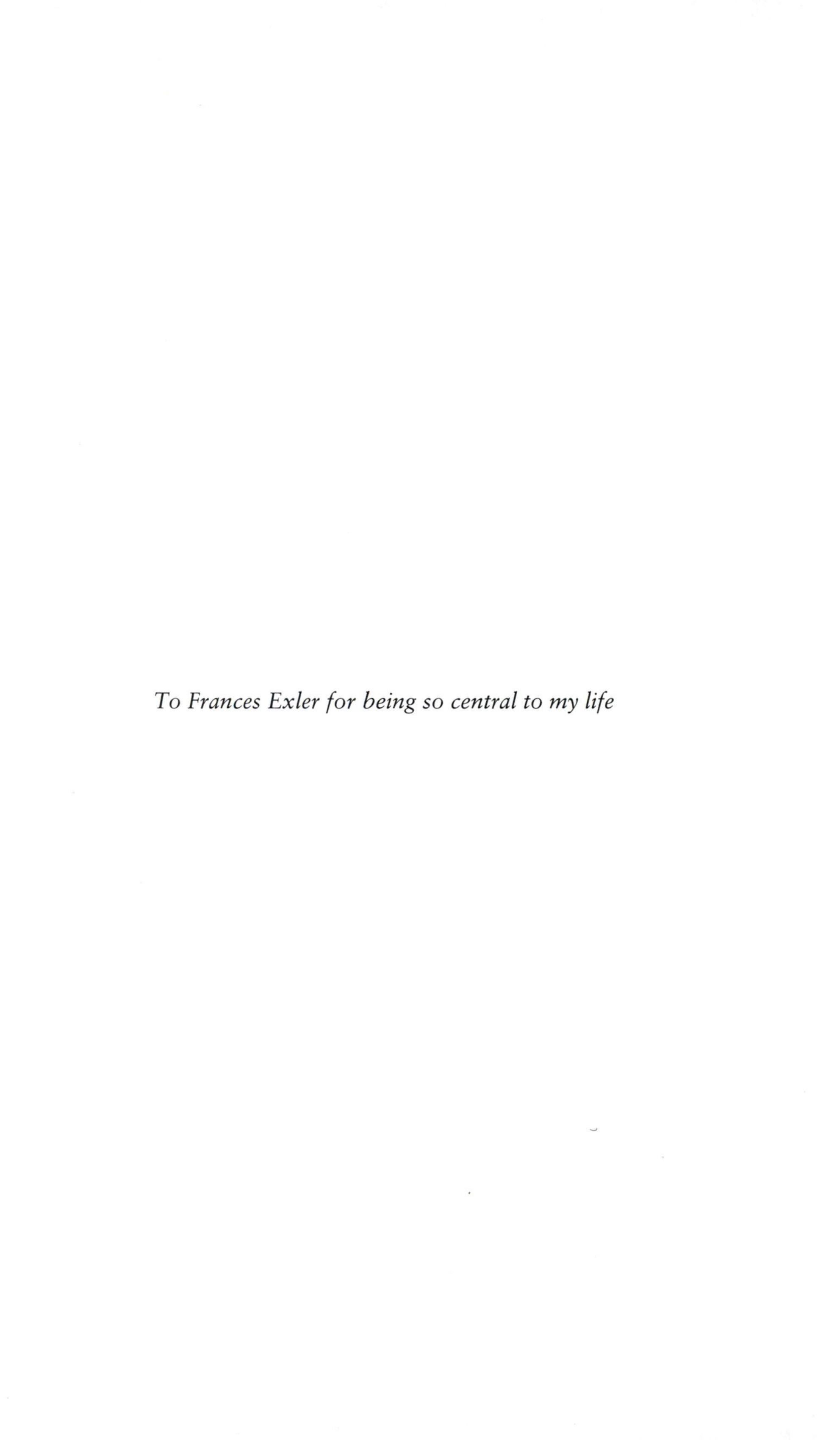

To Frances Exler for being so central to my life

Contents

Introduction

This book is written to introduce social theory to a broad audience in the hope that people will come to understand, as Charles Lemert says, "social theory is a basic survival kit." It distinguishes itself from many other perspectives (such as social philosophy or sociological theory) by its willingness to be both critical and factual and often combines these two approaches. It does not always adhere to strict empirical protocol; yet, its aim is to explore and explain society and culture. Even though social theory seems by its very nature to be abstract and complex, this is not always the case. However, for a book like this one to attempt to present the ideas of Karl Marx in eight pages or the theories of Judith Butler in four is, at the very least, an optimistic if not a quixotic venture.

That said, this book is not so much a traditional introduction to theory as it is a preface to those ideas that underlie some of the most important theories of our time. It is intended to serve up some of these ideas as *hors d'oeuvres* to those hungry enough for a snack but not yet ready for a heavy meal. *Beyond the Enlightenment,* in this sense, is in a class of its own.

Although it might be used for a class in introduction to sociology or in a social theory course to supplement more rigorous treatments of theorists and their ideas, or to introduce students to the personalities and some of the theoretical constructs that brought the authors to the attention of serious scholars, it is also intended as a reference that can be of value to the layperson who simply wants to understand a bit more about a name that is familiar but not clearly connected to ideas. If used in a classroom setting, or in conjunction with other texts, these ideas can be fleshed out by the professor and the teacher and students can enter into interpretation, debate, and exploration of meaning—all of which are essential to understanding ideas.

However, this book is also a social history of ideas. It deals with ideas as an integrated aspect of the social world from which they've emerged. Theories are presented in historical context. Ambitiously, it covers a period from the early nineteenth century to the end of the twentieth century and into the twenty-first.

This work presents a few thoughts of prominent social theorists by way of biography. Often the lives of theorists can give us wonderful insights into why they thought what they thought and how their ideas evolved. Because history is crucial to the development of social theory, this book is also intended to look at the intersection between the theorist as a social actor and the product of the theorist as a reflection of his or her time. Sociologist C. Wright Mills has spoken of the importance of this intersection. Today, history has become too unimportant for many, especially for theorists themselves.

As social theorists, these people whose lives are examined in this text, looked at the issues surrounding them. They explored phenomena including: class, race, gender, technology, language, culture, capitalism, the media, deviance, and more. It is the social world that they explored that makes their work so appealing and so connected to all of us as human beings.

In this volume there is an obvious crescendo of male voices over those of women. Women have been traditionally denied access to the established outlets for theoretical discussion. When they did attempt to contribute, they were often ignored and marginalized by those males who controlled the discussion. This is still true today to a very great extent. Feminist theory, in part, has been a response to such intellectual disenfranchisement. Now, some of the most exciting and innovative thinking has come from feminist theorists and scholars. But this project did not set out to research those voices. Although this is an important project, many talented historians of social theory have already done this. This book is intended to deal with those voices that were made central to the discussions of the last century in the dominant annals of the intellectual establishment. Most of these privileged voices emanate from men, mostly white, mostly European, mostly bourgeois. Thus, this book might be seen as reflective of that male, middle-class, Eurocentric bias.

Many people who should be represented here are not, and some of this has to do with availability of space and publishing budgets than any reasonable standard for omitting them. Names like Thorstein Veblen, Louis Althusser, George Mead, Alasdair MacIntyre, Melanie Klein, Daniel Bell, Margaret Mead, Erich Fromm, Susan Bordo, Jessica Benjamin, and Gilles Deleuze come to mind immediately. There are dozens more. But this lack also has to do with the nature of this project. This is not an encyclopedia or dictionary. In a sense, this book represents a sketch of the social theoretical landscape of a particular point in time. I'm sure many will disagree with the assortment of thinkers offered here and my own perspective on them for many and various reasons.

This said, *Beyond the Enlightenment* hopes to be both informative and entertaining. It is not meant to compete with excellent "theory books" such as those by George Ritzer, Randall Collins, or Jonathan Turner. It is a book written to make accessible important ideas that helped to shape twentieth-century thought—ideas that, in most circles, have significance today. In a sense, it is a book about ideas that too many people have only heard about, but know little or nothing about. Hopefully, it is a book that will motivate the reader to delve into the deeper end of the pool of knowledge available in the library or even on the Internet. This is something that they might have been reluctant to attempt before reading this. I have intentionally kept readers in the shallow end of the pool.

Theory is open to interpretation, much like philosophy. The reading of theory is often a dialectical process, and usually a very personal one. For many of us, there is no turning away from it. It provides us with ways of looking at life and better understanding it. Social theory is sometimes more interesting than the social phenomena it portends to explain, at times imbuing meaning into a seemingly meaningless world. It is a dynamic, creative force let loose by the human mind and creative spirit. It is with this in mind that we begin the journey.

ACKNOWLEDGMENTS

This book could not have been written without the encouragement of my wife, Sandi. Friends and colleagues have also been very helpful with suggestions and advice. Most of all, this book was inspired by my students. I am especially thankful to Pace University's Scholarly Research Committee, which provided me with release time, and I'd like to thank the editors at Praeger for all of their assistance and their belief in this project.

BIBLIOGRAPHY

Lemert, Charles, ed. 1999. Social theory: its uses and pleasures. In *Social Theory: The Multicultural and Classical Readings*. Boulder, CO: Westview Press.

———. 1997. *Postmodernism Is Not What You Think*. Malden, MA: Blackwell.

Mills, C. Wright. 1977. *The Sociological Imagination*. Oxford: Oxford University Press.

Ritzer, George. 1996. *Sociological Theory*. New York: McGraw-Hill.

Turner, Jonathan. 1991. *The Structure of Social Theory*. Belmont, CA: Wadsworth.

1

The Enlightenment and Beyond

Ideas are not only products of the people who formulate them, they are also consequences of history, class, and culture. This chapter presents foundational ideas of Enlightenment and Post-Enlightenment thinkers—those who were greatly influenced by the dynamically changing European landscape in which they found themselves.

Although the intellectual movement referred to as the Enlightenment is often associated with eighteenth-century thought, its origins actually predate this. The roots of what we now refer to as the Enlightenment can be traced back to the Renaissance as well as the work of sixteenth- and seventeenth-century European scientists and philosophers, thinkers ranging from Galileo to Descartes. The term *Age of Enlightenment* has been used to distinguish itself as a period distinct from the so-called "Dark Ages" in which people supposedly lived in feudally bound worlds ruled by spirits, myths, and politically powerful religious forces. In actuality, medieval societies were close to nature and their people were highly interdependent and communal. With the defeat of a monolithic Roman Catholic Church by the Muslim Crusaders of North Africa and, subsequently, the disintegration of that Church through the Protestant Reformation, nation-states rose to fill the power vacuum that had emerged throughout Europe. By the sixteenth century advances in technology and in communications and the emergence of global mercantilistic networks set the stage for burgeoning market capitalism; the European world was radically changing.

For the most part, Enlightenment thinkers were a small group of European males who came from the newly emerging bourgeoisie class—one brought into existence by the decline of papal and aristocratic authority. They were educated, propertied people who not only challenged the centrality of religion, but also encouraged the use of science and reason to explore and control nature and to question what had previously been accepted as true. Many of these thinkers, such as Condorcet and Rousseau of France or Hume and Smith of Great Britain, put forth the idea that people had rights and that governments should work to secure and protect the rights of individuals. Although few agreed on how this would work, many saw a need for a complete overhaul of traditional systems of despotic authority. In general, Enlightenment thought included the following elements:

- a belief that the universe is fundamentally rational and can be understood through empirical science and reason;
- an assumption that all of nature is knowable and that human experience and thought are the only avenues to truth;
- a conviction that religion has no place in explaining the physical world;
- a belief that knowledge serves to improve human life and that ignorance is the cause of human misery and immorality;
- an expectation that there is both epistemological and moral unity that integrates and governs the world; and
- the thought that there is but one universal, discoverable truth and it alone is the key to endless human progress.

Not all of these elements were subscribed to by all Enlightenment thinkers. In fact, the Enlightenment took on a different form in Scotland and England than it did in France and Germany. Still, proponents of Enlightenment thought advanced the notion of *one* truth, *one* reason, and *one* morality. But often buried under its gloss of universal intellectualism was class and cultural bias that provided little space for otherness. Although Enlightenment thinkers espoused the notion of individual freedom, this was applied only to the so-called civilized peoples of the world—typically people of their same social rank, ethnicity, and gender. Enlightenment thought was inherently bourgeois, racist, and phallocentric in this regard. It was, above all, northern European.

FOUNDATIONS OF ENLIGHTENMENT THOUGHT

Because the Enlightenment was something of an intellectual movement, it had specific founders and advocates. To locate these early influences one must look to France and to the work of Voltaire (1694–1778), Montesquieu (1689–1755), Rousseau (1712–1778), and Diderot (1713–1784). These were essential Enlightenment theorists who helped set an agenda and organized what has come to be called the Enlightenment project. They referred to their own time as "*le siecle des lumieres*" or "the century of the enlightened." It was their romance with reason and science that laid the groundwork for modern social and cultural discourse.

Outstanding among Enlightenment proponents was Voltaire whose real name was François Marie Arouet. Voltaire was a French playwright, philosopher, essayist, novelist, and amateur scientist. His travels to England between 1726 and 1729 impressed him positively, and he carried back to France, and to Continental Europe, ideas taken from the work of Isaac Newton, Francis Bacon, and John Locke. He was intrigued with Newton's study of the physical universe, and held in high regard Bacon's empiricism and Locke's ideas on individualism and liberal democracy. He was taken with the British position on religious tolerance. Many of these elements became building blocks for the French Enlightenment.

Voltaire was both anti-Christian and anti-clerical. He deplored despotic monarchies and the enormous powers of the Church; he called for tax relief for the business class and advocated the ascendency of the bourgeoisie to the position of greatest power. He displayed contempt for the peasant classes and the poor. His writings were frequently controversial for their time, and he often suffered periods of exile and imprisonment. Still, he was elected to French Academy in 1764—a great national honor.

France was indeed the center of culture in Continental Europe, and most educated people spoke French no matter where they lived on that continent. Even though Great Britain also contributed more directly to Enlightenment thought, its thinkers were respectively influenced by the French writers and intellectuals. Rousseau was exceptionally influential there. Those who were referred to as the Scottish moralists, most notably Adam Smith and Adam Ferguson, borrowed from the French Physiocrats, and became advocates of modern market capitalism as the embodiment of Enlightenment principles.

The *Philosophes*

The relatively small cadre of influential French thinkers who referred to themselves as the *philosophes* were the heart of the European Enlightenment. *Philosophe* did not literally mean philosopher, but rather "man of letters." These men all advanced the cause of social progress by emphasizing the need for tolerance, knowledge, and an end to blind-faith. Like Rousseau whose *Social Contract* promoted an agenda of equality and democracy and Montesquieu who put forth new models of governance to replace the traditional monarchy, Denis Diderot called for a revolution in knowledge. It was Diderot, who with the help of the humanist mathematician Jean d'Alenbert and nearly one hundred other essayists and thinkers, put together and edited a new twenty-eight volume encyclopedia. The purpose of this project was to free the minds of men, to advance the cause of human reason, and to perfect the methods of the Enlightenment by applying them to an ever-widening range of pursuits. It was a complete alphabetical organization of the whole field of human knowledge complete with ironic, and often irreverent, cross-references. Article topics ranged from mathematics to manners.

L' Encyclopedie became the vessel for the philosophes' attack on the politics of absolute monarchy and religion. It advanced the causes of science, atheism, and anti-clericalism. It promoted the growth of more liberal and humane political institutions—nonreligious education and a synthesis of the arts and sciences. It constantly challenged outdated traditions and superstitions. For this, it was met with hostility by the Church and the entrenched aristocracy.

For the philosophes science was the source of all knowledge. There was no domain in life to which it could not be applied to produce human progress. Through it would come understanding and the total control of the natural world. *L' Encyclopedie* represented this belief. More than 50 percent of the 25,000 copies of its various editions were sold outside of France by 1789. In fact, the term "Encyclopedism" came to represent the Enlightenment value of a refusal to accept knowledge uncritically. Nearly all of the philosophes contributed to the work and its seventeen volumes of text and eleven volumes of technical drawings and illustrative plates.

Other Enlightenments

While France and Britain glowed in this new intellectual movement, Germany was another case. The Prussian empire was viewed by the French and British as notoriously backward. Its universities were often in shambles. Censorship was much tighter in Protestant states where new ideas were often discouraged. Still, Germany would contribute in its own unique way to the Enlightenment, simultaneously calling into question some of the original assumptions that the Enlightenment was built upon. Although one can start with any number of revolutionary German thinkers, it seem most appropriate to begin this discussion with the ideas of Immanuel Kant.

It must be stated that Immanuel Kant was very much influenced by Newton, Rousseau, Voltaire, Hume, and the other important thinkers of Britain and France. Even though he did not see things in the same way, Kant helped to define the Enlightenment (*Aufklarung*) for Germany. In his classic essay "What Is Enlightenment?" he proceeds to discuss the relationship between reason and individual freedom. It is Kant's assertion that individuals need to free themselves from reliance on the intellectual imperial judgments of others, especially religious authorities. For him this personal retreat from the responsibility of reason reduces human potentiality.

He views the nature of humans as selfish and self-serving, as lazy and uninspiring. Paradoxically, like Rousseau, he believes people need powerful rulers who will force them to be free. He advocates duty to state and a strict adherence to secular authority in order to maintain social stability and to maximize freedom for all.

Kant's influence on Enlightenment thought and Post-Enlightenment thought was enormous. Although he opposed wars of liberation and class struggle, his ideas were revolutionary on many levels. To begin with, it is essential to examine perhaps his most important work, *The Critique of Pure Reason.* It is here in which he displays his Enlightenment roots by advocating what he refers to as a "Copernican Revolution" in thinking. He wants to unify rationalism and empiricism by looking at them anew. Just as Copernicus revolutionized astronomy by advancing the proposition that the earth revolved around the sun, disputing the long-held religious doctrine that the sun revolved around the earth, Kant rejects the long-held notion of an objective, universal reality that all struggled to discover. This had been an essential Enlightenment enterprise. For Kant, instead of being observers of the objective world around them, people actually construct reality through their senses and cognitive processes. This is to say things do not exist in themselves in some objectified form awaiting discovery, rather one's senses causes one to see things in a certain way. What appears to us as finite form and substance seems so only because of our unique processes of cognition and internal categorical structures, universal in nature, that help organize what we experience. The object, therefore, is a product of sensory response and abstract thought. He goes on in detail to explain how this works.

In short, true knowledge comes from experiencing the world. It is the apparatuses of human sensibility and understanding that give structure and form to the material world we encounter. This world is part of us, internally, but at the same time it comes from outside of us. We mold our experience of the so-called objective world. This is how we know. Therefore, it is not possible to truly know anything that lies outside the range of our senses and any attempt to try to understand will only lead to inconsistency and error. He, therefore, rejects speculative metaphysics or philosophy as worthless. Knowledge can only come from an action-oriented engagement with the material world through one's senses. However, Kant makes a distinction between postpriori truth based on such experience and apriori truth that exists independent of experience. He recognizes that both must exist. The former is achieved through empiricism and reason and the latter through speculation. To this latter realm he assigns religion, freedom, and morality. It is a place of human values.

Although these ideas might not appear strange at first glance, they were indeed radical if we take into consideration the time and place in which they were formulated. Kant is able to synthesize the work of the British empiricists and the ideas of the French Enlightenment thinkers and produce an entirely new way of understanding that fits within his domestic conservative culture. It is a system of reason that relegates religion to the speculative arena, along with issues of morality and freedom. Yet, it doesn't deny these nonmaterial objects. Thus, Kant remains quite conservative in his worldview.

Kant was certainly the bridge to Post-Enlightenment thinking. His philosophy, although quite conservative, inspired a new wave of critical and radical theorists and paved the way for both critical and interactionist sociology and cultural studies. Actually, much of this thought would lead to more revolutionary ideas of Hegel, Marx, and, much later, Foucault. His thoughts became primary ideas that had to be addressed by other philosophers and social critics before they could move on.

The Enlightenment in Perspective

In his paper on the meaning of enlightenment, Kant helped to define its boundaries. For him, people were not living in an *enlightened age,* but rather in *the age of enlightenment.* It was a period that called into question, often in radical terms, that which had come before it. It was a shedding of light, through the power of imaginative inquiry, on that which was previously unilluminated. The European Enlightenment, philosophically, launched the individual into the position of center of the universe, as an interpreter of the world and as both a discoverer and a creator of reality.

French Enlightenment thinkers and writers sparked a revolution in art and literature; they helped to create a new *Encyclopedie* that would organize information into an accessible, readable format—expanding the dissemination of knowledge. Many of the more radical political ideas eventually would lead to the French Revolution and inspire democratic liberalism.

As we will see later on, however, the Enlightenment led to the vivisection of the natural world, and to an emphasis on specialization and systems at a cost of dehumanization. To be sure these were not a part of its original agenda; however, what was seen as a quest for knowledge would degenerate into a cult of facts; what was viewed as the idealization of reason would be transformed into an acceptance of bounded rationality and instrumental thought. The Enlightenment's focus on materialism and its embrace of capitalism would further corrupt its more noble aspirations.

BIBLIOGRAPHY

Cassirer, Ernest. 1968. *Philosophy of the Enlightenment.* Princeton, NJ: Princeton University Press.

Gay, Peter. 1996. *The Enlightenment: An Interpretation.* New York: W.W. Norton.

Israel, Jonathan Ivan. 2001. *Radical Enlightenment: Philosophy and the Making of Modernity*. New York: Oxford University Press.

Kramnick, Isaac, ed. 1995. *The Portable Enlightenment Reader*. New York: Penguin.

Porter, Roy. 2000. The *Creation of the Modern World: The British Enlightenment*. New York: W.W. Norton.

2

Georg Hegel: Foundations of Modern Social Thought

One nineteenth-century philosopher who had an enormous impact on the development of modern social thought in the West was Georg Wilhelm Friedrich Hegel. Hegel was born into an upper-middle-class family in Stuttgart, Germany on August 27, 1770. He was one of three siblings who survived into adulthood; originally there were six children. His mother died of what was called "bilious fever" when he was only eleven. It was a disorder that afflicted many in Stuttgart and nearly claimed his life and that of his father, both of whom contracted the disease concurrently with his mother's illness. According to Terry Pinkard, a biographer of Hegel, his mother's death was to have a major impact on his life and, most particularly, his relationship with his father. It was to leave the young boy with a speech impediment and put some emotional distance between him and his remaining parent. Even though both of them survived the fever, there was no doubt that the loss of the central woman in their lives affected them enormously, leaving them with feelings of detachment. Hegel was to suffer from lifelong bouts of depression.

The Hegel home was characterized by Protestant Pietism. The house was filled with books and learning. His mother, Maria Magdalena Fromm, came from a well-established local family and a long line of Protestant reformers. Her father was a lawyer in the High Court of Justice. She was well educated for the times and taught young Hegel Latin. His father, Georg Ludwig Hegel, had a degree in law and served as a secretary to the local revenue office of the local court, a civil service position. His family had a very strong religious tradition and descended from notable Lutheran clergy. Although he had no similar inclination for himself, it was expected that young Hegel would enter the ministry.

As a boy, Hegel attended a German School at the age of three and Latin School at age five. In 1784 he began attending the local Gymnasium or preparatory school, which stressed both Enlightenment thinking and humanistic learning. The curriculum included science and mathematics as well as the Greek and Roman classics. Hegel graduated top in his class. In 1788, he received a scholarship to Tübingen University where he took a course of study that was to prepare him for the ministry. It was there, however, that he would come into contact with his early intellectual influences, and it was there that he matured as a thinker. His roommates were none other than Friedrich Wilhelm Joseph Von Schelling (1775–1854), who was to make a reputation for himself as a major figure in German Romantic Philosophy, and Friedrich Holderlin, who became one of the most important German poets of this era. (It seemed like every male in Germany had at least one Friedrich in his name!!) Hegel and Holderlin became lifelong friends.

Even though Tübingen was a university in name, at this time it was little more than the Protestant seminary. The other facilities and schools were meager. The Law School from which Hegel's father received his degree was in shambles, and the Seminary, itself, seemed to be an artifact of the Middle Ages. Students were treated like monks; they were required to wear long black coats, they were regularly scrutinized, and their time was strictly regulated. The rules were rigidly enforced, and infractions punished. There was even a jail cell for violators. And Hegel himself was to wind up there—at least once. This type of environment ran counter to his Enlightenment inclinations and his professed love of personal freedom. His new friends Schelling and Holderlin also shared his aversion to this system.

The three young men joined together socially and in their studies. All decided in due time that the ministry was not for them. Later in their lives Hegel and Schelling would coedit the *Critical Journal of Philosophy*. It was the study of ideas that interested them most. As students, they frequently neglected their studies to read things they found more stimulating. They also visited taverns, cut classes, and played cards. Though cloistered, these young men were plugged into the social and political ideas of the day. Hegel had just started in at Tübingen when the Bastille was stormed. He became an enthusiastic supporter of the French Revolution as did Schelling and Holderlin. The times were changing and the old aristocracy was beginning to collapse under the weight of modernization.

In 1797 Hegel graduated from Tübingen. Although he had wanted to change his course of studies to philosophy, his father insisted that he remain at the seminary. Still, upon graduation he went to Berne, Switzerland and became a private tutor for Karl F. Steiger; he did not seek a position in the Church. There he was granted full use of the family's extensive library. He delved deeply into the philosophy of Kant and Fichte and expressed a profound interest in works of Rousseau. This same year, however, his father died. Hegel came home for a short while, but soon took another tutoring job in Frankfurt. Having been left a substantial inheritance by his father, he thereafter took up residency at the University of Jena where he emersed himself in further study, tutoring on a part-time basis. Schelling, his friend, helped him to secure this unpaid position here; and it was at Jena where Hegel was to meet Fichte.

Johann Gottlieb Fichte (1762–1814) was strongly influenced by Kant's division of knowledge into two types: theoretical and practical. Fichte believed that Kant did not adequately prove his assertion of a separation between the conceptual (or theoretical) and the practical understanding. For Fichte there was only one type of knowledge and it was unitary. All knowledge was the product of an active and indivisible ego, which was the only true source of knowing. Consciousness of the I (or ego) was not a thing-in-itself, as Kant had suggested, but rather it existed only through its own self-awareness. Fichte insisted that all consciousness of the ego is a product of reflection and that all reflection can only exist through its own limitation; and limitation can only exist if the ego is posited against something it is not—some otherness. Thus, Fichte established the idea that knowing is a dialectical process—a concept Hegel would further develop. Friedrich Schelling, Hegel's old friend and past roommate, was also inspired by Kant. He proposed, however, that nature could never be subordinated to consciousness, and that even though there was a difference between nature and mental life, there was an ultimate mind and oneness of knowledge—an Absolute. Hegel was to build his theory of knowledge not only on the foundation laid by Kant, but also on these ideas developed by Fichte and Schelling.

Hegel befriended Goethe, the prominent romantic poet and writer of the time. Goethe had been appointed minister of culture in Weimar and was responsible for developing the University of Jena as a center of learning and thought. The two men corresponded over the years and became close. It is obvious that Goethe inspired much of Hegel's sentiments—especially those that focused on feelings of personal loss and detachment. Hegel visited Goethe on several occasions. The relationship, though not a very close one, was to last throughout Hegel's life.

While at Jena, Hegel wrote his most important work, *Phenomenology of the Spirit* (1806). In this ambitious undertaking, he attempts to establish a means for understanding the developmental history, current workings, and future evolution of the universe. This work was to have a profound effect on modern philosophy as well as psychology, sociology, and the other social sciences and would establish Hegel as a central intellectual figure from the nineteenth century forward. His impact on modern and postmodern world is still being felt today.

THE PHENOMENOLOGY OF THE SPIRIT

Although *The Phenomenology of the Spirit* was a totalistic or grand theoretical scheme for making sense of things, it contained a number of elements representative of modern philosophy—elements that some of the most brilliant thinkers had to discuss before moving on to their own theoretical formulations. Like Kant, Hegel put forth the notion of subjective knowing. However, unlike Kant who claimed that we can only rationally know what we experience for ourselves and anything else we take as truth is based on trust or faith, Hegel countered with the idea that there is only one thinking substance in the universe—only one coherent, indivisible truth. This, of course, was an extension of Fichte's ideas. To Hegel, this truth is the same as reality and in essence the same as the Absolute Being; thus, there is but one holistic reality as there is only one God. The whole of nature is merely objectification of the Absolute Being. How one uncovers the truth of this Being is through a process he refers to as dialectics. Thus, Hegel's ideas are indebted to Kant, Fichte, and Schelling.

The word *dialectic* was taken from the Greek word *dialegein* meaning to discourse or to argue. Hegel proposed that the truth was revealed through a process of successive contradictions by which an initial proposition, a *thesis* if you will, is shown to be inadequate for explaining some phenomenon and, therefore, another proposition (perhaps an opposite) emerges to challenge its place. This might be called an *antithesis*. They run side by side, challenging each other. Soon, however, this new proposition proves to be weak or inadequate and so the best elements of each—the most rational elements—form a *synthesis*. This process of consolidation is referred to as *sublation* wherein the weaker elements are absorbed or consumed into the stronger thesis. This new synthesis becomes a new thesis and this triadic system repeats itself through time until an ultimate total, comprehensive truth is arrived at. What he refers to as Absolute Truth is but a collection of all possible triads in the universe. Although Hegel held out little hope for the ultimate discovery of Absolute Truth, he insisted that the quest for it was essential to human evolution and development. He posits that all history has evolved through these triadic progressions: thesis, antithesis, synthesis—the latter forming a new thesis.

Hegel furthermore proposes that everything that exists is a product of the mind; all reality comes from the mind. Even though we may perceive objects to be separate and independent of it, they are not. They are totally dependent on thought for their existence. But this is difficult to fathom. Once we have discovered this, however, once we become aware that our mind is the source of an objectified world, we become estranged from that world and from our objectified selves. Hegel speaks of language as being a force that both identifies this world and alienates us from it. In any event, progress evolves from a state of primary consciousness wherein there is no sense either of connection or disconnection, through self-consciousness and a sense of disconnection, to the advent of Absolute Reason or total integration. It is only through knowing the world we have created that we can ever come to know ourselves. But this can only be achieved through dialectics. History is the study of the dialectical unfolding of truth.

Subject-object relations play a significant role in this philosophy. Hegel combines this with his dialectics to present a model that will be used time and time again in the analysis of power relations. Accordingly, as people evolve in consciousness, they desire mastery over their perceived external environment—over objects, over people, even over themselves. Mastery over things is an elementary form of control, but mastery over others is a highly complex affair. Similar to his notion of dialectics, there is a desire on the part of the self to negate otherness, to destroy it, to consume it, or to take it into the self. However, the other has the same attitude. It seeks to assert its selfhood over the otherness it perceives. It wishes to destroy, negate, or sublate it. This process is explained through what Hegel refers to as the Master-Slave Parable.

This tale describes how when two so-called *others* see themselves in opposition a battle ensues wherein compromise is impossible. It is a fight to the death. But to save oneself, one submits to the other and becomes the other's slave. However, in enslaving the opponent, the conqueror becomes defined by the very person enslaved. The slave becomes engrossed in work in the world in the service of the master, and the master becomes dependent on this individual both for work and for identity. In fact, even though the slave defines and creates a self through work, the master must define or create a sense of self through dependence on the slave. Also, the slave can see the world first hand, the master only second hand. In being denied independence, the slave becomes more introspective and develops an internalized measure of self-worth. Slavery forces the enslaved to gain insight into the mind or consciousness of the master. One must be able to anticipate how the master views the world, but must also view it from the vantage of a slave. Thus, the oppressed are closer to knowing the truth about the nature of human kind and are far less alienated than their oppressors.

Of course, this view of the world is one grounded in the romance of the Protestant Ethic in which hard work is esteemed and brings one closer to God. It is a view that embraces individualism as the key to knowledge; a bourgeois Christian conviction that the oppressed are gaining something spiritually through their suffering. It is a position eschewing class conflict, something Karl Marx will take up later. In sanctifying subject-object relations as a means to a better end, Hegel reflects a particular class and cultural perspective while blindly claiming the universality of his approach.

VALUES IN THE FACE OF REASON

When the Napoleon's army captured the city of Jena, Hegel was forced to flee. He relocated in Bavaria where he became editor of the Catholic newspaper *Bamberger Zietung* in 1807. The newspaper was rather second rate, containing stories gathered from other papers. Despite his anti-Catholic sentiments, Hegel was able to embrace many of the paper's more conservative perspectives. The *Bamberger Zietung* was politically supportive of Napoleon, as was its new editor who looked at the French despot as a heroic figure. But Hegel's journalism career was short-lived. With the help of a friend, Hegel moved to Nuremberg in 1808 where he assumed the Rectorship of a Gymnasium. It was there that he was to meet Marie von Tucher who would become his wife in 1811. The Tuchers were a prominent Nuremberg family. Marie was twenty years Hegel's junior. Although he is known to have had a child with his landlord's daughter in Bamberg, it was in Nuremberg where Hegel would begin his so-called legitimate family.

That Hegel found himself on the side of Napoleon during the Franco-Prussian Wars and married into an aristocratic family cannot be trivialized here. He often romanticized the warrior. He embraced nationalism as a dialectical step toward Absolute Truth. And he frequently espoused racist and sexist sentiments. Writing in *Philosophy of History* he posits:

> The Negro as already observed, exhibits the natural man in his completely wild and untamed state. In this character there is nothing that reminds one of the human. This is perfectly corroborated by the extensive reports of the missionaries. Therefore, the Negroes get the total contempt of human beings. . . . This character is not capable of development and education. The Negro is destined to end up a slave.

And in his discussion of women in *Phenomenology,* Hegel writes:

> Women are capable of education, but they are not made for activities which demand a universal faculty such as the more advanced sciences, philosophy, and certain forms of artistic production. Women may have happy ideas, taste and elegance, but they cannot attain the ideal . . . women correspond to plants because their development is more placid. . . .

Hegel's views on society and politics are clearly made in his discussions of morality and social ethics. For Hegel, although right and wrong are outcomes of individual conscience, social ethics such as duty require adherence to a general will that can only emerge from the state. Membership in the state is one of the individual's highest duties. He views obedience to the general will as an act of individual rational choice. Hegel sees the state as serving a higher power, and believes that the state would someday be worshiped as the will of God. For him, like Kant, the ideal form of state would be a constitutional monarchy.

CLOSE OF HIS CAREER

In 1816 Hegel published his *Science of Logic* and received an offer to teach at the University of Heidelberg. Under considerable protest from his wife, he moved his family there. By this time he had two young sons and arranged for his son from his affair to move into the household. Although the University of Berlin was interested in his work, they sent an observer to one of his lectures who returned with a report of "false pathos, shouting . . . digressions (and) arrogant self praise. . . ." Nevertheless, Hegel embarked upon writing a text for his classes at Heidelberg and assigning it to his students. It was the *Encyclopedia of the Philosophical Sciences in Outline*. It proved to be a success, and changed the minds of those in Berlin. Therefore, in 1818 Hegel was offered a professorship there where he remained teaching and writing for the remainder of his career.

Aside from producing *Philosophy of Right* in 1821, Hegel did extensive lecturing and traveling. But on November 13, 1831 he succumbed to a bout of cholera that was sweeping Germany. Even though he was expected to recover, he did not. After only one day of noticeable illness, he died in his sleep.

CONCLUSION

Hegel's contribution to modern social thought was significant. He and many of his contemporaries subscribed to and challenged some of the foundations of Enlightenment thinking while proposing views steeped in the romance of reason and individualism. Admirers of his works have been divided between radical and conservative camps. Not only did he greatly influence the work of Marx and the critical theorists, but he also had a major impact on Freud and the eventual development of psychoanalysis. He was fascinated with mental disorders, since it epitomized the opposite of reason. His life was in many ways tragic. His own depression frequently curtailed his writing. Hegel's younger brother did not survive him and died fighting in the Franco-Prussian wars, and although his sister did outlive him, two months after Hegel's death she took her own life.

Hegel's ideas would help shape the course of poststructural and postmodern social discourse. His emphasis on objectification and alienation, and his focus on subject-object relations would help to catalyze existential philosophy.

BIBLIOGRAPHY

Butler, Clark. 1977. *G. W. F. Hegel*. Boston: Twayne.

Hegel, G.W.F. 1977. *Phenomenology of Spirit*, trans. by A.V. Miller. Oxford: Oxford University Press.

Hook, Sidney. 1994. *From Hegel to Marx*. New York: Columbia University Press.

Lauer, Quenten, ed. 1977. *Essays in Hegelian Dialectic.* New York: Fordham University Press.

Loewenberg, J., ed. 1957. *Hegel Selections.* New York: Charles Scribner's Sons.

Lukács, Georg. 1976. *Young Hegel: Studies in the Relations Between Dialectics and Economics.* Cambridge, MA: M.I.T. Press.

Pinkard, Terry. 2000. *Hegel: A Biography.* Cambridge: Cambridge University Press.

Seidel, Georg J. 1976. *Activity and Ground: Fichte, Schelling and Hegel.* New York: G. Olms.

Solomon, Robert. 1987. *From Hegel to Existentialism.* New York: Oxford University Press.

3

Auguste Comte: The Origins of Modern European Sociology

The origin of sociology is usually associated with the Enlightenment and the belief that science can be applied to gain a better understanding of the world in which we live. But the beginnings of sociology as a distinct discipline in the social sciences is somewhat of a paradox. This is because Auguste Comte, considered by many to be the founder (and so-called "father") of sociology, saw himself as quite more than a mere Enlightenment thinker. He viewed himself as the equivalent to a priest and viewed sociology as a new religion—aimed at improving the world by scientifically addressing the social problems in it.

Comte was a brilliant man but also at times quite mad. He was born on January 19, 1798 in the city of Montpellier in the south of France. His given name was Isidore-Auguste-Marie-François-Xavier Comte. His early familial existence was comfortable and orderly with a loving mother and father, and two siblings.

Throughout his childhood and into his adult years, France was reeling from the aftermath of the Revolution—the Reign of Terror had been imposed by Robespierre who marched thousands of people to the guillotine. Paris appeared to be in chaos, and the surrounding countryside suffered severe economic depressions related to structural economic shifts. Montpellier, particularly, had been a stronghold of royalist Catholics who had opposed the Revolution. The more active political opponents were frequently routed from their homes and taken to prison. Some paid for their opposition with their lives. Comte had witnessed an anticipated new democratic order turn into a series of despotic insurrections. Napoleon overthrew the unstable new government in a bloody coup and eventually installed himself as Emperor. This was followed by a series of successive but equally unsuccessful changes in government often brought about through violence. Still, Comte frequently seemed more perturbed by the rebellions than the despotism.

Comte believed that the Enlightenment and the French Revolution were responsible for this state of anarchy. He was highly critical of those intellectuals and writers whom he believed had led France into a war with itself. The making of Comte's conservative ideology emerged from his traditionalist Catholic family, and particularly his father—a high-ranking civil servant.Yet Comte was sympathetic with many of the Revolution's liberal goals. In fact, he eventually came to reject his parents' royalist ideology and became a republican, giving up his Catholicism along the way. In doing this he remained emotionally and personally loyal to both his parents, and a good part of him stayed committed to his inherited class ideology.

Auguste Comte was a precocious child and regarded as a brilliant student by his teachers and friends. As a boy he excelled in his studies at the local *lycée* in Montpellier. His keen mind and extraordinary memory were admired by his teachers. He did well on competitive admissions examinations and gained entrance to France's most prestigious technical institute—the École Polytechnique. At age sixteen he went to Paris to study in an intensely competitive academic atmosphere. Students (only boys could be admitted to study here) took classes nearly twelve hours each day, undertook military training, and immersed themselves in the sciences and mathematics. Comte, who was always attracted to the sciences, excelled here.

He was well liked by his fellow students and had a full social life. Still, there was considerable personal conflict with some of his teachers. Students at the École Polytechnique were quite rebellious, and most espoused antiroyalist sentiments.Yet there was a great *esprit de corps* centering around a shared love for science and their resentment of conservative authority. In Paris, students found themselves connected to a world of culture and ideas. Comte, who had already rejected his faith and much of his conservative background before leaving Montpellier, became somewhat of a rebel. His arrogance frequently got him into trouble. He flaunted the rules of curfew. He argued with his professors. While France underwent a form of royalist revisionism, the school was becoming a hotbed of republican, antiroyalist sentiment. The administration, taking its lead from the State, cracked down on rebellious students and dismissed the entire student body in 1816. Even though it might have been true that there was a spirit of political opposition fermenting at the school, Comte was much more of a behavioral problem than a political one. The only protest in which he was embroiled was about the bad manners of one of his professors.

Comte worked in Paris as a journalist and a tutor after dismissal from the École Polytechnique. But it was a financial struggle. He was soon introduced to Henri de Saint-Simon by one of his professors and would begin a seven-year-long tumultuous relationship working in his employ.

COMTE'S EARLY INFLUENCES

There were numerous influences on Comte's intellectual and ideological development, but none more powerful than that of Saint-Simon. While Montesquieu had already established that society could be studied systematically and Tugot suggested that there were particular stages of social development and understanding, Saint-Simon focused much of his attention on the basic elements of social organization and promoted the importance of science as a tool for both understanding and solving the problems of society. He laid an intellectual foundation for much of early sociology.

In 1817, Comte was hired by Saint-Simon as his secretary. Claude-Henri de Saint-Simon was from an aristocratic family. Thirty-eight years Comte's senior, he was worldly and seasoned in diplomacy and business. He had served in the French Army in the American Revolution and was much closer to exigencies of the French Revolution than Comte. Frequently described as an opportunist, he narrowly escaped the aristocratic purges of the Revolution and spent his time amassing a small fortune by purchasing confiscated lands of fellow aristocrats who were fleeing France or who were beheaded for their royalist positions. His political connections and his statements in opposition to the king kept him safe. Still he loved money. Arrested as a suspected enemy of the Revolution, he managed to keep his life and his wealth until the rise of Napoleon in 1799.

Saint-Simon is perhaps most famous for his modest republican positions relative to the aristocracy and their value to the state:

> Suppose that France suddenly lost fifty of her best physicists, chemists, physiologists, mathematicians, poets, painters, sculptors, musicians, writers; fifty of her best mechanical engineers, civil and military engineers . . . bankers, two hundred of her best businessmen . . . best farmers . . . eminent scientists. . . . It would immediately fall into a position of inferiority compared with the nations which it now rivals.
>
> Let us pass on to another assumption. Suppose that France preserves all the men of genius that she possesses in the sciences, fine arts and professions, but has the misfortune to lose in the same day Monsieur the King's brother, Monseigneur le duc d'Angouleme, Monseigneur le duc de Berry, Monseigneur le duc d' Orleans. . . . Suppose that France loses at the same time all the great officers of the royal household, all the ministers (with or without portfolio), all the councillors of the state, all the chief magistrates, marshals, cardinals, archbishops, bishops . . . all the civil servants and judges, and, in addition, ten thousand of the richest proprietors who live in the style of nobles.

> This mischance would certainly distress the French, because they are kindhearted, and could not see with indifference the sudden disappearance of such a large number of their compatriots. But this loss of thirty-thousand individuals, considered to be the most important in the state, would only grieve them for purely sentimental reasons and would result in no political evil for the state.

Saint-Simon espoused the importance of work. He called for a system of meritocracy wherein each would be awarded according to his or her ability. This was predicated on his view of a "natural inequality of people." He promoted the virtues of hard work, science, and engineering, and called for a national governing council comprised of businessmen, scientists, and intellectuals. For Saint-Simon and most other functionalists, he believed in the inevitability of progress.

Comte worked closely with Saint-Simon first as his secretary and later as a collaborator. Their association lasted for about seven years. Yet many of Comte's ideas were appropriated by his senior who included them in his papers and public addresses. Some of Saint-Simon's notions found their way into his assistant's later works. Nevertheless, both men benefited from their association. They parted company in 1824 after a number of disagreements. Most of these centered around intellectual differences and credit for authorship or what we now call *intellectual property rights.* Thus, it is difficult for most historical scholars to determine which of these men should be credited with ideas developed during the period of their collaboration, which lasted from 1817 to 1824.

COMTE'S CENTRAL IDEAS

Upon leaving his position with Saint-Simon, Comte sought out intellectual alliances with varying degrees of success. Financially, however, he fell onto hard times. He attempted to eke out a living by giving public lectures, grading entrance examinations, and writing for newspapers. However, he barely survived. He petitioned kings and magistrates throughout Europe to sponsor him and his intellectual efforts, but he was turned down repeatedly. In 1825 Comte married Caroline Massin, a woman he claimed to have never loved. Later in his life Comte openly declared that she was a young prostitute he met upon an evening visit to Galeries de Bois of the Paris Royal in 1821. While his story is somewhat suspect, their marriage was indeed a difficult one.

Although his public lecture series on positivist philosophy had gained a modest following of disciples, it was not enough to keep him financially solvent. He began having severe bouts of depression, fits of mania, paranoia, and occasional breaks with reality. Before he would complete his planned lecture series he would be confined for a while at Charenton asylum in 1826. Still, it was from these lectures that Comte developed his classic *Course of Positive Philosophy,* which was eventually published between 1830 and 1842. His ideas influenced an entire generation of thinkers and found a receptive audience among some of Europe's more influential thinkers including John Stuart Mill and Herbert Spencer.

In his *Positive Philosophy* Comte provided the ground work for what he would term *sociology*—the science of society. He emphasized that all phenomena, including those sociological, were subject to *natural laws*—laws inherent in nature. (This was a premise in keeping with the Enlightenment ideology of his day.) It was up to the sociologist to discover the laws that regulated societies. Thus, sociology was not so much concerned with cause and effect, but rather with the laws that describe and dictate basic relationships in the social world.

Among his own most important findings was his self-proclaimed "great discovery of 1822." This was an idea that Comte conceptualized when he was still working with Saint-Simon and it is known that his employer had developed a substantial part of it. He referred to this discovery as *the law of the three stages.* Here Comte explained that human understanding evolved over time from a less sophisticated method of comprehension to a more highly developed one.

Accordingly, all primitive knowledge has its origins in magic and religion. This is the first way we come to understand the world and everything in it—including ourselves. Spirits are thought to be omnipresent, giving life and meaning to all things. Eventually religions form and myths develop to establish causes and explanations. This stage he refers to as theological. It is the most unsophisticated stage of knowing, but one that is still common throughout the world. This stage is socially structured around slavery and military despotism. This passes to the next stage—the metaphysical stage. Here the physical nature of things become abstracted and conceptualized. Understanding is through categorization, basic logic, sophisticated conjecture, and philosophic insight. Socially this stage is identified with the establishment of laws and legal-political systems. Finally, the third stage is positivism. Understanding is gained through the application of logic, science, and empiricism. For Comte, this is the highest and most sophisticated way of knowing. It is socially connected to industrialization and engineering.

Like most theories of its time, this was inherently developmental—meaning that there were progressive stages of development with the clear assumption that succeeding stages were somehow better. Of course, there was some overlapping. This idea was very much in line with the Newtonian science of his age in that it was mechanistic and linear. It was functionalist in that it saw these stages as a naturalistic progression of growth operating with a life force of their own.

Comte saw this evolutionary hierarchy as present everywhere. Societies, themselves, could be placed on a continuum and ranked from the most primitive to the most advanced. The same could be done with the sciences. In fact, he developed a hierarchy of sciences predicated on this hypothesis. He asserted that the sciences evolved from their most simplest form to their most complex through this natural progression. At the simplest level each discipline evolves in complexity to arrive at the positivist stage. For Comte, sciences emerge in developmental stages from mathematics to astronomy to physics to chemistry to biology to sociology. Sociology is seen as the most complex and abstract and, therefore, the most advanced of the sciences.

Comte's doctrine of positivism repudiated all reliance on religious or speculative knowledge. All knowledge must be grounded in science—contained within its boundaries. Thus, philosophy also must give up any pretense of attaining knowledge. However, scientific knowledge was relative, not absolute. Absolute knowledge was unattainable according to Comte. Whatever questions cannot be answered by scientific methods must be left permanently unanswered. Only science could reveal the natural laws governing the social order. Therefore, positivism was characterized by the notion that only science could bring about benefits to society, address its social ills, and solve its problems.

To further this end, it was the duty of each scientist to develop abstract principles through the use of scientific method including observation, experimentation, comparison, and historical analysis. Social knowledge could be gained only by looking at the *totality* of society. For Comte this totality was "organic." By this he meant that societies were made up of interrelated components that stood in relation to each other like organic components of any living system. Each part was interdependent. Thus, there could be no understanding of society by studying its elements in isolation. This notion was an essential ingredient of early functionalism.

Comte, in his more general discussions of sociology, proposes that part of the sociological agenda should be the understanding of social change. Sociologists should set out to discover the laws of *social statics*—what holds society together, and *social dynamics*—what causes society to change. Although he understood that structures of society simultaneously remain constant and change over time, he believed that there were inviolate principles at work here.

Politically, Comte must be described as suspended somewhere between pale liberalism and crackpot conservativism. He found it difficult to put his faith in the peasants and working class, although he occasionally romanticized them. He stood in opposition to the demands of labor and liberal intellectuals and was horrified by the social revolutions taking place around the world. He makes clear his misgivings toward egalitarianism in a letter written to Tsar Nicholas:

> The collective revolt of modern thinkers against all authorities of former times has gradually produced in each individual an habitual insurrection of the mind against

the heart, tending to destroy all human discipline. The whole West is thus drifting toward a savage communism in which true liberty would be crushed under degrading Equality.

It is clear that Comte had severe mental problems for most of his adult life. Many of the symptoms described by his biographers indicate signs of what we today would call schizophrenia. His problems seem to have become manifest in his early to mid-twenties. As he grew older, his writing became more manic and bazaar. Upon his release from the asylum, he displayed disturbing breaks with reality. His biographer, Mary Pickering, notes:

During the first week at home, Comte made no improvement. Somber and uncommunicative, he would often crouch behind doors and act more like an animal than a human. He still had many fantasies. Every lunch and dinner, he would announce that he was a Scottish Highlander from one of Walter Scott's novels, stick his knife into the table, demand a juicy piece of pork, and recite verses from Homer. He often tried to scare Massin by throwing his knife at her. Once he even grazed her arm. One day, when his mother joined them for a meal, an argument broke out at the table, and Comte took his knife and slit his throat. The scars were visible for the rest of his life.

In 1827 Comte attempted suicide by throwing himself into the Seine River. Even though his mental state was further deteriorating, he was able to secure a position as tutor at École Polytechnique. He taught there between 1832 and 1842 until he quarreled with the director and lost his post.

LATER IDEAS

The clarity and logic of Comte's earlier work gave way to more muddled and curious ramblings toward end of his life. He separated from his wife in 1842, blaming her for much of his unhappiness and distress. In 1845 he met and fell passionately in love with Clothilde de Vaux, a middle-aged woman who had been deserted by her bourgeois husband. Although their relationship was platonic and short-lived, Comte saw it as deeply romantic. Less than a year after they met, de Vaux was diagnosed with tuberculosis and died. Even though Comte's physical advances had been turned away, he literally worshiped de Vaux. He spent her last dying moments alone with her in her bedroom. Comte had secured a lock of her hair and upon her death he began a series of ritualistic devotions to her.

In his four-volume *Systems of Positive Polity*, published between 1851 and 1854, one can easily discern his emotional break with reality and the impact of de Vaux on his life. In this work, aside from recapitulating many of his earlier thoughts, he proposes to reconstruct society on the basis of a new spirit of religion, the Religion of Humanity. Now, it must be noted that numerous utopian thinkers of his age attempted to bring about some synthesis between religion and science. Saint-Simon, in fact, had also called for a new Christianity of social harmony and a utopian community founded outside of Paris that subscribed to this idea of religion in the service of science.

Nevertheless, parts of Comte's *Systems of Positive Policy* are unintelligible and highly charged with emotion. Comte advocates love as the unifying force of humanity, and refers to society as the "Great Being." He proposes this new religion of science based upon the love of humanity—inspired by the moral superiority of Clothilde de Vaux. Furthermore, he meticulously plans for its organization, modeling it on the hierarchial structure of the Catholic Church. He develops a calendar of rituals to be performed on specific dates by Church members and establishes himself as High Priest calling upon his disciples to establish churches (which actually many did). He proposes that the Pope will step down and allow him to lead this new religion.

CONCLUSION

Auguste Comte died of cancer in 1857 and was buried in Pêtre-Lachaise. His life seems rather paradoxical. Here was a man of science who invented a new way of seeing the world. Yet, his great emphasis on rationality was later wedded to a peculiar array of mystical ideas. His madness or illness did not prevent him from making solid contributions to philosophy and social science or from winning for himself followers and admirers around the world ranging from John Stuart Mill to George Eliot to Herbert Spencer.

Comte's quest was the elevation of science to the status of religion, eclipsing the authority of all traditional religions. Few in the West can doubt the powerful influence of science in this regard today. His contribution to sociology was very significant in that he viewed the study of society as both reflexive and essential to our understanding of everything else.

Comte laid down a rather conservative intellectual and conceptual foundation for sociology. Even though he called for rights of women and the disenfranchised poor, he wavered between viewing sociology as a unique way of knowing and seeing sociology as a tool of social control. For Comte sociology would become the science of an elite class of priests, people with sacred knowledge who could use scientific research to direct the course of the world and keep it from social fermentation.

Comte's sociology helped to reify society, making it something separate and apart from people, giving it a natural life of its own. His intellectual categories reflected a particular set of class interests. Still, this influence was profound.

BIBLIOGRAPHY

Comte, Auguste. 1853. *Positive Philosophy*, trans. and ed. by Harriet Martineau. New York: D. Appleton.

Lenzer, Gertrud, ed. 1975. *Auguste Comte and Positivism*. New York: Harper and Row.

Pickering, Mary. 1995. *Auguste Comte: An Intellectual Biography*, Vol. I & II. Cambridge: Cambridge University Press.

4

Herbert Spencer: Survival of the Fittest

Even though August Comte coined the term sociology, British social theorist Herbert Spencer was the first to write a comprehensive text on the subject. Unlike his European counterparts, Spencer was more pragmatic a theoretician and far less schooled in classical literature and refined philosophic thought. Still, he displayed an inordinate degree of inventive thinking and intellectual eclecticism. Despite the fact that he would go down in history as a primary advocate of laissez-faire capitalism and survival of the fittest, he was very much a radical for his day. He was also a man of intense moral and intellectual contradictions.

Herbert Spencer was born in Derby, England on April 27, 1820. His father, George Spencer, was a teacher and school master who had inherited a school from his father, Matthew Spencer. The Spencers were originally ascetic Methodists, but George later turned toward Quakerism. He, like his son Herbert, displayed radical liberal sentiments for the time and was profoundly anticlerical. A man interested in ideas, George Spencer became honorary secretary of the Derby Philosophical Society, which had been founded by Erasmus Darwin, Charles Darwin's grandfather. He imparted to his son the importance of learning.

Herbert Spencer was one of nine children, but the only child to survive past the stage of infancy. His mother, Harriet Holmes, was a quiet and unassuming person; both Herbert and his father viewed her as intellectually inferior, if not mentally challenged. Yet, she appeared to be kind, unassuming, and altruistic. For these qualities she was held in considerable contempt by her husband and also by her only son. She occupied a subordinate position in the household that was far from a warm and loving place. There is some evidence that she suffered from depression. Biographers note that young Spencer was frequently left on his own to an unusual degree. There appeared to be no close bond between mother and son. Although such conditions promoted self-reliance, they also laid the foundation for insecurities. Spencer's attitude toward women was significantly shaped by his relationship with his mother. Despite his friendship with the author George Eliot and his early advocacy for women's suffrage, he viewed women as innately inferior to men and less evolved physically and intellectually. He never developed more than cerebral relationships with women—relationships he considered to be more civilized than deeply emotional or romantic ones.

Young Spencer was not provided with formal training in Greek and Latin, which was the custom with children from middle-class families, but he did attend local day school. Still he was constantly challenged by his father and encouraged to explore the natural world surrounding their home. At thirteen, Spencer was sent to the Hinton Charter House near Bath where his uncle, Reverend Thomas Spencer, was curate. Thomas Spencer, a temperance agitator and strict disciplinarian, was put in charge of Herbert's education. The young Spencer found the intellectual confinement and corporal punishment not to his liking and ran away from school, returning to Derby. When he eventually came back to Hinton, he got along much better with his uncle, and completed three years of study there.

Spencer's education was rather nontraditional. Although the curriculum at Hinton provided little in the way of history or literature, he became rather adept at mathematics and mechanics. He never became a reader—certainly not a reader of philosophy or the classics; he knew little of art and foreign language, but he did like music. The books he used to form judgments about the ideas of others were frequently secondary sources. He drew upon these as though they were reference texts. His thinking was often mechanistic, but he held his own intellect in very high regard. His biographer, James G. Kennedy, noted: "One can admire Herbert Spencer's pleasure at solving a theorem on circles at twenty and publishing his demonstration as one hitherto unnoticed. Yet it is disconcerting to find that Plato solved the theorem two thousand years before."

After his formal studies Spencer tried his hand at teaching, but he was not very good at it. Realizing that his son was not cut out for this work, George Spencer helped to secure him a job through one of his former students who was working with the London and Birmingham Railway. Herbert Spencer was hired as an assistant engineer and soon was promoted to the position of civil engineer. In his spare time he dabbled in inventions that never amounted to much. He worked with the railroad for nearly ten years, but as he worked he developed more compelling interests in geology, natural history, and the biological theories of evolution. He read, or some would say misread, Lyell's *Principles of Geology.* When his engineering job was finally terminated, he turned to a career in writing and journalism.

In 1842, living off the savings he accrued from his engineering post, Spencer was able to publish a series of letters in a newspaper at which his uncle had some connections, *The Non-conformist.* These letters reflected ideas he had discussed with Thomas Spencer and his father. In these pieces Spencer argued that government was a threat to individual freedom, and as such its functions had to be curtailed. He condemned the government's role in social policy, in education, in health, and in human welfare. He viewed government involvement in these areas as standing in the way of progress and justice. Government's only true function was to ensure justice—something he did not venture to expound upon.

Though Spencer fancied himself somewhat of a philosopher and could quote Jeremy Bentham and J. S. Mill, he was not well versed in Kant, Hegel, Marx, nor the most important ideas of his day. After reading a second-hand description of their ideas, he would frequently dismiss their entire body of work because he took exception with their premises. He felt that extensive reading would only confuse him and cloud his ideas.

During his hiatus from paid work, Spencer became active in political causes and joined the Complete Suffrage Movement. Despite his philosophy of *laissez-faire,* he strongly supported the rights of all to participate in the electoral process. He became an assistant editor of *The Pilot,* the official organ of this organization. However, he only remained connected to it for a little more than a month. During this time Spencer supported communal ownership of land, suffrage for workers, and women's and children's rights. He later deserted these ideals.

Financial need and not being able to find income-producing employment in journalism led him back to engineering work for the railroad. This venture, however, was short-lived when the proposal he made for rail improvements was turned down by the government. Spencer tried on occasion to market some of his inventions such as a unique paper clip, but with no practical outcome. He also began reworking some of his ideas that would combine his interests in evolutionary theory to his study of society. All the while he applied for positions in writing and journalism.

In 1848, Spencer was offered an assistant editor post with *The Economist* in London. This was the break he had waited for. While working there he befriended John Chapman, the man who would become his publisher and introduce him into a small circle of London intellectuals including Thomas Huxley, Marian Evans (George Eliot), and Thomas Carlyle. In his spare time he worked on his manuscript, which became his most important work, *Social Statics.* Published in 1851, *Social Statics* amplified his ideas on individualism and *laissez-faire* capitalism and planted the foundation for what was to later become social Darwinism.

THEORY OF SOCIETY

Social statics was a term Spencer borrowed from Comte. It defined the conditions of social stability as opposed to change—social dynamics. Like Comte, Spencer was an empiricist. He asserted that all knowledge needed to be grounded in empiricism and social science. As he saw it, the focus of science was not merely the accumulation of data from which to make sense of the world, but also the discovery of basic universal principles and natural laws that could be only be deprived through empirical scientific discovery. Thus, Spencer rejected the notion that knowledge could in any way be subjective; it had to be based on rational empirical outcomes.

Having been influenced by theories of evolution developed in biology, particularly those theories of Lamarck, Spencer attempted to show how society itself was an organism subject to the same natural laws as the biological entities that comprised it. Like all living things, societies seemed to evolve on a trajectory from the simplest primitive form to the most refined state. People did the same; there were primitive peoples and those who were highly developed. Of course, the primitive peoples were biologically and socially inferior. Spencer latched on to quasi-scientific ideas such as phrenology to support his assertions. His reification of societies as living organisms also included the notion that social institutions that comprised them emerged naturally, functioning without human control similar to the circulatory system in the human body. Nation-states and capitalism, therefore, were phenomena that emerged from nature and were far superior to those social institutions associated with so-called simpler, more primitive societies.

Although Spencer differed with the population theorist the Reverend Thomas Malthus in many respects, he embraced *laissez-faire* as a naturalistic phase of advanced societies. Like Malthus, he asserted that there were superior and inferior human beings and that this system of noninterference on the part of the State would lead to a cleansing of substandard ones through mass die-off and starvation. This was merely a natural law of survival of the most capable. Echoing Malthus, Spencer believed that those who are less stimulated by sexual needs (such as himself) would be driven to improve their mental and physical output while those of excessive fertility would become extinct.

As Spencer became more familiar with the work of Charles Darwin, he moved further away from the Lamarckian notion of evolution, which appeared to completely deny the principle of natural selection. As his work became more accepted, he corresponded with Darwin and sent him samples of his own writings. He saw many parallels between his vision of society and Darwin's vision of the natural biological world. Darwin in turn shared with Spencer the manuscript of his later editions of *Origin of Species*. In fact, it was from Spencer that Darwin borrowed the term "survival of the fittest." Of course for Darwin, it was meant to describe genetically inherited traits that would be passed on through a process of adaptation and natural selection. For Spencer, it meant somewhat more than this—it suggested that those who were well off economically and intellectually, those who had accrued power and wealth, had become that way because of an their innate superiority. Those who were poor or disempowered, those who were slaves, were primitive peoples who were innately inferior. In the natural order of things, everyone got what they deserved.

OTHER WORKS

Herbert Spencer was a prolific writer. He wrote volumes including controversial texts in biology, psychology, and sociology. Much of his work was serialized in popular magazines of the day. Although he was not formally trained as a scientist or as a scholar, his thoughts had wide appeal. His later studies were so popular that the income they generated allowed him to give up his journalism career. Nevertheless, they were not as original undertakings as his earlier projects. They were continuations of his earlier ideas, and popularization of others that he seemed to agree with. They were frequently refinements of notions he had previously put forth in other works.

After the publication of his *Principles of Psychology* in 1855, he began suffering from what his biographers described as a condition of poor mental and physical health. He seemed to have long periods of depression and despondency. In his attempts to deal with these problems he became a regular user of morphine, a drug his father overdosed on and died from. Eventually, Spencer became addicted to opium. Still he was able to travel and led a relatively active life. There were periods when he would go for months without seeing anyone, or without writing a word.

Spencer's *Synthetic Philosophy*, which was published between 1862 and 1893 in nine volumes, was his attempt to merge his limited knowledge of biological evolution with his more limited knowledge of history and the social sciences. Even though it was put forth as a comprehensive philosophical tract, it was considerably less than this; it was more a compilation of speculative social thought taken from *The Principles of Biology* (1867), *The Principles of Psychology* (1872), *The Principles of Sociology* (1876–1885), and *The Principles of Ethics* (1891–1893). This work was forever to mark Spencer as a classic functionalist. Ironic as it might seem, this man who saw himself as a radical was above all a New Age Tory, espousing a form of liberalism that was grounded in biological determinism. His romance of science and misinterpretation of many of its principles led him to celebrate the new world order of capitalistic development. So much so was this the case that Andrew Carnegie wrote him fan letters, calling him a master teacher.

Spencer was particularly influential in American sociology. His espousal of individual egoism as the height of human achievement struck a resonant chord with American millionaires who built universities and hired scholars to send forth the message—the rich were superior people and deserved what they had while the poor and working class were inferior human beings who deserved to starve. The new world order of survival of the fittest was to them a scientific fact, and Spencer had proven this to the world.

Spencer's works were used at Harvard, Yale, Columbia, and the University of Chicago—an institution of higher learning built by John D. Rockefeller. American sociologists who were often unfamiliar with the complex theories of European thinkers found the utilitarian emphasis, the simplicity of the ideas, and the English language refreshing. Here was indeed a theory that espoused the dignity of individual freedom and the ethic of materialistic egoism. Here was a system of thought that justified industrial capitalism as the height of social advancement. Also, Spencer seemed to have found a biological construct upon which to nail sociological ideas. This made sociology more legitimate in the eyes of many shallow thinkers.

The view of the social world as a living organism with its own morphology, metabolism, and life cycle encouraged a radically conservative sociology to emerge in the United States. Racist policies around the world, policies of eugenics, forced sterilization, and ethnic cleansing drew upon Spencer for justification. Scholarship, particularly American and British social scholarship, would become increasingly empirical and would draw generously from biological models and make extensive use of organic metaphors. Those who attacked *laissez-faire* would be seen as reactionaries.

SOCIAL DARWINISM AS A WAY OF LIFE

Spencer became locked into a reactionary approach to society by marrying his sociology to biology and to what Weber would later term instrumental reasoning—a narrow range of rational thought. The belief that social arrangements are naturalistic and that there are universal natural laws determining them was never empirically justified. But it was comforting to many. Although Spencer had many supporters, he had numerous detractors who viewed his work as not only simplistic, but also as highly dangerous. Still, his desire to put forth a theory of world order and evolutionary progress was welcomed by those who saw in this work the foundational principles for sociological study. In a world that seemed so disorderly, it was nice to feel that there was a rational purpose and a scientific way to better understand the chaos.

The systems approach to viewing society that Spencer articulated comprises the organizing basis of most American textbooks in sociology.

Systems, subsystems, and network theories owe much to Spencer. Yet it is unlikely that a man who at one point in his life called for the nationalization of land and universal suffrage would find himself defending powerful elites and attempting to justify social and economic inequality. More ironic is the notion that a man raised in a Quaker family, who found himself opposed to militarism and the military function of the state, would see war as a naturalistic means to social cohesion and progress. Social Darwinism was to have a life of its own, being used to justify both imperialism and war. Near the end of his career Spencer used much of his time to both defend and reformulate his positions.

Toward the end of his life, Spencer was very much alone. After a visit to the United States his strength seemed to wane. He was able to complete a number of projects, but he was constantly tired. He seemed pathologically void of affect. He lived in various boardinghouses in London and eventually took up residence in a house on the East Cliff at Brighton. He spent much of his time there listening to music and looking at the sea. He died the morning of December 8, 1903.

BIBLIOGRAPHY

Elliot, Hugh. 1917. *Herbert Spencer*. New York: Henry Holt & Company.

Hudson, William Henry. 1916. *Herbert Spencer*. London: Constable and Company.

Kennedy, James. 1978. *Herbert Spencer*. Boston: Twayne Publishers.

Peel, J. D. Y. 1971. *Herbert Spencer: The Evolution of a Sociologist*. New York: Basic Books.

Spencer, Herbert. 1969. *The Principles of Sociology* [abridged edition]. Hamden, CT: Archon Books.

———. 1954. *Social Statics*. New York: The Robert Schalkenbach Foundation.

———. 1904. *Autobiography*, Vol. I & II. London: Williams Norgate.

———. 1888. *The Principles of Psychology*, Vol. I & II. New York: Appleton & Company.

———. 1884. *Principles of Biology*. New York: D. Appleton.

———. 1880. *First Principles*. New York: H. M. Caldwell.

5

Harriet Martineau: Feminist Sociologist

A woman who significantly influenced the early development and dissemination of sociological thought in the mid and late nineteenth century was Harriet Martineau. It was Martineau who translated the work of Auguste Comte into English and spread the gospel of positivism throughout Great Britain and the United States.

Martineau was born on June 12, 1802 to upper-middle-class parents. Her father was a successful textile manufacturer and devout member of the Unitarian Church. Her mother, a well-read, self-educated woman who cared for the educational well-being of her children. Harriet was the sixth of eight brothers and sisters. Although her family was active in an elite social circle in the city of Norwich, a major center of manufacturing in England at the time, the emotional environment of the household was puritanical and rigid—even repressive. In fact, Martineau's autobiography draws attention to her childhood sense of emotional rejection. She felt disconnected and ignored by her parents; she dreamed of suicide as a means of getting people to care for her once she had died by securing some emotional recognition of her absence.

The Victorian society in which she grew was indeed an emotional desert. Feelings were to be hidden away and repressed. As an infant, Harriet was placed into the care of a wet nurse, which was common for children of her class. From this wet nurse she received little in the way of emotional nurturance. And there are references in her autobiography to early remembrances of cravings for physical contact. Such early experiences were to have a significant influence on her quest for connection through her writings.

The conservative social and political climate of the day had a profound impact on her work. Although she was one of the first to speak forcefully for universal suffrage and the abolition of slavery, she was an outspoken apologist for British colonialism in India and a defender of free-market capitalism. Among her intellectual heros were David Ricardo, Thomas Malthus, and Adam Smith. Although she supported the rights of workers to form unions, she opposed laws protecting laborers, and disputed most child labor laws. She called for the elimination of the Speenhamland (a form of direct-payment welfare) and called on Parliament to place the poor into work houses. In fact, she believed that welfare in the form of supplemental income was the chief cause of poverty. She looked upon capitalism and free markets as means to salvation.

Martineau received little in the way of formal education, but more than most women. She was highly intelligent and primarily self-schooled. She read Milton's *Paradise Lost* at age seven and Shakespeare when she was only ten. She read French and Latin and could translate Tacitus. She and her sister Rachel were sent to study at a local Unitarian school, which made an exception in the general policy of not admitting girls. She loved school and clearly resented the fact that as a girl she watched her brothers attend universities while she and her sisters were trained in needlework. Her love for reading and for ideas led her to writing critical essays, some of which were published in local Unitarian publications when she was barely out of her teens.

Harriet Martineau was not a well child. She was plagued by all sorts of illness, but none as severe as the constant ear infections that left her with a substantial hearing loss by the time she was fifteen. As an adolescent this compounded her insecurities and her concern that she was considered unattractive by friends and relatives. In her twenties she needed to use an ear trumpet.

In 1825 the economy of Norwich sunk into a deep depression. Her father was beginning to suffer serious financial losses, which in turn aggravated his health. In an effort to ensure his daughter's future, he helped to encourage her marriage to John Worthington, a college classmate of Harriet's brother James. But before the marriage could take place, her father would die, and his death was soon followed by that of Worthington, who was to succumb to a brain illness. Harriet, in some ways, appeared relieved at Worthington's death and moved on with her life.

By 1827 the Martineau family was nearly bankrupt. The business was sold to its debtors and Harriet began to find ways of keeping herself and her family solvent. Even though she was a skilled seamstress, she had a flair for writing. Despite her mother's discouragement, she pursued this latter talent. Between 1827 and 1828, Martineau struggled to publish her work and even traveled to London in an effort to be more connected to publishers. This venture was unsuccessful. Her brother James encouraged her to enter a contest sponsored by the British and Foreign Unitarian Association. It required contestants to write essays to attract Catholics, Jews, and Muslims to the Church. Martineau wrote all three prize-winning essays and launched her career as a professional writer.

Martineau's next venture was a series of small books in political economy. The work that helped to bring her fame and financial stability was *Illustrations of Political Economy* (published between 1832 and 1834). This was a series of relatively short narrative pieces, fictionalized stories, illustrating the workings of natural law and the ideals of *laissez-faire* economics. Based on the works of classical capitalist writers, Martineau devised moral tales to show how these principles work in contemporary life. The books made complex ideas accessible and theoretical ideas simple and concrete. Needless to say, the work was quite popular among those in Parliament. *Illustrations of Political Economy* endeared Martineau to many of the more conservative social thinkers.

Martineau was more successful as a popularizer of ideas than she was as a theorist. John Stuart Mill's book *Principles of Political Economy* (1848) sold merely three thousand copies within four years of its initial publication, but Martineau's series in political economy sold ten thousand copies each month in 1834. The work gave Martineau greater visibility as an author and made her quite wealthy.

She was now able to move to London and settle into a life as both a journalist and writer of fiction. Inherent in her opinionated essays was a sense of naturalism that guided the universe. She saw an intrinsic fairness to the free-market system, which could serve the interests of reason. She was captivated by the work of Adam Smith. She would also find a fascination in the work of Jeremy Bentham and Auguste Comte. Bentham's utilitarianism complimented her cultural proclivities for order and progress. Comte's work romanticized both, yet called for the strict adherence to science as key to understanding. Within these writers' works she would find the yearning for industrial progress, social betterment, and a romance with the new.

MARTINEAU'S SOCIAL PHILOSOPHY

It is indeed difficult to categorize Martineau's social philosophy. Her ideas changed considerably over time. Her support for the principle of *laissez-faire* and disdain for socialism put her far to the right of many of her contemporary progressives. Beyond this, she found in the ideas of classical liberalism a justification for a more open society, something she espoused but never fully participated in. Like Adam Smith, she believed that each person in pursuit of his or her own interest would best serve society. She also clung to a view she attributed to John Locke and Joseph Priestley—namely, there are universal laws of nature that not only apply to the workings of the planet, but also guide the interactions of those who live on the planet. Everything is a direct consequence of an immutable causality. And she believed that there was a scientific calculus in all of this.

Although Martineau was an outspoken and articulate advocate of abolition and a promoter of women's rights, she was not a deep thinker. In fact, many of the political positions taken by Martineau would be considered shallow and reactionary by some today. Valerie Pichanick, her biographer, views her philosophy as somewhat "simplistic." Even though Martineau avowedly denounced greed and avarice, she could not help but be swayed by arguments put forth by Ricardo and Malthus that condemned governmental interference to help those in need. Although she condemned the Corn Laws as unfair restrictions on free trade, she condoned the British undermining of the Indian textile economy. The Irish problem was their own creation, too many babies encouraged by the Church. If we were compare this to Marx's analysis of the Irish problem, we can see the superficiality and apologistic nature of her understanding. To her, Adam Smith's notion of the invisible hand made much sense.

To her infatuation with free markets she combined an admiration of Jeremy Bentham and the whole notion of utilitarianism. She certainly believed in the greatest happiness for the greatest number of people. But she saw this happiness evolving from unrestrained capitalism.

What comes closest to her socio-theoretical view of the world can be summed up in the doctrine of necessity. As alluded to before, this doctrine was one of causality; it complimented her attraction to classical liberal economics and to Comte's positivism. Within this doctrine is the idea that there are unchanging laws in the universe that dictate the behavior of nature, society, and the individual. That although individuals are said to have free will, it is really not free. This is because all actions have been predetermined by antecedent events, and by current circumstances over which one has no control. Even thoughts and motives have extrinsic causes. Thus, freedom of choice is a sham—such freedom is circumscribed and all action has predetermined outcomes. Accordingly, the universe we inhabit cannot be significantly altered by humans or even by God. Although God might be considered "the first cause," he is equally constrained by the unwritten laws of the universe, which he, himself, authored. Like Priestley, Martineau saw prayers as unanswerable since God cannot change the natural course of things that he set into motion. She eventually gave up her belief in God.

For Martineau this position was simultaneously liberating and frightening. It was liberating because there is security in the belief that unwritten rules guide our lives and the future of the world. For the same reason it was frightening; even if science allowed us to understand these laws, we had no ability to change them nor the natural evolutionary course of things. Still she believed that understanding these laws was within the grasp of human comprehension. Some have referred to her position as a type of "evolutionary naturalism." This is a perspective that holds that evolution is key for comprehending change, that human behavior is dictated by causal relations, and that all knowledge is constructed and verified by human experience. Even though Martineau became an atheist, her philosophy remained deeply rooted in her Unitarian faith, which had a reputation in Britain for being somewhat iconoclastic. Although she gave up her faith, she never gave up the idea that one's purpose was to attempt to do good in the world.

THE SOCIOLOGY OF MARTINEAU

There can be no doubt that Martineau was instrumental in the promotion of sociological thought within the English-speaking world. She and Herbert Spencer were very much aware of the work of Auguste Comte. Martineau, however, was much more in touch with this work because of her mastery of French. In her early twenties she was captivated by the work of Saint-Simon and attended lectures by some of Comte's students. She was attracted to his evolutionary position on the development of knowledge. She read Comte, and although she disagreed with much of what he had to say, his naturalistic inclinations appealed to her. She shared his quest for order and progress and his thirst to discover the laws regulating social behavior. Even though she had more democratic inclinations and obviously detested his blatant racist and misogynistic views, she overlooked these and never called them into question. She also ignored much of his later work, which called for the establishment of a positivist church.

Martineau translated five volumes of Comte's work, *Positive Philosophy,* which was mainly a collection of lectures. Her translation edited out the book's redundancies and made the language more accessible to a broader range of the public. Comte was so impressed with her enterprise that he translated her version back into French and re-released the book.

The prolific nature of Martineau cannot be overstated. She engaged in her own sociological research for her book, *Society in America.* On a two-year trip to the United States she recorded her observations and reflections on the culture. She observed the horrors of slavery and the discriminatory treatment of women. She noted the disparity between the democracy that America professed and the reality of its existence. These became central points of her book. Although the work cannot stand as a classic in sociology, it is an interesting curiosity—a mixture of anecdotes and personal observations. Certainly, Alexis de Tocqueville's *Democracy in America* (1835) had a much more profound impact.

In *How to Observe Morals and Manners,* she wrote what might be considered the first social methods essay. In it she stressed the inherent tendencies toward ethnocentrism in most research including her own. She devised methods for observation and classification. Her contributions were vast, but did not have the same impact on sociology as that of her contemporary, Friedrich Engels.

CAUSES AND CAREER

Her success as an author of popular social commentary was not fully translated into accomplishment as a novelist and a writer of children's books. Even though she was nowhere near a failure as a writer, she could not challenge the more dynamic literary talent of Charlotte Brontë, George Eliot, or even Charles Dickens, with whom she had worked. Her novel, *Deerbrook,* seemed melodramatic, even for her time. Her work was often overly moralistic.

After her two-year tour of the United States, Martineau returned to England. She focused on her writing and attended Queen Victoria's coronation in 1838. She then began a European tour during which she became quite ill; she was diagnosed with ovarian cancer. Martineau returned to England and settled in Tynemouth. Her pain was so great that she became addicted to opiates. Through her social contacts, however, she discovered mesmerism as a way of dealing with the pain from cancer. In 1844 she wrote of her positive experience with the treatment in *Life in the Sickroom.*

Martineau's tenacity kept her working. In 1846 she bought a home in the Lake District not far from the Wordsworths whom she befriended. The same year she traveled briefly to Egypt. Upon her return, she began writing regularly for the *Daily News* and worked on her translation of Comte.

She became an outspoken champion of women's rights. She maintained the education of women could better serve men, and she was critical of marriage and called for the opening up of formal education to girls and young women. This was quite radical for her day. She called not only for improving women's skills as homemakers, but also for promoting arithmetic for women so that they might one day enter fields like accounting. Martineau advocated college for women. She was among the first to call for equal pay for equal work.

Despite her most conservative attitudes toward sexuality, she opposed England's Contagious Disease Act as a law that discriminated against women prostitutes but allowed their men customers to avoid control and penalty. In fact, Martineau worked hard to oppose this act, which forced women suspected of being prostitutes to submit to a forced physical examination.

CONCLUSION

Harriet Martineau helped to bring sociology to the English-speaking world. Although she elaborated principles for sociological investigation, she was quite far from the value-free scientific researcher we now associate with positivism.

As a writer she was exceptionally influential. As a social theorist she was not. Yet as a woman in Victorian society where there was enormous discrimination against females who saw themselves as intellectuals, she carried her own. So the issue raised by many who looked at her career is the extent of Martineau's role in shaping sociology. For many this role was exceptionally significant; for others it was less so. Many contend that her potential as a founder and shaper of sociology was undermined by the patriarchal nature of the society in which she lived. It was indeed a society that "wrote women out" of the canon and made credible only male perspectives. Needless to say that had there been less bias again women, her role could have been even more significant.

BIBLIOGRAPHY

Hill, Michael R., and Hoecker-Drysdale, Susan. 2001. *Harriet Martineau: Theoretical and Methodological Perspectives.* New York: Routledge.

Martineau, Harriet. 1877. *Autobiography with Memorials by Maria Weston.* London: Smith, Elder and Co.

———. 1838. *How to Observe Morals and Manners.* London: Charles Knight.

———. 1837. *Society in America.* London: Saunders & Otley.

Pichanick, Valerie Kossew. 1980. *Harriet Martineau: The Woman and Her Work, 1802–76.* Ann Arbor, MI: The University of Michigan Press.

Thomas, Gillian. 1985. *Harriet Martineau.* Boston: Twayne Publishers.

6

Karl Marx: Capitalism and Human Exploitation

During the nineteenth century, many European cities experienced an array of physical and social problems brought on by the Industrial Revolution and the decline of feudalism. Cities were filling up with peasants forced from rural areas by real estate speculators and landlords. Most of these rural exiles were in need of jobs. Violence, crime, and child abandonment increased. Men, women, and children were forced to live under conditions of extreme environmental degradation. In some urban quarters narrow streets became open sewers filled with disease and devastating poverty—not unlike what might be found in parts of the so-called "developing world" today.

Laborers were forced into factories to work for subsistance wages, earning just enough to pay for their own survival. Those who could not find work (including very young children) were often consigned to work-houses where they became unpaid laborers or found lives in prostitution. British writers like William Blake, Samuel Coleridge, and Charles Dickens painted gloomy literary portraits of the horrible conditions under which poor people lived—conditions generated by the greed of that era. Although many liberals condemned such conditions and called upon capitalists to be more sensitive to the social conditions around them, others like Karl Marx demanded a violent revolution against the system that generated these conditions.

THE YOUNG MARX

Karl Marx was born in Trier, Prussia (now Germany) on May 8, 1818. His father, Hirschel Marx, was a wealthy middle-class lawyer from a long line of religious Jews and rabbis. His mother, Henriette Presbourg, was the daughter of an important rabbi from Nymwegen in Holland. Because state discrimination in Prussia prohibited Jews from holding public office or practicing in professions, Hirschel Marx, a liberal nonbeliver, converted to Christianity and had his children baptized in the Evangelical Church. He himself joined an influential local church in which he made his business and social connections.

Karl Marx was one of eight children. He was an intelligent boy who loved to read. He was sent to the local *Gymnasium* as a child and from there he won entry to the University of Bonn where he spent only two semesters. At Bonn he gained a reputation for being not only politically radical and outspoken, but also gained renown for his excessive drinking, gambling, and womanizing. He wrote a lot of bad poetry, was involved in a duel from which he received a scar, and carried a gun to class. He was nearly dismissed from the university for this. With his father's help, he transferred from Bonn to the University of Berlin, which had a reputation for being an intellectual and cultural center of the day.

Marx's career as an intellectual begins here. Even though he self-selected the classes he attended, he was considered brilliant by most of his teachers. Aside from taking course work in philosophy and law, Marx dedicated himself to the study of Hegel. He joined the Young Hegelians' Club and read everything he could get his hands on by and about the philosopher. Marx found much to criticize in Hegel's philosophy as did many of those he associated with there. His solitary studies were often accompanied by cheap cigars and lots of beer. He also loved to join his friends in the local saloon for a discussion of the political events of the day and deeper social issues. Revolution seemed to be on the minds of many. After five years at the university he left Berlin without a degree. His dissertation, *The Differences between Democritean and Epicurean Philosophy,* was accepted at the University of Jena even though he never took a course there.

Marx entered the field of journalism in 1842 becoming the youngest editor-in-chief of the *Rheinsche Zeitung,* a new newspaper in Cologne. He spoke out for freedom of the press and for the rights of workers. However, when he defended the rights of poor peasants to gather wood for fuel from privately owned forests to warm themselves during one of the coldest winters on record, he was dismissed from his position.

In 1843, two months after losing his job, Marx married Jenny von Westphalen with whom he lived until his death. She had been a childhood friend and neighbor. Jenny was the daughter of an aristocratic family. Her father, a liberal baron, knew Marx as a young boy and allowed him into his library to delve into his classics in literature and philosophy. He was a neighbor to the Marx family and discussed books and liberal politics with Hirschel Marx.

The newly married couple used their wedding money and what Marx had earned at the newspaper to travel to Paris where he eventually found work as co-editor of a radical magazine, *The Franco-German Annals*. Paris was teeming with radical thought of the day. There the couple came into contact with the ideas of Pierre-Joseph Proudhon, Louis Blanc, Saint-Simon, and others. While in Paris, Marx also delved into the work of the classical British economists and moralists such as Adam Smith and David Ricardo. The *Annals* became a vehicle to disseminate his own work and that of his friends. It was in Paris, through his editorship of the *Annals*, that Marx met a young man, a fellow German, who was to become his lifelong friend and collaborator, Friedrich Engels.

The days in Paris were difficult ones, but rewarding on many levels. Marx found himself connecting through salons with important thinkers and fellow radicals. Unlike the reactionary atmosphere of Germany, France seemed more intellectually liberated. He befriended the poet Heinrich Heine who was quite famous at the time and developed a coterie of bohemian friends. He began working on his early manuscripts that centered on the relationship between capitalism and alienation, and he coauthored a book with Engels, which was titled *The Holy Family*.

Marx was eventually expelled from France at the urging of the Prussian government and the French police who found him to be promoting political insurgency. He traveled to Brussels where he wrote a book on the philosopher Feuerbach and collaborated with Engels on his now infamous *The Communist Manifesto*.

The Communist Manifesto was a proposed program of action for two small but important political groups. In Brussels, Marx founded what he called the Communist League, a small political party consisting of only eighteen people, including himself, his wife, Engels, and his brother-in-law. Although it was originally designed to be a real political party, it remained only a modest group of friends who talked about revolution. The League of the Just, located in London, was another group of would-be revolutionaries. In fact, it was a small group that had a history of revolutionary politics, but it could not seem to find a voice. Marx was asked to become that voice. It was to these two groups that *The Communist Manifesto* was originally addressed as a proposed political platform. Shortly after its publication in January, 1848 Marx was arrested by the Belgian police for using most of the money he inherited from his father's estate to purchase rifles for Belgian workers. Both he and Jenny were sent to prison.

The world seemed to be in turmoil. In February of that year unemployed workers demonstrating in Paris were fired upon by soldiers. The city broke into riot, the king abdicated, and his government collapsed. Similar revolts broke out in cities all over Europe. The streets were ablaze with revolution. Although details are not clear, Marx and Jenny were released from prison and put on a train to Paris with their two children. However, by the time they arrived, the revolution had already failed there. They turned around and headed for Cologne where Marx became editor of yet another radical newspaper, the *Neue Rheinische Zeitung.* The brilliantly written newspaper took the side of workers. In Cologne, Marx was accused of incitement to armed rebellion, but he was acquitted by a jury. He was now certainly a target of authorities. He escaped to London via Paris and was prevented from ever returning to Germany again.

Marx settled into London and stayed in the city the remainder of his life. While he, Jenny, and the children lived in relative poverty, Marx continued to write. He eventually found a quiet place to author his work—the British Museum. There he emersed himself in the work of economists and political scientists, spending eight- to ten-hour days there; he sealed himself away from family and learned to write acceptable English.

The domestic situation went from bad to worse. Jenny discovered that their maidservant was giving birth to Marx's illegitimate child and she became severely depressed, threatening to leave. Beyond this, their own little girl, Franziska, who was born in the same year, died of bronchitis and malnutrition. Jenny had to borrow the money for a coffin from a friend. Still Marx refused to tear himself away from his work and find a paying job.

It was during this time that he produced work that would challenge the very foundation of Western capitalism—work that helped inspire revolution in much of the world. Among these works would be *Das Kapital.* It was also during this time that Marx would help to organize what became the First International. This was a collection of labor representatives from all over Europe, but particularly France, Germany, Great Britain, and Italy. Marx became its spokesperson.

MARX'S SOCIOLOGY

Marx's contributions to sociology were indeed vast. It is safe to say that he radicalized much of the field and pushed sociologists to recognize the importance of social class and political economy. In fact, sociology is still reeling from his impact. It is also safe to say that he helped to polarize it and divided it into various camps. Without Marx, there would not be much of a conflict perspective in sociology. Given his major influence on this field and the vastness of his work, it is impossible within several pages to cover even his most central ideas. However, it is important to address a few.

Perhaps the notion of dialectical materialism is one place to begin. Although Marx never used the term, it is important to understand his frame of reference as a philosopher and social scientist. Marx wanted to make philosophy more real, to give it purpose and consequence. By this he meant to make it more grounded in the affairs of everyday life and everyday social relations. His argument with Hegel's ideas was that these ideas were not based in material existence. Hegel was much more theological and psychological in his orientation to theory. He saw the world as a consequence of this psychic or spiritual forces in the universe, forces that were dialectical in nature, shaping the course of history and the nature of humanity. Marx on the other hand proposed the opposite. "It is not the consciousness of men that determines their existence, but, on the contrary, it is their social condition that determines their consciousness." For him, the dialectic that contributes to the evolution of thought and being is neither an inherently psychic nor spiritual phenomenon, it is rather a historical-material process. For Marx the history of the world is a history of struggles for material position and power. It is a battle for physical survival. It is this struggle that gives shape to the psychic and spiritual manifestations of internal consciousness. This is why many Marxists found the work of Freud so reactionary, a liberal intellectual apology for unequal material relations.

However, Marx's work was far from being void of psychological analysis. His earliest work centered on the process of alienation that, to him, was associated with the modern development of capitalism. His work was to influence a large number of psychoanalysts who shared this view. Later on some intellectuals developed a perspective that would connect psychology to the material dialectic. This was the Frankfurt School.

In some of Marx's earliest writings he spoke about the relations of the means of production to the individual's psychic being. He spoke of true consciousness and false consciousness. He spoke about the individual estrangement from the self; the commodification of the self in the service of capital. He also spoke about the fetish of commodities and the role they played in furthering the alienation of the self from his or her being and the lives of others. These elements form much of the basis for Marx's sociology and, therefore, it is important that we survey some of them.

Class struggle became a central theme in Marx's work. All history, he tells us, is the history of class struggle. In positing this notion he uses the term *class* in a historical sense and in a modern one. Class has to do with structured inequality. In class struggle, one group rises up to dominate a less powerful one and to exploit that group. For Marx, history moves in a developmental dialectical manner. Like Enlightenment thinkers, he proposed that the world is getting better and better. Capitalism is just the stage before socialism, which will sweep in a new communal order characterized by a greater sense of human dignity and material equality, an order wherein there will no longer be classes.

Marx does not totally excoriate capitalism. In fact he praises the wonders that it has produced in the world both technologically and politically. It was a major revolutionary force that overthrew the entrenched aristocracy that dominated Europe. It challenged those who were resistant to change by force. Through a process of creative destruction and innovation, it displaced feudalism and slavery in many corners of the earth. However, it was merely the latest in a historic line of class systems that was put into place by a new aristocratic group. A self-serving clique—a small number of people who would control power to exploit a much larger group and gorge themselves on the fruits of this exploitation. This group or class would command control by commodifying the world and owning virtually everything in it. Everything under capitalism goes up on sale! And by so doing, they construct and control the development of culture and how people think about themselves and the world.

CLASS AND CLASS CONSCIOUSNESS

Marx looks at capitalism as creating only two major classes: the bourgeoisie and the proletariat. Literally, the bourgeoisie means city-dwellers in French (most of the wealthy business classes lived in the city), and proletariat is a term he borrowed from history. It was originally used to identify part of the class system of Imperial Rome—a group one rung up from the slaves. These groups were capitalists and the workers, respectively. The bourgeoisie were owners of the means of production; the prolitariat worked for them.

The bourgeoisie were different from the aristocracy in that the origin of their wealth was not strictly found in social lineage. Although many inherited wealth, they were forced to invest it in order to make money. Much of the money of this group came from family earnings. Although some were former aristocrats, many came from the merchant class and invested their money to make more money. Marx makes some room for what he refers to as the petite bourgeoisie—those who have substantial earnings like shop owners and professional people. However, one distinguishing feature is the idea that the bourgeoisie own the means of production. Most do not need to work because it is through the investment of capital that they become rich and maintain their wealth. Everyone else works for them. Also, the argument can be made that lawyers, doctors, and small shop owners (a group now rapidly disappearing) merely serve the needs of capital that has been invested. They all work for the bourgeoisie to keep the machine running.

Now Marx proposes that it is class, more than anything else, that determines one's consciousness. This is to say that one sees the world through one's class position and acts accordingly. The bourgeoisie understand that they need to pay workers low wages to make greater profits, and so they can act in behalf of their own best interests by doing so. They realize their position, who they are, and what they are doing. On the other hand, the proletariat has no such power and no understanding of their own potential. For the most part, they feel fortunate to be exploited and to have a job. Because the jobs at which they work are for the most part in the service of someone else and not themselves, they only get validation of who they are and what they are worth through their paycheck. They see themselves as powerless and, therefore, need to take on the consciousness of the bourgeoisie—the consciousness of their oppressors. They become what Malcolm X referred to as "house slaves." The majority identify with their oppressors and thus do not view themselves as exploited workers. By private ownership of the media, the government, and the educational system, the bourgeoisie keep workers in a fog, never allowing them to be truly educated or to realize their full potential.

ALIENATION AND COMMODIFICATION OF LABOR

In his *Economic and Philosophic Manuscripts of 1844,* Marx spoke eloquently about the alienation of the worker. Some of the central points made in his essay on estrangement include the idea that under capitalism the worker becomes just another commodity whose primary social and personal value is determined by the forces of market. How much one earns determines one's status, one's identity, and how well one can provide for his or her children. The money economy, itself, is inherently alienating. Capitalism separates labor from the laborer. This is to say that most of one's life is spent in the service, not of the self, but in attempting to satisfy the need of some other—often an invisible other who determines the workers' wages. A large segment of one's life is taken away; a life that could have been used for self-development. Instead it becomes a life dedicated to generating profit. And profit means one's own exploitation. The more one works, the more one produces, the less value is one's labor in the marketplace. The harder one works, the greater the exploitation, the more oppressive the system becomes using the worker's value to sustain itself and grow. Thus, the worker pays for an elaborate police state and military that are used to further exploit and oppress workers for the benefit of the bourgeoisie.

The entire process of exploitation is dehumanizing. People become extensions of machines and begin to think like machines. Workers find themselves physically and psychologically ruined in order to make enough money to survive. They go into debt buying products that enrich the lives of their exploitors rather than enriching their own existences. The near totality of their lives is spent in the service of their own exploitation and for the benefit of the bourgeoisie. They are exploited by landlords and banks who own their homes; they are exploited by the products they own. Also, they are taxed by governments that use the money to defend the privileges of the upper class.

In his later studies of commodification Marx talks about the fetishism of commodities. By this he means that things we buy take on a magical significance, a significance not based in reality. Each product is imbued with meaning both by those who produce it and those who consume it. We learn to associate products with happiness or adventure or strength. We associate products with things that have been alienated from our lives. We work for money to buy things that promise to put these values back into our lives. But capitalism can only survive on personal discontent and the promise of happiness. So, the products mostly fail to deliver and if they do deliver some abstract happiness, it will usually be short-lived. There will always be another product. For Marx, this was a brilliant trap.

CONCLUSION

Karl Marx was both a revolutionary and a romantic. He was a brilliant scholar and theoretician. He despised liberals almost as much as he hated the bourgeoisie. For him, capitalism would self-destruct. It was an avenue to socialism, which would be a more humane and democratic system, one that would eliminate class distinctions.

The self-destruction of capitalism would be brought about through a combination of massive business mergers, consolidations, and resulting unemployment. It would decay from its own greed for more and more profit. Workers would find in the misery a true consciousness, an understanding of their exploitation, and their own power to do something about it. But the bourgeoisie would not give up easily. The world would see a revolution, massive and bloody. But capitalism was bound to fall.

In 1881 Jenny died of cancer. The next year his eldest daughter died. He was never the same. Marx died in his armchair in his study on March 14, 1883—thirty-four years before the revolution that was to change the face of the twentieth century.

BIBLIOGRAPHY

Bottomore, Tom; Harris, Laurence; Kiernan, V. G.; and Miliband, Ralph, eds. 1983. *A Dictionary of Marxist Thought*. Cambridge: Harvard University Press.

Hook, Sidney. 1994. *From Hegel to Marx*. New York: Columbia University Press.

Lefebvre, Henri. 1982. *The Sociology of Marx*, trans. by N. Gutterman. New York: Columbia University Press.

Marx, Karl. 1967. *Capital*, trans. by S. Moore and E. Aveling. New York: International Publishers.

———. 1956. *Economic and Philosophic Manuscripts of 1844*, trans. by M. Milligan. Moscow: Foreign Languages Publishing House.

Marx, Karl, and Engels, Friedrich. 1967. *The Communist Manifesto*, trans. by S. Moore. New York: Penguin Books.

Payne, Robert. 1971. *The Unknown Karl Marx*. New York: New York University Press.

Wheen, Frances. 1999. *Karl Marx: A Life*. New York: W.W. Norton.

7

Emile Durkheim: The Eclipse of Community

More than Comte, more than Spencer or Martineau and much more than Karl Marx, Emile Durkheim viewed himself first and foremost as a sociologist with an important agenda. His task was to change the way people looked at the world. In fact, the emergence of sociology as a legitimate method of scientific investigation and analysis would not have been possible without him. Durkheim gave sociology academic and scholarly integrity by dedicating his life to the advancement of the field.

David Emile Durkheim was born on April 15, 1858 in Epinal, France in the Lorraine region. His father, Moise Durkheim, had been a rabbi in the town for over twenty years. His grandfather, Israel David Durkheim, was also a rabbi as was his great grandfather. His mother, Melanie neé Isidor, was the daughter of a merchant. Although not formally educated, she encouraged the education of her children. As the wife of a rabbi, she contributed to the meager family income by opening an embroidery workshop. Emile was the youngest of four surviving children. He had an older brother and two older sisters. He attended the local schools, including the *Collège d' Epinal* where was awarded a *baccalauréats* in Letters in 1874 and one in the Sciences in 1875.

Durkheim grew up in an orthodox Jewish home and some biographers note that it was anticipated that he would enter the rabbinate and follow in his father's footsteps. However, there is no real evidence of these kinds of pressures on him. His older brother entered business and his secular interests did not cause conflict within his family. Emile Durkheim's life was to take him away from formal religion although he would maintain an academic interest in it. His focus was instead on science and its application to the study of human behavior.

EARLY INFLUENCES

There is very little available to the reader on Durkheim's childhood and not much on his personal life in general. Most of his biographers can contribute little to our understanding of his early influences aside from commenting on broad historic issues that affected his era such as the Franco-Prussian War or the anti-Semitism connected to the Dreyfus Affair. We do know from accounts of his friend, Georges Davy, that he appeared to be somber and serious. His upbringing was austere. Some have suggested a hint of Calvinistic self-denial in his overarching dedication to his work even as a child. We do know that his family struggled financially and were sometimes targets of discrimination.

The Franco-Prussian War (1870–1871) brought the German occupation of Epinal, which in turn brought festering anti-Semitism out into the open as Jews were blamed for their lack of patriotism and weak allegiance to France. The war was the result of German imperialistic attempts to unify its aligned states and crush opposition to its development as a superpower. It led to the German occupancy of France with the exception of Paris, which hosted a rebellion against the French surrender to the German forces. This became known as the Paris Commune. These resistance fighters, which included communists, anarchists as well as local business people and clergy, were defeated by a combination of German and French forces, which later executed most of the rebellious survivors. The war was an embarrasment to France and was responsible for conceding large stretches of territory to the Germans and for pushing governance of France even farther to the right while promoting the search for scapegoats. Jews became the target once again. It was the Dreyfus Affair, the trial of a young Jewish officer in the French army for the crime of treason in 1894, however, that got Durkheim to speak out against racism and anti-Semitism in France.

Durkheim's conservative upbringing was reflected in his concerns for law, order, and social stability. His functionalism, similar in many respects to that of Comte's, reflected the so-called liberal ethos of his day. Despite his distaste for Marxist theory and his strong dedication to republicanism, he sometimes considered himself a socialist. Of course, his socialism was not the radical brand. It was based upon what he considered to be "scientific morality." Morality for Durkheim was what held society together.

As a functionalist, he viewed social problems as a result of social disintegration brought on by heterogeneity and, particularly, moral differences. He believed that in order for society to be free there needed to be a central mechanism of social control. His socialism was similar to that advocated by Saint-Simon, Comte, and other early sociologists. For him, Marxism was far too radical in its call for a revolution of the proletariat. Although he claimed not to be a nationalist, he believed in the moral centrality of the state. He believed in orderly progressive change and believed that stability could only be imposed from above.

Upon graduation from secondary school he went to Paris to prepare for entrance examinations for *L'Ecole Normal Superior.* This training would allow him a license to teach in the French high schools. While in Paris, his father became ill. Durkheim made several trips from Paris to Epinal while preparing for his entrance examination. He failed the admissions test twice, passing it only on his third attempt.

Durkheim was admitted to *L'Ecole* in 1879. Among his schoolmates were future illuminaries in philosophy including Henri Bergson. Bergson became world renown for his vitalist philosophy and his study of time and evolution. He also won the Nobel Prize for literature in 1927. Unlike Durkheim, Bergson was highly suspicious of scientism. Durkheim's studies in Paris were spent in scholastic reclusiveness. Due to nerves, he developed a severe skin disorder. He was a serious and often elusive student, so serious that his peers referred to him as "the metaphysician." Although he enjoyed his studies, he found the school's emphasis on the Greek and Latin classics quite distasteful; he preferred a more modern scientific emphasis. Even though he did well in his first year of study, he completed his program, ranking last in his class. But he did manage to pass his licensing examination, *l'agrégation,* which allowed him to teach in high school.

Beginning in 1882 Durkheim began teaching philosophy in schools in and around Paris. He was now twenty-four. He took a serious interest in pedagogy and was awarded a scholarship by the Ministry of Public Instruction to tour Germany and become familiar with university education there. While in Germany, he was exposed to the work of psychologist Wilhelm Wundt, which formed some of his later ideas in moral philosophy.

TEACHING AND SCHOLARSHIP

Upon his return from Germany he resumed his teaching in public high schools. He also began writing about the German educational system. In much of his writing, Durkheim was very supportive of a free system of national education that could help promote social solidarity and moral order. A number of his articles, particularly those that emphasized the important role of the social sciences in Germany, came to the attention of university officials in France. In 1887 he was appointed to the faculty at the University at Bordeaux to teach in the area of secondary school preparation, but his appointment also allowed him to teach "social science." This was the first time that sociology entered a university curriculum anywhere in the world. It was here in Bordeaux that Durkheim settled in to devote himself to furthering the study of the discipline. He would go on to write his classic works including *The Division of Labor in Society* (1893), *Suicide* (1897), and *Elementary Forms of Religious Life* (1912).

Durkheim was married to Louise Dreyfus in 1887. She had come from Wissembourg in Alsace. Her father operated a foundry in Paris. The couple had two children together, Marie and André. Louise Durkheim not only kept house but ensured his privacy and his scholarly productivity by assuming every responsibility of running a household. According to his nephew, Marcel Mauss, she even collaborated with him in his work, copied manuscripts, and corrected proofs. To Durkhem's solemnity she added a lightness and good humor.

The first few years at Bordeaux were a struggle. Durkheim worked long hours and needed to defend sociology from its detractors at almost every turn. Here he was in a university that emphasized the classics, teaching a course that was both disparaged and perceived as threatening academic integrity. He enlisted the help of philosophers and legal scholars in his cause and in 1898 founded the *Année Sociologique*. This was the first social science journal in the history of France. Even though his main responsibilities as a teacher and a scholar were to promote the theory, history, and practice of education, his Saturdays were spent giving public lectures on the social sciences, including specialized talks on kinship, incest, crime, suicide, and the like. His books won much critical acclaim.

In 1902 Durhkeim was offered a chair at the Sorbonne in Paris. His detractors claimed that it was a means of appeasing Jewish intellectuals who were hurt and offended by the Dreyfus Affair travesty. He was now forty-four years of age. Nevertheless, the appointment was a great honor and a substantial recognition not only of his work as a brilliant scholar, but also of the importance of sociology itself. Durkheim was given the rank of professor. Eventually, the name of his chair or position would become the chair of "Science of Education and Sociology."

In Paris, he still had opponents, most of them were on the political right. Still his lectures were enormously influential. His courses were obligatory for all students seeking degrees in philosophy, history, literature, and languages. He trained future high school teachers and instilled in them the value of the sociological perspective and what he referred to as a rationalist morality as opposed to a religious one. He assumed power by serving on the university council and the French Ministry of Public Instruction. He was accused of managing appointments and creating chairs in sociology throughout the public university system.

ANOMIE AND THE COLLECTIVE CONSCIENCE

Where Auguste Comte promoted the idea of empirical sociology, Durkheim actualized it. It was Durkheim who conducted some of the first important statistical studies of social phenomena. As a functionalist, however, his call for order, consensus, and progress reveal a strong discomfort with the forces of modernization. There are few references in his work to issues of social class. In fact, some of his work contains direct attacks against Marx and his followers.

The Division of Labor in Society is proposed as a complement to and an extension of the work of Adam Smith. In this work Durkheim ignores the inequities generated by capitalism and focuses instead on the impact growing specialization has on human relationships and the degree of moral consensus. He uses the terms *mechanical* and *organic solidarity* to distinguish between traditionally organized societies—those organized around a low division of labor and united by a high level of consensus, and its opposite, which he terms organic solidarity.

Mechanical solidarity versus organic solidarity is constructed as a binary opposition similar to Ferdinand Tönnies' *Gemeinschaft* and *Gesellschaft*. In each of these models the traditional, communal society is contrasted to the impersonal, rationalistic one. Underlying each is a notion that moral homogeneity and community cohesion gives way in modern life to a heterogeneity and weakening social unity. Durkheim's mechanical solidarity is characterized not only by a low division of labor but also by a high level of what he terms "collective conscience" or shared understanding of the world and thus a shared moral perspective. In mechanically organized societies people are held together by their similarities; in organic ones, they are held together because of their differences, their specializations that complement each other.

Traditionally organized societies emphasize laws of retribution (swift and harsh punishment) for those who violate norms, but more modern organically organized ones stress laws of restitution or means for making amends. There is little if any individualism, little personal freedom, in mechanically organized societies and a much higher level of freedom and individualism in more heterogeneous, modern ones. However, modern societies suffer the consequence of anomie—a lack of moral consensus, a confusion of norms and values. The traditional society displays a higher level of collective conscious and consciousness. Thus, the challenges posed by modernity have little to do with personal psychology or economic disparity. It is the structure of society that determines how people behave.

SUICIDE

Durkheim's study of suicide was an important extension of his work on anomie. But more than this, it was a comprehensive theoretical and empirical study of a phenomena that had traditionally been the realm of psychology. At first examination, why a person takes his or her own life might be viewed as due to a highly individualistic set of reasons and circumstances. However, Durkheim contends that this is only a small part of the story. Not all societies emphasize individual choice. The concept of the individual is a particularly modern one. More traditional, more communal societies have little in the way of suicide. Those with more impersonality, those with greater levels of anomie, have higher suicide rates.

Durkheim spends a considerable amount of time in his book providing statistical evidence for his position. He looks at religions in the West and finds that Jews, because of their moral cohesiveness, have little suicide compared to Protestants who emphasize individualism even more than Catholics do. Other variables also appear to correlate with the likelihood of suicide, including occupation, age, and marital status.

Durkheim develops a typology of suicides including egoistic, anomic, altruistic, and fatalistic. Each has to do with the quality of personal group integration and attachment. For instance, egoistic suicide is more common in modern societies and results from a sense of individual estrangement or alienation from the group. Anomic suicide, on the other hand, results from a breakdown of the regulative powers of the society. There is nothing holding people together, no common morality. The giving up of one's life for others or altruistic suicide can be caused by a strong group cohesion. Suicide bombers who die for a cause are reflective of this. Fatalistic suicide is an act of desperation resulting from a real or imagined fear of inevitable doom or disaster.

In all of these types the structure of society is the important determining factor or predictor of suicide. This is not to dismiss the psychological or economic reasons frequently associated with it. Durkheim makes the point that social analysis is critical to our understanding of this problem and others.

TOTEM AND THE COMMUNITY OF GOD

In *Elementary Forms of Religious Life,* Durkheim discusses not only the earliest forms of religion and religious worship, but he also locates the origin of community in the totem. Here is another extension of his moral cohesion hypothesis.

The early totem faiths focused tribal worship and ritual on a sacred animal that has come in some ways to represent the tribe itself. If a tribe worships a fox, it espouses the importance of such qualities as quickness and cunning, qualities associated with the fox. Rituals bring members together to offer sacrifices to it, to elevate it in the consciousness of tribal people.

But it is important to note, Durkheim insists, that the worship of the sacred animal is really a worship of the tribal values. The tribe reconfirms its collective conscience in its celebration of the totem. It is the values that hold the tribe together and allow for it to survive, the animal is only a symbol of these values. Thus, the tribe imbues the animal with sacredness, makes it into a god. When they worship it, they worship those qualities that enable them to survive as a group.

As tribes turn into nations, cohesion becomes much more of a challenge. There is less consensus on values and on their importance. Heterogeneous values often drive people apart. Monotheistic societies that are intolerant of other gods attempt to ensure conformity.

Durkheim makes much of the difference between the sacred and the profane. On one level he appears to lament the passing of the sacred world. On another, he views that passing as a healthy sign. He is a product of the Enlightenment and, therefore, suggests that God is a social construction, not a spiritual one. For him, God is constructed in the image of people, and not the other way around. It is the people who differentiate between those sacred things and those that are not.

CONCLUSION

Durkheim set the tone for modern sociology. His conservative nature made his work much more acceptable to the French establishment. Still many of his contemporaries considered his work to be far too radical. Certainly, he was no Marx. Yet, he helped to build an important sociological perspective that influenced subsequent generations of scholars.

The functionalist perspective in sociology owes a major debt to him. He had a profound influence not only on European sociology, but also on American social science. His work was both revealed and enhanced by such theorists as Talcott Parsons and Robert Merton. It became central to much of the theoretical research in criminology, deviance, and sociology of religion. His concept of anomie remains an essential theme in modern sociology. His contribution to the development of methods of social research has been enormous.

BIBLIOGRAPHY

Durkheim, Emile. 1984. *The Division of Labor in Society,* trans. by W.D. Halls. New York: The Free Press.

———. 1951. *Suicide,* trans. J. Spaudling. New York: The Free Press.

———. 1915. *Elementary Forms of Religious Life,* trans. by J. Swain. New York: The Free Press.

Thompson, Kenneth. 1962. *Emile Durkheim.* London: Travistock.

8

Max Weber: Reason and Bureaucracy

The story of Max Weber is one of brilliance and tragedy. It is a tale of intellectual achievement and mental despair.

Max Weber was born in Efurt, Germany on April 21, 1864. He was the first of eight children born to Max Weber, his father, and Helene Fallenstein Weber, his mother. His parents were both descendants from a long line of Protestant refugees who had settled near Weimar in an attempt to escape Catholic persecution in Salzburg. Both parents came from commercially successful families. His father was an accomplished lawyer and very active in local politics. His mother looked after the interests of the family. The couple took up residency in Berlin, a center of culture, commerce, and academic life.

We are told by John Patrick Diggins, his biographer, that baby Max was born with an astoundingly large head, much too large for his small, frail body. As a boy, young Max Weber was filled with nervous pecularities and anxieties. He feared being thrown into the ocean by his mother. He also dreaded his father's anger. Young Weber was often sickly. Later, in his adolescence, he was tormented by thoughts of his own death. A darkness would eventually settle over his great mind and for months, and even for years at a time, he would not be able to function normally.

The Weber household was socially alive. His father was very much involved in public life and enjoyed the company of academics and politicians. He was a lover of music, art, food, and drink. His personality was outgoing, yet he had highly emotional outbursts with frequent mood shifts.

His mother was a quiet person, a staunch Calvinist with strong religious beliefs. She never challenged her husband and his unflinching authoritarianism. It was she who conveyed to her son the notion of Christianity as a dogma of unwavering responsibility, duty, and self-denial. Growing up in this household was difficult for Max Weber, a boy of intense sensibilities, whose work would come to reflect these very interpersonal dynamics.

The Weber home was upper middle class. It was comfortable though not lavish. Young Max was an avid reader, but reports from his teachers frequently noted his disrespect for their authority and lack of discipline. Nevertheless, he read the works of great Greek and Roman thinkers such as Herodotus and Cicero in their original Greek and Latin. Also, he was very familiar with the works of Kant, Goethe, and Spinoza before entering the university.

At eighteen years of age he enrolled at the University of Heidelberg. Like his father he studied law, joined the same dueling fraternity, and drank beer with his schoolmates. Still, he remained an ardent reader and displayed the makings of a great scholar. He was particularly attracted to the study of medieval history, philosophy, and economics. After three terms he left the university to serve in the military, and in 1884 he returned to Berlin where he continued his studies at the University of Berlin. His interests now led him more into economic history. Weber's doctoral thesis was on the history of commercial societies in the Middle Ages.

He spent most of the 1880s living at home, financially dependent on his father for whom he was to increasingly lose respect. He never saw his mother stand up to her husband who verbally abused her, and Weber found this emotionally troubling. His father seemed content in life with his position and wealth. He was at one time a man of high political ideals but now was a passive supporter of Bismarck and benefited from his overt cronyism. Weber detested this. He disliked his father intensely. Upon graduation, he took a position as a junior barrister in the Berlin courts and later accepted a job as an unpaid lecturer at the University of Berlin. But he remained financially dependent on his father.

Weber continued his studies, took postdoctoral work at Berlin and wrote extensively. He wrote important work on Roman agrarian history and a study of the conditions of East Elbian agricultural workers. He worked long into the night while continuing to toil as a barrister for the courts during the day. In some sense, he took on the characteristics of an ascetic scholar, working tireless hours in the day in the courts and locking himself in his room at night to work on his manuscripts and edit a journal for the *Verein fur Sozialpolitik*. Release, in a sense, came to him with his marriage to Marianne Schnitger, a cousin on his father's side of the family. Prior to this marriage in 1893, he had been engaged to another cousin, Emmy Baumgarten, whose illness confined her to a sanitarium. They had been seeing each other for nearly six years but never consumated the relationship physically. Thoughts of Emmy haunted him much of his life as he abandoned her in the sanitarium to pursue his life.

Marianne Schnitger was also a brilliant thinker—a feminist writer to whom Max Weber was deeply attracted. She was twenty-two when they married and he was twenty-seven. But here also a sexual relationship failed to materialize. The expression of Weber's sexual passion was to come in the form of an extramarital affair when he was in his late forties, shortly before World War I. Marianne would always remain his confidant and source of strength.

CAREER AND MENTAL DECLINE

Max Weber was awarded a teaching position in economics at the University of Freiburg in 1893. His work there brought him international renown and in 1896 he was offered a chair in economics at the University of Heidelberg. His career was now on a rapid upward trajectory. He was gaining the independence and status he had always wanted. At the same time he was honing his skills as a scholar.

But in 1897, he and his father had a highly charged emotional encounter during which Weber verbally attacked his father in front of his mother and his sisters, who were visiting his home in Heidelberg. He blame his father for destroying his mother's life, for abusing her emotionally. At one point Weber demanded that his father leave his house and not return. A door was slammed. The intensity of the exchange was to leave each man with unresolved bitter feelings toward the other. One month later, however, Weber's father died of a gastric hemorrhage. We are told by biographers that it was in all likelihood this event that led Max Weber into a severely dark depression from which he could not escape for several years. It was a malaise characterized by social withdrawal, an inability to sleep, a loss of appetite, and an inability to concentrate on his work. For hours at a time he would stare into space, and eventually sought retreat in a sanitarium, resigning his professorship in Heidelberg.

In 1903, a shaft of light seemed to pierce the darkness. He suddenly began working again. But not at the old pace. He became editor of a journal with Werner Sombart, another famous sociologist, and was invited by a former colleague who was now teaching at Harvard to come to the United States and present a paper at a meeting in St. Louis. Since his youth, Weber had a fascination with America. He admired much about the American spirit and wanted to experience it firsthand. His trip was rewarding in several respects. Aside from experiencing the St. Louis World's Fair, he traveled with his wife for three months across the United States and learned much about the influence of early Protestant groups on America's values, particularly its glorification of capitalism and individualism.

Upon his return to Germany he wrote what many consider to be his most important works, among which was *The Protestant Ethic and the Spirit of Capitalism,* published in 1904. This book articulated his fascination with the relationship between Calvinism and the rise of an individualistic form of capitalism in the West.

Because Weber was a liberal, he found radical ideas disturbing. On some early occassions he had dismissed the work of Karl Marx as impractical, if not misguided; yet toward the end of his career he professed that the ideas of men like Marx and Nietzsche had laid much of the groundwork for modern thought. He admitted their important influence on his own work. Weber's cadre of friends now included both liberals and radicals. Among his friends and associates were Georg Simmel, Robert Michels, and Georg Lukács. Yet, his most important intellectual influence was his wife, Marianne, whose radical feminism had a significant impact on his writing and who helped to edit (if not to write) some of his works while he suffered with depression.

A VASTNESS OF CONTRIBUTIONS

It is in no way possible to survey the totality of Max Weber's contributions to sociology in a short chapter such as this. However, it is important that those who are about to read him bear in mind that his knowledge and interests were vast. His work ranges from ancient history to the culture of modernity. His studies include factory workers, political revolutions, accounting procedures, and religions of the world. They include sociological research methods and ethics. There is hardly a topic that he failed to make his own.

Some of Weber's more important "discoveries" have been conceptual. *Versheten* and *ideal types* are but two. The former concerns a type of understanding gained from subjective knowing, conceptually placing oneself in the position of another in order to gain a sense of how the other perceives or understands. Weber believed that each individual sees the world through a set of cultural and personal filters. They shape what people see and how they react to things. This focus on individual perception gave Weber's work an interactionist bent. On the other hand, ideal types have to do with categorical constructs that reflect the essential elements of a distinct social unit. Thus, Weber gives us what he sees as the essential elements of bureaucracy: hierarchy of authority, specialization, rules, impersonality, and professional development.

Weber's extensive study of the types of authority also reflect the ideal type focus. With precision he makes distinctions between traditional authority, charismatic authority, and legal-rational authority. Many who have written on Weber's life believe that this focus on authority is related to his attempts to understand his father and the autocratic German society in which he lived.

Unlike Marx who viewed social class as based on a structural division between capitalists and workers, Weber advanced the idea that it was much more complex. He asserted that one's position, even in capitalistic societies, was not determined by one's relation to the means of production alone. One's prestige and access to power could, and often did, emerge from nonmaterial things as well. For instance, great leaders could have spiritual or value legitimacy, which had little to do with their wealth or lack thereof. Greedy capitalists were often required to seek the blessings of the Church or other representatives of the people in order to legitimatize their power. Thus, religion could advance a set of values opposed to the avarice inherent in the capitalist ethos that Marx had described.

Weber's work on bureaucracy and modernity had a profound influence on those who became known as the Frankfurt school theorists. He also has had a significant impact on many postmodern sociologists, such as Zygmunt Bauman. For Weber the world was becoming more and more bureaucratized. Although he admired bureaucratic efficiency, he was also disturbed at its impact on human sensibilities and creative thought. The notion of instrumental reasoning, a type of bounded rationality limited by the confines of the bureaucratic structure, was creating human automatons—unfeeling, nonreflective actors without souls. This construction would be a danger to Germany and to the rest of the industrialized world.

Weber articulated a distinction between means-end rationality and values rationality. The former was eclipsing the latter in almost every corner of public and commercial life. This form of practical reasoning was based on pragmatic and egoistic interests that seemed to displace more primal forms of thought associated with traditional societies.

To this end Weber viewed the process of modern history not so much as Enlightenment, but as "disenchantment." The world was being gradually bleached of its color and vitality. The once enchanted world, a world full of mysteries and spirits, was giving way to a rationalistically organized society—a machine manned by lifeless, hollow souls.

CAPITALISM AND THE PROTESTANT ETHIC

Although Marx attributed the troubles of modern societies to the institutionalization of Western capitalism, Weber disagreed. Religion, particularly Protestantism, had created the values that seemed to underlie the "spirit" of modern capitalism. That capitalism and Protestantism shared many of the same values was no accident of fate.

The Protestant ethic meant that work was good for the soul. The harder one worked, the closer one was to God. Hence, work was the key to salvation. Without this work ethic Western capitalism could not have come into dominance. Furthermore, individualism is central to most Protestant dogma in which the individual is responsible for his or her own soul. The

Catholic Church in western Europe under feudalism had emphasized communal life. God's grace came only from the Church. Its channels of distribution were tightly controlled and the person could only find redemption through ministers of the Church. The old Church looked on wealth with suspicion, perhaps something that might challenge its authority. It called for those with wealth to give it to the Church. But the new faith was more accepting of accumulated wealth.

It was decentralized and because it had little wealth of its own and no centralized power base, it was in no way threatened by such accumulation. Individualism served its needs and purposes, as well as the needs and purposes of a blossoming form of modern capitalism. In the eyes of the Protestant Church, particularly Calvinism, the wealthy man was in all likelihood destined for heaven—God had smiled upon him for his hard work and personal efforts. However, an important part of this new faith was asceticism. To lavish oneself with worldy goods was sinful. Saving was therefore encouraged. Calvinism promoted capital accumulation and economic industry. The self-made man was the hallmark of this faith.The unequal distribution of wealth was viewed as the will of God.

New Protestant faiths de-emphasized the mystical elements of Church teaching. Its priests were nearly secular, far from the monasticized breed associated with Catholicism. Faith became more "rational" in some sense. All of these elements helped to promote the rise of a particular type of Western capitalistic spirit. It was only in Western Protestant nations that industrial capitalism came into full bloom. Catholic nations lagged behind. The reason that capitalism failed to take root in China, for instance, was because of the deeply embedded familial traditions that controlled economic activities there. Also, according to Weber, Confucianism militated against capitalism and modern change in that it promoted ancestor worship and was resistant to the changes needed for industrial development.

CONCLUSION

Weber's theories and studies launched sociology into the modern age. He was able to connect macro-order issues with micro-order ones. Through his own expansive scholarship and his renown as a scholar, he was able to draw others to the importance of sociological concerns. His public lectures were always full. People came from around the world to hear him.

During World War I he worked with the German military as a reserve officer to run nine military hospitals in Heidelberg. Toward the beginning of the war he remained a loyal supporter of Germany and the kaiser. But as the battles raged, he became more and more disillusioned with the German political leadership and the position of Germany in the world. He saw the war as causing future problems that would threaten his country's economic stability.

Between 1918 and 1920 he became politically active, writing articles and commentaries for the German press. In 1918, he returned to teaching and taught at the University of Vienna for one semester and then went on to the University of Munich the following year. He served as an advisor to German delegation at the Versailles Peace Conference and participated in drafting a new constitution for Germany after the war. He kept busy writing and worked on a substantial draft of *Economy and Society,* which was published posthumously.

In June of 1920 he contracted pneumonia and died on June 14 of that year.

BIBLIOGRAPHY

Coser, Lewis. 1977. *Masters of Sociological Thought.* New York: Harcourt Brace.

Diggins, John Patrick. 1996. *Max Weber: Politics and the Spirit of Tragedy.* New York: Harper Collins.

Mitzman, Arthur. 1969. *The Iron Cage: An Historical Interpretation of Max Weber.* New York: Grosset and Dunlap.

Weber, Marianne. 1975. *Max Weber: A Biography,* trans. by H. Zohn. New York: Wiley.

Weber, Max. 1978. *Economy and Society,* trans. by Fischoff and Gerth. Berkeley, CA: University of California Press.

———. 1956. *Sociology of Religion,* trans. by E. Fischoff. Boston: Beacon.

———. 1930. *The Protestant Ethic and the Spirit of Capitalism,* trans. by T. Parsons. London: Unwin.

9

Sigmund Freud: The Unconscious Civilization

Few theorists can ever claim the magnitude of influence on modern social thought as Sigmund Freud. His ideas dominated the entire twentieth century. Although considered the quintessential psychologist, Freud's impact was felt well beyond the scope of his professional discipline. As a social theorist, Freud was steeped in the work of psychiatry, and immersed in the important ideas of biology, philosophy, anthropology, literature, and sociology.

Sigmund Freud was born in Fribourg, Moravia (part of Austria-Hungry) on May 6, 1856. His father, Jacob, was a textile dealer; his mother, Amalia, was from a middle-class family that valued education. Jacob had children from a previous marriage, but Sigmund was Amalia's first born. According to Freud, she cherished him and held him in great esteem often referring to him as her golden boy.

Amalia was twenty years younger than Jacob and was close in age to two of her husband's sons (Freud's stepbrothers). Freud would sometimes be overcome with panic that one of his brothers had actually sired him.

Freud's given name was Sigismund Schlomo Freud; he was to be called Sigmund early on in life. He was raised in a Jewish household; however, he had a Catholic nanny to whom he was very attached. Still, his mother catered to his every need. She saw him destined for great things. He recounted joyfully playing in the nearby woods, but by the age of four his early happiness would come to an end. He was forced to give up his home due to his father's failing business. The family was required to relocate and settled in the Viennese neighborhood of Leopoldstadt, a quiet Jewish enclave. At this time Vienna was truly the heart of Europe. The city was a cultural mecca, a center of art, music and intellectualism. Young Sigmund Freud was often inspired by the city and he frequently returned to play in the woods of Fribourg.

EARLY LIFE AND WORK

As a child, Freud lived a sheltered life. His mother was extremely protective of him. A story is told that when he complained of not being able to study because of his sister's constant piano practice, she arranged to terminate the piano teacher. In return she expected much of her son. He was an outstanding student and entered the Sperl Gymnasium (a secondary school) a year ahead of schedule. He constantly ranked first in his class. He loved the classics and was deeply interested in law, philosophy, and biology. He had a good command of several languages and could read Shakespeare when he was eight. In 1873 he graduated *summa cum laude,* being recognized for his excellent command of the German language. After hearing a lecture on Goethe's famous essay, *On Nature,* he decided to pursue the study of medicine. This was a field open to Jews at the time.

Freud entered the University of Vienna in the fall term of 1873. He attached himself to his studies with vigor. His course load included such subjects as chemistry, botany, physics, physiology, biology, and even Aristotelian logic. He worked long into the night. While at the university he encountered a number of incidents of antisemitism to which he responded with anger. Jews were being blamed in Vienna for many of the country's economic problems. He attended frequent lectures by some of the best minds of his era, including a series of talks by Brentano. Freud eventually attached himself to Ernst Brücke and received a grant to work with him in his laboratory where he was investigating sex glands of anguillas, or eels, and nerve cells. Brücke saw Freud as a rising star and took him under his wing. In Brücke's research circle, Freud was to meet Josef Breuer who would become a major influence on him.

In his last year of study, Freud attended lectures by Theodor Meynert on psychiatry. He was attracted to and excited by many of these ideas, especially his neurological findings. After taking a one-year leave to meet his military obligation, Freud passed his final examinations in 1881 and received his medical degree. At the urging of Brücke, he accepted a position in residence at the Vienna General Hospital. Even though he was particularly drawn to research, he was not in a financial position to give up the more lucrative fields of medical practice. He would remain at Vienna General for three years where he would try his hand at surgery, internal medicine, as well as psychiatry. Throughout this time he dabbled in his own research. Eventually, he would marry Martha Bernays and leave his hospital work to set up a private practice in psychiatry and neurology.

Freud was constantly in search of innovative treatments for mental disorders. He himself dabbled in cocaine for a while, experimenting on himself and recommending it to others as a treatment for mild depression. He prepared a manuscript on its use. Also, Freud attempted to make use of W. Erb's electrotherapy. This too met with little success. Also, while at Vienna General, Freud took a leave to study with Jean Charcot in Paris. He had been impressed by the French neurologist's work in hypnotism to treat hysteria and other mental disorders. Freud experimented with hypnosis for a while, but found that its effects were short-lived. Nevertheless, Freud was impressed with Charcot's work.

It was Josef Breuer's work that impressed him the most. Breuer, also trained in hypnosis, had discovered that by encouraging hysterical patients to talk uninhibitedly about their earliest symptoms and onset of their conditions, symptoms began to subside. Freud commenced working with Breuer to both identify various forms of neuroses that had their origins in trauma and to develop treatments that would enable the patient to tap into his or her unconscious to recall and confront the problem head-on. Freud and Breuer published their findings in 1895 in a paper entitled "Studies in Hysteria."

Breuer eventually took issue with Freud's heavy emphasis on the sexual origins of neurosis and they parted company. Breuer had been a major support to Freud throughout his early career, giving him guidance in his research, relating experiences from his own patients (such as Anna O), and even loaning him money. Nevertheless, Freud threw himself into his work without Breuer and further developed what's come to be called psychoanalytic theory. The culmination of his efforts was a self-analysis in the form of a book entitled *The Interpretation of Dreams.*

EMERGENCE OF PSYCHOANALYTIC THEORY

Freud's *The Interpretation of Dreams* is today considered a classic. However, when it was first released in 1899, it was met not only with a sense of scandal, but with a degree of intense hush in professional circles. In the Talmud it is written: "A dream which is not interpreted is like a letter which is not read." Freud was not the first to see the dream as a window into the unconscious, but his work made him the most important advocate of this notion.

Between 1886 and 1897, Sigmund Freud was settling into his practice in Vienna and embarking upon a project of self-analysis. His father had died in October of the previous year, and he had recurring dreams that he interpreted as responses to his father's death. He spoke regularly about these dreams with his friend Wilhelm Fliess who became his sounding board for his self-analysis. During the book project, Freud appeared to be undergoing an emotional crisis that gave rise to many of the dreams that he experienced. There were glimpses in his dreams of sexual arousal in his infancy by his nanny, visions of his mother's naked body as she undressed on a train journey, and an infantile sexual attraction toward her. Freud recognized fear of his father's power, jealously over his mother's relationship with him, and relief at his death. In this dynamic he found the seed of the Oedipus complex. He also attempted in his dreams to come to terms with his own inner struggles between his despair and his sense of accomplishment. Thus, the book was part psychoanalytic theory and part autobiography. But it sold only 351 copies. His ideas were still not accepted in the professional community of his peers. However, in his first book he had planted the seeds for a new and innovative way of looking at psychic life. It was to be a book that would revolutionize psychology.

Although the unconscious was nothing new, he elaborated on its structure and function. He looked at examining repression as a means of better understanding the current suffering of his patients. Analysis became both a method of research and an innovative therapy. The book was soon followed by *Psychopathology of Everyday Life* (1901) and *Three Essays on the Theory of Sexuality* (1905). His essays on human sexuality even made him more of an iconoclast. In this book he made the case for sex being the most powerful of human drives. Also, it was here that he shocked the world with his discussion of the sex lives of infants and further developed his ideas on the Oedipus complex.

Freud divided psychic life between primary and secondary process. The unconscious mind and its workings and the conscious mind. For Freud, the unconscious terrain was a significant determinant of the conscious life. The conscious life only represented a fraction of who people are and what they are feeling. In the unconscious were housed not only the innate biological drives including hunger, sex, and destructive instincts, but also those things relegated to it—experiences, memories, and feelings that did not or could not find conscious expression. It was described as a shadowy place of taboo thoughts and feelings, things that were hidden away—sometimes deeply buried. For Freud, it was the charge of the therapist to help the patient unearth these mental artifacts in order to better come to terms with the pain and distress the individual was feeling as a consequence of them.

There is great imagery here. Freud would later discuss the structure of the personality as conceptually comprised of an id, an ego, and a superego. The id would reside in the unconscious, dark, violent, and sexual side of the individual—a cauldron of taboos and unbridled passions. As part of the unconscious, it was the source of feelings and drives, most of which Freud viewed as destructive in nature. The ego was the conscious self, functioning to satisfy one's needs, yet complying with societal demands. And the superego was comprised of society's prescriptions for order. The biological energy or drives that comprised the innermost recesses of the animal self was seen as primitive, irrational, and guided by impulse.

THE SOCIOLOGY OF FREUD

In a very real sense, Freud's concept of the human psyche was a transmutation of some of the social, political, and economic dimensions of the world in which he lived. For the most part, it was a world characterized by a Hobbesian notion that humans were innately destructive and lazy and in need of patriarchal control; a world in which women were oppressed both sexually and economically, and a world promoting a false dichotomy between modern civilization and primitive savagery—a place where primitives needed to be controlled for the betterment of human kind. This patriarchal worldview reflected the interest of an elite class. His apprehension about that world caused him to look inward.

It should come as no surprise that Freud's patients were primarily from the bourgeoisie or the petite bourgeoisie. These were people with money who could afford the time to speak with him about their problems. In addition, their problems resembled narratives that writers such as Flaubert and Dostovesky had described in their popular novels. His talk therapy, though borrowed from Breuer, yielded some dramatic prose and important human insights. At a time the world was becoming more impersonal, Freud personalized it. At a time when the world was being made void of spirits and ghosts, he brought them back into town. He had a flair for the dramatic. Early on, he had come to terms with his need to make money as opposed to his desire to be a scientist.

His book did not accrue to him the celebrity he sought; in fact, it made him more suspect in the eyes of his professional colleagues. Although it made him no money, in 1902 Freud received a university appointment. It was made possible for him by a wealthy and influential patient. At the University of Vienna he organized a group of like-thinking men who could intelligently discuss the various facets of psychoanalysis. This group became his inner circle, or as it was formally called the Vienna Psychoanalytic Society. Its members included Alfred Adler and Carl Jung. He was able to work with these and others to organize the first International Psychoanalytic Congress that was held in Salzburg in 1908. By this time, both he and psychoanalysis were becoming more respectable.

At home his wife Martha steadfastly supported him. She bore six children, the youngest of which would be named Anna. Anna would become a renown child therapist and the favorite of her father. The Freud home was nonreligious. Even though his paternal grandfather was a rabbi and his mother a religious woman, Freud demanded to be married in a civil ceremony and refused to keep a kosher home or allow Martha to even light the Shabbat candles. For the most part, Martha played the role of a supportive wife and kept the children a distance from their father.

As his popularity grew, Freud was invited to lecture in the United States at Clark University in Massachusetts in 1909. He was well received by his American audience who appeared to be fascinated with his graphic discussions of sex and violence. For the next several years he continued to lecture, write, and maintain a small practice. The fame he sought gradually became his.

Freud's sociology is an outgrowth of his libidinal theory. It was his notion that the social repression of the sex drive leads to the emergence of civilization as we know it in the West. Much of this is based on Freud's model of tension reduction in which the demands of moralistic society restrict the natural release of sexual and aggressive energy emanating from the body and this restrained energy builds up, attempting to find release. Sublimation (what Freud identifies as a defense) becomes the means of converting this energy into something more acceptable. Still, because the individual never achieves unrestricted release, civilization is characterized by lots of neurotic disorders representing the cost or toll of this conversion. In a very practical sense, Freud is a conflict theorist. Civilization is achieved as a result of a constant tension between *Eros,* the drive for life or pleasure, and *Thanatos,* the death instinct and between the id, representing the mostly destructive libidinal drives, and the superego, which houses societal demands. It is Freud's idea that the quest for erotic connection is associated with the release of sexual energy, so pleasure can only result from tension buildup and release. However, the ultimate quest for pleasure, the ultimate release from all tension is death. This is where death and love meet up. Orgasm, or, as the French put it, *le petite mort,* is the point at which tension disappears after a series of contractions and releases. It is the apex of serenity. Cigarette anyone?

To socialize a child meant keeping his or her destructive instincts in check. Freud believed that the id was kept at bay by diligent parenting. Parents were responsible for imposing societal demands on their children. Children were in turn responsible for self-restraint and developing a conscience as an internalized mechanization of control. Much of this would be predicated on the idea that only the caregiver could care for and give the child what was needed to survive. Without the caregiver there could be only pain and discomfort. Therefore, the child would come to understand absence of mother as a threat to its own survival and a loss of the primary object of pleasure. The child would have to suppress its destructive drives to gain such love and take on societal and parental values. But this would take place at her direction. Any failure to do this could result in withdrawal of love, which ultimately could be understood as being abandoned by the source of comfort and life. Freud identifies this loss as associated with guilt. Guilt is a type of anxiety resulting from a lost love object; it is a fear that the mother might not return with food—with her breast. But the suppression of this energy results in the buildup of sexual and aggressive tension. The focus on childhood, therefore, is an extremely important component of Freudian thought. It is from childhood where most adult problems emerge.

In *Civilization and Its Discontents,* Freud's last major work, he describes the neurotic legacy of sexual repression. This is indeed a sociological masterpiece for many reasons. It ties together many of his concepts to more fully examine the nexus between the social and the sexual dynamics. More than this, it examines the tensions that characterize the world as he knew it.

SEX AND SOCIETY

The reason why we associate Freud with sex is that his work focused on it. Not only did he see sex as the basis for personal development, but he also saw it as an unconscious undercurrent responsible for the tensions that invade modern life. The repressed libido came in many forms. For Freud, all people were sexual beings. He believed in the polymorphous sexual nature of humans. That is, sex was a biological drive that could potentially be released or expressed in a variety of ways. Sex could take an inordinate number of forms. However, it was restricted to "acceptable" sex by the rules governing society. Because perversity is a social construct, people were innately polymorphously perverse. Although they could naturally express themselves sexually in any number of ways, sexual expression was strictly controlled by society.

Freud was writing in Victorian Europe, during which anything outside of heterosexual intercourse between a married man and woman was considered perverse. Thus, homosexuality, bisexuality, sex outside of marriage, extra-marital sex, and even masturbation were deemed perverse. Freud was well aware that sexuality around the world took many forms. Restrictions were not the same from culture to culture. Could this mean that people in other cultures were perverse? Freud, as a social scientist, backed away from this question.

That children had sex lives replete with wishes and fantasies shocked the Victorian world. Yet, Freud cobbled together a sophisticated theory relating the child's sexual development to personality formation and adult character. Through careful study and observation, he hypothesized that there were five stages of psychosexual development: oral, anal, phallic, latent, and genital.

Like other theorists of his era, Freud looked at the "developing" nature of a phenomenon. Children developed in stages both physically and cognitively. They also developed sexually. The oral stage, the first stage, was referred to by Freud as the "cannibalistic" stage. Here the child, who has not yet distinguished himself or herself from the rest of the world, relies heavily on the mouth for discovering, exploring, and ingesting it. The sucking reflex is used both for exploration and pleasure. At this stage, the mouth is an erogenous zone. The baby, toward the end of this stage, begins biting and becomes oral-sadistic, fluxuating between sucking and biting.

The anal phase in sexual development focuses on the anus as the erogenous zone. Feces become the center of much activity—feeling them, playing with them. The child perceives excrement as an extension of the self. Toilet training and bowel control become part of parental training, and this is seen by Freud as the essential basis of all other imposed measures of self-control and restraint. It is seen as a primal basis for civilization. This is followed by the phallic stage.

During the phallic stage, the penis and clitoris are the erogenous zones. Through mother's washing and autoeroticism, the child experiences sexual pleasure. Here, too, the Oedipus complex emerges for boys. The boy's desire for his mother and resentment and fear of his father (castration anxiety) is later resolved by the boy identifying with his father and repressing his wish to kill him. But at the latency stage, around age five to twelve, children appeared to lose focus on sex while exploring the external world. They only gain a renewed interest in puberty or the genital stage. The last stage, the genital stage, has to do with finding erotic fulfillment by connecting to another.

According to Freud, successful passage through these stages is important in the process of psychic maturation. However, there are impediments to achieving a successful mastery and transition. It is here where the psyche can run aground or crash on the jagged rocks of social inhibition, resulting in a failure to achieve healthy maturity. In fact, some personality disorders are seen as resulting from an unsuccessful navigation through these currents. The notion of "fixations" is one way of explaining these. For example, a child undergoes trauma by being weaned too early from the mother's breast. Because of this he or she might develop an oral fixation—finding pleasure primarily in and through the mouth: smoking, sucking on candy, or chewing gum—not being able to move on to the next stage. Constantly chewing on pencils, a fixation on oral sex, even overeating, or talking constantly have been referred to as "oral fixations." Anal fixations can result from trauma at potty training. Being yelled at for a bowel movement at an inappropriate time in early childhood can result in anal retentive personality traits later on in life. Anal retentive people have difficulty "opening up" or "letting go," people who are "tight-assed," or "neat freaks." Anal expulsive personality traits, on the other hand, are sometimes seen as the result of inadequate restriction on the child, or inadequate attention by the parents to bowel control of the child. Here we have sloppiness, disorganization, and anarchy.

PSYCHOANALYTIC SOCIOLOGY

Many of the social issues that we confront can be looked at through a psychoanalytic lens. This is to say that Freud's ideas about such things as the emergence of the superego, the problems resulting from the unresolved Oedipus complex, and the stress in modern life to repress socially unacceptable feelings have been at one time or another converted into practical social theories.

Take, for example, the issue of juvenile crime. Using a classical psychoanalytic approach, one could say that a boy who does not resolve his Oedipus complex is likely to have problems with male figures in authority as he matures. These problems can lead to purposeful acting out against the law, against authority, never being able to hold down a job. Thus, if a boy still is attracted to his mother and resents his father and wants him dead, this feeling can be repressed in the unconscious and emerge in the form of bad behavior revealing that the boy somehow sees all male authority as castrating and emasculating—something he cannot admit to see in his father. In fact, no permanent father figures in the lives of many juvenile offenders has frequently been viewed as a cause of delinquency. This is not merely because there is no one to keep them in line, mothers usually do this; but, it might be a consequence of not developing a strong superego, which Freud saw as bestowed from the father onto the son. Weak superego can result in sociopathic behavior through which the child cannot feel guilt or remorse—where there is no fear of withdrawn love.

Too strong superego is not a healthy matter either. It usually means that the individual has repressed way too much. As the individual suppresses and suppresses his or her destructive urges, tensions mount, often resulting in a catharsis or explosion of emotions—frequently violence for men.

For many Freudians, the basis of our social problems resides in the psyche. However, this explanation reeks of the type of determinism we discussed in an earlier chapter in which all problems, regardless of their complexity, can be traced to one cause. Although psychoanalysis offers many insights, it is not the only tool needed to examine and assess the world's condition. In fact, this paradigm has little efficacy in non-Western, non-European places. It is unlikely to be the way of addressing the global social conditions that we see before us today: racism, poverty, and human injustice.

CONCLUSION

Due to his notorious cigar smoking, Freud was diagnosed with cancer of the jaw in 1923. He was sixty-seven years old. Over the next sixteen years he would have thirty operations. In the 1933, the Nazis rose to power in Germany. Books authored by major Jewish intellectuals were burned at their rallies, including Freud's work. By 1938, the Nazis had taken over

Austria and his passport was confiscated. Because of powerful friends, he and Martha were allowed to leave for London. He lived there until his death in 1938. By that time, his impact on the intellectual and artistic world had been enormous.

BIBLIOGRAPHY

Freud, Sigmund. 2000. *Three Essays on the Theory of Sexuality,* trans. by James Strachey. New York: Basic Books.

———. 1999. *The Interpretation of Dreams,* trans. by Joyce Crick. Originally published in German in 1900. New York: Oxford.

———. 1961. *Civilization and Its Discontents,* trans. by James Strachey. New York: W.W. Norton.

———. 1960. *The Id and the Ego,* trans. by Joan Rivere. New York: W.W. Norton.

Gay, Peter. 1998. *Freud: A Life for Our Time.* New York: W.W. Norton.

Jones, Ernest. 1961. *The Life and Work of Sigmund Freud,* ed. by L. Trilling and S. Marcus. New York: Basic Books.

10

Friedrich Nietzsche: The Will to Power

One of the most vehement critics of the Western Enlightenment and Victorian European society was Friedrich Nietzsche. As a thinker and social philosopher, he challenged the entire course of Western civilization. He condemned what he viewed as a hypocritical faith in God characteristic of his generation. Yet, he also denounced the disenchantment of life and the cultural banality and human emptiness it produced.

Friedrich Nietzsche was born on October 15, 1844 in Röken, a part of Prussia located in rural farmland southwest of Leipzig. His family had a tradition of service to the Lutheran ministry. His father, Karl Ludwig Nietzsche, was a pastor of a small church in Röken and was descended from a long line of clergy. His mother, Franziska Oehler Nietzsche, also came from a family of ministers. For his earliest years, the young Nietzsche lived in a house his father's church provided for the family, which was located adjacent to the sanctuary.

In 1849, when Nietzsche was only five years of age, his father died unexpectedly of a brain disease. Nietzsche's two-year-old brother died six months later. His world was turned upside down by these events. As the eldest boy he was already prized by his mother; now he became the only boy—the treasure of the family. His mother took Friedrich and his sister to Naumburg where they lived for eight years with Nietzsche's paternal grandmother and two aunts. It was there that Nietzsche learned to hate women.

THE EDUCATION OF NIETZSCHE

Nietzsche was surrounded by German prudishness both outside of the home as well as in it. Hard work was demanded and pleasure, particularly sensual pleasure, was stifled. It was growing up in his home that he first experienced the repression that became the subject of much of his work.

At four years of age Nietzsche could read and write. He attended a local *Gymnasium,* but at age of fourteen he was sent to study at a prestigious boarding school at Pforta, just outside of Naumburg. There he became fluent in Greek and Latin and was introduced to the work of Plato and Aeschylus. He was very involved in composing music for piano and writing poetry. His teachers saw him as brilliant. However, he was often plagued by severe migraine headaches and temporary bouts of blindness. In 1864 he enrolled at the University of Bonn where he studied theology and classical philology, sometimes referred to as historical linguistics.

At Bonn, Nietzsche was introduced to the work of some of the leading intellectuals of his time. He spent only one year there and transferred to Leipzig where he discovered the work of modern romantic philosophers such as Schopenhauer and was greatly influenced by his book *The World as Will and Idea.* Nietzsche was also fascinated with the philosopher's radical atheism. He wrote prize-winning papers while at Leipzig, but in 1867 he left the university for the military. There he was assigned to an equestrian field unit. While jumping onto a horse, he slipped and was injured in the chest by the pummel of the saddle. Although he suffered his pain silently, he was eventually forced to give up his commission because of the severity of the injury. He returned to Leipzig and to his studies. He impressed his professors so much that he was recommended to a chair in classical philology at the University of Basel in Switzerland even before he was awarded his doctorate. He was only twenty-four. Upon his acceptance of the position, the faculty of Leipzig immediately awarded him his doctoral degree without ever requiring him to take an examination or write a thesis. In one year he was made full professor at Basel. This was virtually unheard of in the history of the academy.

Nietzsche's serious scholarship begins here. However, it was briefly interrupted by another leave for military service. This time he volunteered as a medical orderly in the Franco-Prussian War. After one month, however, he became exceedingly ill. He developed diphtheria and dysentery and, as some have conjectured, he might have contracted syphilis at that time. When he returned to Basel, he was sick but resumed his teaching and writing. It was at this time that he grew close to Richard Wagner, the flamboyant composer whose music was revolutionizing Europe. Nietzsche had been introduced to Wagner in November 1868 by a colleague. Both men connected immediately. Wagner was just about Nietzsche's father's age and he too had been educated at Leipzig. After moving to Basel, Nietzsche was frequently invited to Wagner's home.

Nietzsche was roused by Wagner's music and looked to him as an inspiration. Like his own work, Wagner's compositions were attacks on the regimentation of nineteenth-century culture. Nietzsche joined Wagner's inner circle of disciples. On his regular visits to Wagner's home, he fell in love with the composer's beautiful young wife, Cosima. A deep and lasting relationship with Cosima failed to materialize.

The relationship between Nietzsche and Wagner was often stormy when the two giant creative spirits clashed ideologically. Even though Nietzsche was enthralled with the hedonism inherent in Wagner's musical spirit, and could do nothing but admire and praise his work, he frequently found Wagner megalomaniacal and reactionary, gravitating more and more toward Teutonic mythology, medievalism, and festering antisemitism.

EARLY WORK

Nietzsche's first book, *The Birth of Tragedy Out of the Spirit of Music,* uncovered what he believed to be an important lie that helped to bolster a false facade of modern European society. Philology was discovering that the historical image of the Greeks as a reserved, refined, and even-tempered was not a completely accurate one. Although Socratic Greek culture was portrayed as rational and constrained, there was another side to the pre-Socratic Greeks that was seldom discussed. There were important groups of Greeks who were much more emotional, more radical, and frenzied in their ways—there were Greek fertility cults and sects that celebrated nature and worshiped the god Bacchus. It was Nietzsche's contention that modern society had all but buried the Dionysian cult to serve its own repressive ends. Where Apollonian society and its self-restraint was supposed to represent a means between extremes of intellect and feeling, it was distorted into an attack against sensuality. Nietzsche's work provided a radical reevaluation of classical Greek culture. He claimed that there were nonrational elements at the heart of all creative work. Reality, for that matter, was a creative undertaking—a product of the unbridled imagination.

The book was published at an important time in European history. It was a time of rampant imperialism and enormous social repression around the globe. Nationalistic myths of cultural superiority and inferiority did not sit well with Nietzsche who assumed the role of a cultural relativist and iconoclast. He eventually gave up his German citizenship and spoke out against the state. When he was not teaching, he was traveling. His views on music and art were nontraditional and based, in part, of his understanding of world cultures.

The early ideas of Nietzsche find themselves at odds with both the rationalist and romantic philosophies of the day. For him, there were no sacred cannons. Upon its release in 1872, *The Birth of Tragedy* gave him something of celebrity status among rebels, but he was shunned by more traditional

Greek scholars whose work he condemned. Upon its release, he was only twenty-eight. The book was dedicated to Wagner.

Between 1873 and 1876, Nietzsche published four meditations, which attacked more traditional thinkers and helped to further his reputation as a renegade. But throughout this period, his health was deteriorating. He took a leave from university teaching in 1876, and further distanced himself from Wagner. He traveled extensively throughout Europe and spent a considerable amount of time in Italy. His eyesight deteriorated and his headaches worsened. In 1879 he resigned his professorship. Nietzsche proposed marriage to a young Dutch piano student, but was turned down. At the age of thirty-seven he began a courtship with Lou Salomé, a student of philosophy who eventually worked closely with Freud. When it was discovered by his mother that he and Salomé were moving to Paris to live with one another, she followed them and broke up the affair.

THE WILL TO POWER

The irony that a man of such powerful personal ideals could so easily quake before the presence of his mother has not gone unheeded by his biographers. Nietzsche's personal life stands in stark contrast to the Ubermensch, or super man, with whom he identified.

Human, All Too Human, The Gay Science, and *Thus Spake Zarathustra* were works that came in quick succession. Each of these books attest to Nietzsche's creativity as a philosopher, poet, and writer of prose and to his importance as a social theorist. *Human, All Too Human* was published in 1886 as a series of aphorisms ranging from two lines to two pages in length. The work was a departure from the typical grand theorizing of the time. Although the work contains the seeds of some of his later ideas, it is primarily a set of reflections on the human social, psychological, and cultural condition. He muses on pleasure and pain and the place of the body in modern life.

The Gay Science, a book whose title was inspired by a French folk song, lays the foundation for modern existentialism. Beginning with the notion that "God is dead," Neitzsche looks at the destruction of God as both an end to the mystical life and the birth of human freedom. It is coping with God's death that opens up an avenue for self-discovery and actualization. It calls for rejecting a world invented by patriarchy. *The Gay Science,* published in 1882, also provides the basis for his own understanding of eternal recurrance, which was taken up in one of his most important works, *Thus Spake Zarathustra,* published in 1885. Perhaps it is here that Nietzsche begins to integrate many of his important ideas into a cohesive philosophy.

This work is filled with naturalistic imagery embedded in the spirit world of the ancient Greeks. A Persian sage becomes the narrator who lays before the reader some of Nietzsche's most profound ideas. Zarathustra takes the reader on a journey of thought and feeling that questions and challenges all that came before. In recognizing the death of a patriarchal God, the human will becomes the sole giver of meaning.

It is important to recognize that Nietzsche's notion of the will is not only psychological, but also physiological and spiritual. It is not merely equated with determination, rather, it creates the world. In this sense the will is highly individualistic—imbedded in the genealogy of existence. The will is the essence of all life. It is innate, vital energy that is simultaneously destructive and creative. Nietzsche does not limit the idea of will to people alone; instead he sees vital energy inherent in the natural world. All matter, organic and inorganic, are struggling for self-realization. For humans, consciousness and everything contained therein are but derivatives of the will. In order to grow, the will must be expressed. But in its expression it must come up against a consciousness that is the product of other wills. It is only through the clash of wills that greatness unfolds.

Nietzsche calls for the abandonment of conscience—a refusal to accept meaning and comply with all values as they are given. One must not accept the consciousness of others and, therefore, must construct a self-consciousness that gives new meaning to the world. He recognizes that the world is articulated by the conflict of powerful wills, not negotiated consensus. Power, therefore, is at the heart of his philosophy. In the clash of wills there can be bloodshed and chaos, but for Nietzsche this is not viewed as a completely bad thing. Only through destruction can creation emerge.

Even in the repression of the will by more devious wills Nietzsche saw value. In the struggle to overcome, in the challenge of advancing despite that range of barricades errected, the will could become that much stronger. The challenge of obstruction is met with creativity and vigor rather than resignation and compliance.

Because God is dead, in that we have literally and figuratively killed him, there is only the vital energy of will to explain the world. Although we might mourn the loss of God, this absence must be recognized as liberating. History is merely the story of the ascent and decline of wills. Societies are stratified because of a will to power. Civilizations rise and fall. For Nietzsche, there are those who express their energy in an effort to create the world and then there are those who assume the passive position; these are people willing to allow the world to be made for them.

Nietzsche vehemently attacks Christianity and posits it as the reason for the rise of autocratic ignorance and slave-like morality. As an advocate of enlightened thought, he claimed that the spectre of repressive religious dogma still haunts the world. Although many claim to be free of religious mysticism, they cling tenaciously to dead moralisms by which individuals were required to sacrifice themselves to a greater good. This good need no longer be God. Thus, the slave values of obedience, subserviance, passivity, altruism, and the like are the legacy of decaying religiosity.

In a utopian vein, Nietzsche calls for personal liberation from the psychological chains that shackle us to the earth. He dreams of human liberation from self-imposed repression and extolls the emergence of a will to power in the form of an Ubermensch, a super man. This is not conditioned by race or nationality. It is a product of the individual will and the energy it represents. It exists by refusing to turn back in order to make amends for the past. It exists by rejecting the pettiness of revenge, which is itself part of slave morality.

LATER LIFE AND WORKS

In 1886 Nietzsche published *Beyond Good and Evil,* followed by *Genealogy of Morals* in 1887. In these works he continues his attack against the elements of Christian morality, such as guilt, that he contends blocks human progress. *Beyond Good and Evil* is a collection of 296 aphorisms dealing with wide-ranging moral issues and containing substantial poetry. *Genealogy,* on the other hand, is comprised of three substantial essays. Here, Nietzsche delves more deeply into the notion of slave and master morality. He views Western morality as a mixture of both. Nietzsche sees no universal morality that is applicable to all. Instead he sees a set of moral principles for each social position or status. There are some moralities appropriate for leading and dominating and others more suitable for following.

Nietzsche remained intellectually productive well into 1888, but his health kept deteriorating. *The Case of Wagner, Twilight of Idols, The Antichrist,* and *Ecce Homo* were all published in that year. Each of these works attest to his brilliance as a thinker and writer. *The Case of Wagner* was a final attack on a man he once held in great esteem. Wagner had been welcomed back into Germany from self-imposed exile. His outspoken antisemitism as well as his growing nationalism presaged the rise of Nazism. For Nietzsche, although a brilliant musician, Wagner's work came to represent both intellectual and social decadence. This book is no mere diatribe against what Nietzsche now viewed as a pathetic figure, it deals with art and its place in the world of ideas and the role of music in culture.

Twilight of Idols, or How One Philosophizes with a Hammer is a book that recapitulates and refines some of his earlier ideas. The title is a parody on Wagner's major opera *Twilight of the Gods.*This book is both an attack on contemporary German society, and an assault against some of the most important intellectual and artistic figures that have profoundly affected Western consciousness. Here is not only a reevaluation of Plato, but also criticisms of Dante, Zola, Darwin, and a whole range of master thinkers. At the same time he praises Caesar, Napoleon, Goethe, Dostovesky and others as more representative of the Ubermensch. *The Antichrist* continues the attack on Western culture by focusing in on the corrupting influence of Christianity and those, such as Saint Paul, who helped to undermine what Nietzsche sees as more noble values associated with the Roman Empire. Finally, *Ecce Homo* is a book of self-praise as well as a review of his own life's work. Although megalomaniacal in its tone, which many attribute to Nietzsche's humor, in it he tries to explain how he came to think, write, and feel the way he did.

THE MADNESS OF NIETZSCHE

Nietzsche Contra Wagner, published in 1888, was his last fully coherent work. Again, he turns to a critique of the man who had long inspired him. Nietzsche's inability to let Wagner go as a subject illustrated his own obsessiveness. For Nietzsche, Wagner seemed to represent his own moral and emotional failures. Wagner was no longer an iconoclast.

It was on a January morning in 1889 that Nietzsche's break with the world would come. The story told is that as he was strolling through the Piazza Carlo Alberto in Turin, Italy Nietzsche noticed a coachman whipping his old horse for what seemed like no reason. As the horse cried out in pain, Nietzsche threw himself in front of the whip and hugged the horse in an effort to save him. He fell to the ground unconscious. When he recovered, he had lost his mind. He would never write another word of his philosophy again.

After a brief stay at a hospital in Basel, he was sent to a sanatorium in Jena. In 1890 his mother took him to her home in Naumburg where he lived with her until her death seven years later. In 1897 his sister Elizabeth, a rabid antisemite, took him in to live with her. With his money she purchased a manson where she stored his original works and the books from his personal library. There she put him on display, charging people to see him.

Nietzsche died in 1890. Through the efforts of his sister, his unfinished notes were edited and published in book form. Nietzsche's works were pitched to Hitler and other Nazis, who were already infatuated with his old friend Wagner and who they saw as the artistic godfather of the Aryan state. Thus, despite his disdain for all that Nazism was to be, Nietzsche was to become a hero to antisemites everywhere.

BIBLIOGRAPHY

Hayman, Roland. 1980. *Nietzsche: A Critical Life.* New York: Oxford University Press.

Hollingdale, R. J. 1973. *Nietzsche.* London: Routledge.

Kaufmann, Walter. 1968. *The Portable Nietzsche.* New York: Viking Press.

Nietzsche, Friedrich. 1967. *Thus Spake Zarathustra.* New York: Heritage Press.

———. 1907. *Beyond Good and Evil.* New York: Macmillan.

Solomon, Robert. 1987. *From Hegel to Existentialism.* New York: Oxford University Press.

11

Georg Simmel: Sociologist as Outsider

Georg Simmel was one of the world's most renown sociologists. Born in Berlin on March 1, 1858, he was the youngest of seven children. His father, Edward Simmel, who had owned a chocolate factory, died when Georg was sixteen, leaving him with a small inheritance. Although Edward and his wife Flora Bodenstein were from middle-class Jewish families, he converted to Catholicism. His children were baptized in the Evangelist Church. Flora, who has been described by Simmel's biographers as a cold and domineering mother, bestowed upon her young son a sense of aloneness—a theme that would work its way into many of his essays.

As a child, Simmel attended the local *Gymnasium,* proceeded to Friedrich Werder secondary school, and then on to the University of Berlin. There he studied with some of the most influential thinkers of his time including the world-renown German art historian, Hermann Grimm. At Berlin, he continued on for his doctorate. Simmel's particular interests were in human psychology and philosophy. Heyman Steinthal and Moritz Lazarus, founders of *Völkerpsychologie* (human psychology), influenced him enormously. His doctoral thesis, *The Nature of Matter According to Kant's Physical Monadology,* brought him the admiration of his teachers and gave evidence of his promise as a thinker and writer.

Upon receiving his doctorate, Simmel taught a variety of courses at the University of Berlin, but he never received a regular appointment to the faculty there. There is significant evidence that he was refused an appointment because of antisemitism at the time. Nevertheless, he was allowed to teach on a fee-for-lecture basis. His lectures on the philosophy of Kant, Schopenhauer, and Nietzsche were heavily subscribed as were his lectures on social psychology and sociology.

Simmel's interest were quite broad. He went from one topic to the next, never landing long enough to settle in completely. His lectures and writings ranged from art history and literary criticism to philosophy. He looked at urban life, at landscapes and ruins; he delved into loneliness, manners, and high fashion. In 1890 he married Girtrude Kinel who was also a philosopher. Together they had one son, Hans, who became a medical doctor. The Simmel home was an important gathering place for intellectual and cultural elites. Simmel, himself, had gained celebrity status. His friends included such eminent twentieth-century figures as Edmund Husserl, Heinrich Rickert, Werner Sombart, and Max Weber. His public lectures were lively and entertaining. The denial of a full-time university position did not stop him from being prolific and engaged. By the time he was forty, he had already authored six books and more than seventy articles. Much of his work was translated into French, Italian, Russian, and English.

In 1900 he published what many consider to be his most important work, *The Philosophy of Money*. Although we will look at some of the ideas in this work later on, in short, it examined the psychological, sociological, and philosophical dimensions of money and its significance to modern life. A central theme in the book as well as a motif running throughout his scholarship was depersonalization, rationalization, and intellectualization associated with modern life. Unlike Marx who saw capitalism as the cause of alienation, for Simmel it was the entire process of modernization.

THE OUTSIDER IN HIS LIFE AND WORK

Shortly after his book on money was published, Simmel was recognized with an official academic appointment to the rank of *Ausserordentlicher* professor, which gave him a title, but still did not allow him full entry into the University of Berlin's traditional professorial rankings. He struggled with his outsider status most of his life. His work frequently expressed this concern.

In much of his writing we see a focus on fragmentation, alienation, and separation from the crowd, and on depersonalization and disconnection. In his essay, "The Stranger," Simmel looks at the outsider as a means of discovering truth. The stranger takes on an almost mystical quality—a wanderer without permanent roots. Simmel proposes that the stranger is often perceived as a danger and a threat to a relatively stable community. Still, strangers and wanderers are people with extraordinary insights given their estranged relationship to the community—emotionally detached from the group and, yet, a part of it. In this way strangers bring in a levelheadedness not found within the walls of an emotionally charged homogeneous grouping. In many instances, they make good judges or fine mediators.

Nevertheless, the stranger is always essential to the definition of the group. He or she is what members of the group are not. The stranger, in this way, helps to define the group. By being an outsider, the stranger can shed light into a closed, and often dark, familiar world. There is almost a heroic quality to the stranger presented in Simmel's essay.

The fleeting nature of the stranger makes the figure a particularly modern one. A lack of bonds leaves the stranger ready to flee at a moment's notice. But in many instances, the stranger lives among those from whom he or she is alienated. Unlike the merchants who are quintessential outsiders entering the community from some distant land and who stay only a short while, there are those who remain, taking on the role of an insider/outsider. Jews were often emblematic of this position. There is both cultural and personal marginalization here.

His discussion of the stranger allows him to deal with the fine line that divides the outside from the inside, the division between attachment and separation. For Simmel, there is a general commonality between the insiders and the outsider. In fact, he goes as far as to contend that unfamiliarity can be an aphrodisiac for romance. The strong appeal of the exotic differences seems undeniable.

Overall, the outsider becomes merely one phenomenon in the complex web of social life warranting greater attention. Simmel was driven to make many of these observations on the interpersonal order. Yet, at no time does he ignore the importance of social structure in determining these relationships. His essays on popular culture and the micro-dimensions of everyday life are frequently related to broader issues such as personal freedom, individuation, and estrangement resulting from modernization. He constantly challenges the illogic of the binary system through which the world is often viewed.

MICROSOCIOLOGY IN A MACRO-CONTEXT

Simmel must be credited with infusing a heavy doses of psychology into the more structurally based field of sociology. His work constantly examined the importance of the individual in the interaction processes. In fact, he saw society as a web of personal interactions. He believed it was his duty as a sociologist to study these patterns of social engagement. By focusing on the micro-order of human relationships, Simmel moved sociology toward a person-centered analysis.

It was Simmel's contention that the macro-order, or the large-scale social structure, was the outcome of intricate patterns of interpersonal relations. Groups, therefore, played an important role in the social order, and the structural makeup of groups determined how participants would behave.

In fact, Simmel was the first sociologist to emphasize the importance of human interaction in groups. In his classic paper "The Isolated Individual and the Dyad," he looks at group size as conditioning both individual and group behavior. In this paper Simmel wants to contrast the group with the individual. For him, the individual was a cognitive unit of experience. It was the group that provided the network of interactions that constituted the basis of society. Still, society was reflective of an ongoing tension between the struggle for individual freedom and the demands of the group.

The isolated individual, he posits, is not really isolated. This is a fiction. Isolation is viewed as a psychological concept. "Isolation is interaction between two parties, one of which leaves, after exerting certain influences," he notes. Although the so-called isolated person might appear to be isolated, he or she remains in the mind of the other party and therefore continues to live and play an active, though indirect, role.

Simmel identifies the dyad (or two-member arrangement) as the simplest of all groups. For him it is the most elementary sociological formation. It contain "the germ and material of innumerable more complex forms." The dyad could be any type of couple: romantic, sexual, business, or social. In such a group the individual is able to achieve a certain level of intimacy that is not possible in a larger group. However, it is simultaneously the most vulnerable of all groups in that the loss of one member destroys it as a group. The threat of termination hangs over this group more than any other group arrangement.

The introduction of only one more person to this dyad radically changes its nature. It become a triad. Now members have three ways of interacting and affecting group dynamics. The third person can play a unifying role, a mediating role, or a divide-and-rule strategy wherein he or she assumes authority over the group.

Group size is a particularly important element in determining both individual and group behavior. Accordingly, large groups increase the opportunity for individual freedom and small groups curtail it. Thus, cities are places in which freedom can be maximized as opposed to small towns. Nevertheless, the individual in mass society is usually consigned to a number of small groups in which freedom is restricted.

IMPERSONALITY AND MONEY

Simmel's *The Philosophy of Money* comes closest to being an entry into macrosociological theory. In this book he reflects on the spirit and meaning of modernity. Unlike Marx, Simmel sees money as a factor not only correlating with alienation, but also related to freedom and objectivity. By ignoring class interests and focusing on how money works in society as a medium of exchange, he is able to ignore the downside of capitalism and to make it a subject of cultural inquiry.

Simmel begins his discussion by examining the notion of value. He proposes that value is created neither by the laborer nor by the market, but by the distance one stands in relation to something one desires. The nature of obstacles set in the way of attaining something made it more or less valuable. Something easy to attain would have less value than something out of reach. However, the idea is more complex than what it appears to be at first blush. Money both distances, or alienates, people from the objects they desire and, simultaneously, becomes the means for transcending this distance. It become an abstraction. It means different things to different people as it provides a personal basis of assigning value.

Unlike Marx who proposed that one gains identity through work, Simmel suggests that one's self is constructed by acquiring objects and making them a part of the self. The self is made complete through these cathexes. He is among the first sociologists to set consumption at the center of all human activity.

It was Simmel's notion that modern capitalism and the money economy ushered in an emphasis on hyper-rationality and personal indifference that in many ways eclipsed the human intuitive and sentimental means of understanding. Money not only depersonalized most relationships, but also emphasized the quantitative over the qualitative ones. People in cities, for example, were more distant and impersonal in their interactions. In his classic essay, "Metropolis and Mental Life," he portrays the modern urban individual as detached, rational, and desensitized to events surrounding him or her. This *blasé attitude,* he contended, was associated with both hightened sophistication and overstimulation. The reserve characteristic of the city dweller was a means of self-protection from overstimulation.

For Simmel, money in cities regulates human existence placing an inordinate value on time and depreciating deep human connections. Thus, money becomes the means of evaluating everything in a detached and matter-of-fact way. Borrowing from Karl Marx, he proposes that all values are translated into money. Nothing can escape such valuation. Time, in cities, was easily translated into money and was elevated in importance.

Philosophy of Money won Simmel recognition among scholars and intellectuals for his intellectual abilities; however, he was much more popular for his shorter essays. In fact, Simmel's essays were translated into English early on and had considerable influence in the United States, particularly on symbolic interactionists and urban theorists working at the University of Chicago in the 1920s and 1930s. His work profoundly influenced the writings of Robert Park, Louis Wirth, and Herbert Blummer of the Chicago school.

LATE CAREER

Affiliation with the field of sociology could be a hazard in Germany at the end of the nineteenth century, especially for an academic. Simmel worked diligently to bring the field a degree of respectability. Along with Ferdinand Tönnies, Werner Sombart, and Max Weber, Simmel helped to found the German Society for Sociology in 1909. Only thirty-nine people gathered for its very first meeting. In 1910, the first sociological conference in Germany was held.

A regular academic appointment was extended to Simmel in 1914 at the University of Strasbourg. Not really wanting to leave the excitement of Berlin, but desiring a formal acceptance into an academic institution, he reluctantly accepted. It appeared to be a mistake. He was separated from the intellectual and cultural life of his home city, and missed his students and friends. World War II broke out right after his move. The lecture halls at Strasbourg were turned into army hospital rooms. Many of his prized students went off to battle.

Interestingly enough, Simmel was an outspoken supporter of Germany and its participation in that war. He gave many patriotic speeches and wrote newspaper pieces defending Germany. He died in 1918.

BIBLIOGRAPHY

Coser, Lewis. 1977. *Masters of Sociological Thought.* New York: Harcourt Brace.

Frisby, David. 1984. *Georg Simmel.* London: Travistock.

Simmel, Georg. 1970. *The Philosophy of Money,* trans. by T. Bottomore and D. Frisby, ed. by D. Frisby. New York: Routledge.

Wolf, Kurt H., ed. 1950. *The Sociology of Georg Simmel,* trans. by K. Wolf. New York: Free Press.

12

W. E. B. Du Bois: Double Consciousness and Race

The Fourteenth Amendment to the American Constitution passed Congress in 1868, giving all former slaves citizenship. It was in this same year, February 23rd to be exact, that William Edward Burghardt Du Bois was born into the small town of Great Barrington, Massachusetts.

If there was ever a sociologist who epitomized the notion of scholar-activist, it was Du Bois. His life would span two centuries of the African American struggle for civil rights. He would make major inroads into the pursuit of justice and equality and, yet, toward the end of his life, would find himself to be an outcast—an enemy of both white liberals and the conservative black leadership.

Du Bois's modest upbringing in a town of 5,000 ill prepared him for the worldwide fame he would accrue and political conflict he would find himself embroiled in later in his life. Born to Alfred Du Bois, an itinerant barber who had migrated from Haiti, and Mary Silvina, a descendant from a hard-working family of farmers and manual laborers of New England, William would look back on his childhood with rose-colored fondness. Although he grew up in poverty, he could only recall how pleasant were his surroundings. Nevertheless, his father disappeared from the home before he reached his second birthday and his mother was left with the parental, and financial, responsibilities for raising him and his older half-brother—a child she conceived before she married Alfred.

Mary Silvina was a woman of particularly strong character. She was strict and religious. Her maternal family was rooted in the Berkshires of

Massachusetts. When Alfred left her, she was forced to move to a run-down house near the edge of town. Soon thereafter she suffered a stroke, which left her partially paralyzed. Nearby family helped as much as they could.

It was in Great Barrington where Du Bois would attend integrated public schools and learn his earliest lessons on racism. He distinguished himself in elementary school and was one of only a few black students from town to go on to high school. There, under exceptional tutorage, he found himself excelling. It was the principal of his high school who identified Du Bois's leadership potential and worked with his teachers to prepare him for college. He took college preparatory classes in Latin, Greek, and the classics. He never missed a day of school. It was in high school where he was introduced to journalism and started writing regular articles for the New York *Globe*. This was a newspaper published by a young black progressive, T. Thomas Fortune. Du Bois had fallen in love with the boldness of the publication that had a national distribution. In fact, he was the Great Barrington distributor of the weekly before he started writing for it. It was an unpaid job, but one in which Du Bois could find expression on issues of race and class. He was only 15.

As he grew into adolescence, Du Bois began distancing himself from the faith of his mother—a rigorous Calvinism that was first associated with the Episcopal Church, but later became manifest in her membership in The First Congregationalist Church in Great Barrington. Still, he regularly attended services there as well as classes in the church's Sunday school. He constantly challenged his teachers.

Just before he was ready to graduate from high school, his mother died of a stroke in March 1885. He was taken in by a relative. He was just 17 years old and his life was radically changing. Although much of his time had been spent in the care of his mother, he was now free of the responsibility.

Du Bois had aspirations for Harvard, but finances and strict admissions standards kept him out. Through the efforts of his high school principal and members of the Congregationalist Church he was awarded a scholarship to Fisk University. Fisk was a Congregational institution for Negroes in Nashville, Tennessee. Although it was not his first choice, he did see it as a challenge. Du Bois had only read about the blatant racism many were experiencing in the South. He read stories about lynchings and activities of the Klan in the *Globe*. Now he would observe all of this close-up.

EDUCATION AND SCHOLARSHIP

Fisk was an important turning point in Du Bois's life. The college provided a classical liberal arts education to sons and daughters of former slaves. These were young men and women from around the country—bright, articulate, and industrious. By the time Du Bois entered his freshman year, admissions standards at Fisk were quite high. Many of his classmates came from poverty; many were sons and daughters of ministers; others came from wealth.

Du Bois took up residence in the men's dorm. By the end of his first year there, he was already a contributing editor to the Fisk newspaper, the *Herald,* and editor of the Fisk literary magazine. He did well in his studies and became a favorite of many of his teachers, all but one of whom were white.

In an effort to support himself through college, Du Bois found employment as a school teacher in the rural countryside far from the Fisk campus during the summers. It was a challenge working with the locals, but one from which he gained more knowledge about race and race relations. Racism was rampant in the South, and lynchings of young black men were at epidemic proportions. His experiences bolstered his dedication to politically confronting the issue of race in the United States.

Upon graduation from Fisk, Du Bois applied for admission to Harvard. He received a scholarship and settled into the life of Cambridge. Taking classes with William James, the leading American pragmatist and psychologist, he developed a keen interest in social psychology. He would also take courses with the philosophers George Santayana and Max Eastman, and American poets T. S. Eliot and Robert Frost. He worked hard at his studies and soon was awarded a bachelor's degree, a master's degree, and a doctorate. Although he excelled at Harvard, he found himself socially estranged from the institution. He would often say that he was "in" Harvard, but not "of" Harvard. Still, he was the first African American to receive a Ph.D. there. Before being awarded his doctorate, however, he won a scholarship to study at the University of Berlin. His interest in economics and sociology led him to Max Weber, with whom he maintained a continued correspondence after leaving Germany. Weber sparked in Du Bois a new concern with perception and cultural understanding.

Du Bois's dissertation, *The Suppression of the African Slave Trade to the United States of America, 1638–1870,* was an important historical study. Although it received little critical acclaim, it was a well-documented, comprehensive view of the United States violation of international law banning the Atlantic slave trade and its historic role in the economics of slavery.

Upon completion of his graduate studies, Du Bois found a teaching position at Wilberforce College in Ohio. Wilberforce was surrounded by Ohio farmland. He spent two years there teaching Greek and Latin while polishing articles written for various journals. It was at Wilberforce that he would develop a cadre of strong friendships and would eventually meet Nina Gormer. Gormer was the daughter of a hotel chef from Grand Rapids, Michigan. She was a student in one of Du Bois's classes. They were married on May 12, 1896.

At age 28, Du Bois received a one-year teaching appointment at the University of Pennsylvania. He and Nina happily moved to Philadelphia where they settled into a one-room apartment. It was in Philadelphia that he would conduct one of the most important social surveys of urban African Americans, *The Philadelphia Negro*. This was a comprehensive study of the black population of the city's Seventh Ward. Over five thousand respondents were interviewed. It was published in 1899. The book constitutes the first major work in African American sociology, or, what would later be called "Black Studies."

Winning him considerable notoriety, Du Bois was offered a teaching position at the University of Atlanta. There he served as an assistant professor in the economics department. Later in his career, between 1924 and 1934, he served as chair of the sociology department. Atlanta became a base of operations for Du Bois's intellectual life as well as his political and social activism. In 1903, he published his most influential work, *The Souls of Black Folk*. Part autobiographical, part scholarship, part theoretical, and part poetry, the book proclaimed that "the problem of the twentieth century is the problem of the color line." Here he attempts to understand the meaning of that problem personally: its significance to African Americans as a group, its importance to white people, and its influence on the contours of American society. In this book, he begins developing a most important idea that will run through his later works. This idea has to do with race and consciousness.

THE VEIL AND DOUBLE CONSCIOUSNESS

Perception was key to understanding the role of race in the United States. Du Bois had often reflected on the powerful dynamic of growing up as a person of color in a predominantly white society. In fact, for Du Bois, the African American not only saw the world from the vantage point of a member of American society, but also from the perspective of a marginalized race. That is to say, African Americans shared a double consciousness, one of the American and one of the black American. This bifurcated identity was a product of both overt and covert discrimination. The African American, therefore, had a "twoness" of being—two souls; two selves warring against each other; two very distinct identities. Throughout life, suggests Du Bois, there is a struggle to heal the split in identity, to merge the two parts. However, assimilation would only result in the loss of black identity and the "bleaching of the African soul." And America could not stand becoming Africanized.

Those of color seemed to be separated from the white society by a veil. This veil formed an unbreachable barrier separating the two groups. Du Bois speaks of this in terms of a sense of alienation and estrangement. But, again, the veil also speaks to a distorted communication and perception characteristic of two groups. The separation and segregation between white and black meant that there was little likelihood of mutuality, or what we might now call intersubjectivity. Yet, to be an African American has almost always meant to look at oneself through the eyes of others; to evaluate oneself through standards not of your making.

The veil is also emblematic of a certain type of insight for Du Bois. "The Negro," he claims, "is a seventh son, born with a veil and gifted with second-sight in this American world—a world which yields him no true self-consciousness, but only lets him see himself through the revelation of the other world." But what of this second sense? What of this gift of second-sight? The double consciousness has buried within it something redeeming. This is the ability to see the world through the eyes of others, through the eyes of the oppressor. Although this sense might be available to others, it is particularly associated to those who have been objects of discrimination, particularly, those who were thrust into the position of slaves.

Certainly, there is Hegel, Marx, and Weber making their presence known in this expostulation about consciousness and the veil. There is the Hegelian master-slave struggle for identity and consciousness; there is the sense of alienation and estrangement present in both Hegel and Marx, the sense of true and false consciousness. There is also Max Weber's notion of *Verstehen,* or insight that one can only have as an outsider who is inside.

It is Du Bois's position that double consciousness becomes a means of self-survival. It is essential for the preservation of African Americanism in a sea of racism and intolerance. Although there was no telling of what might transpire in the future, it was necessary for African Americans to hold on to their identity and not trade it in for some compromised whiteness. These theoretical suppositions were cornerstones for much of Du Bois's social activism.

THE STRUGGLE FOR CIVIL RIGHTS

These ideas that called for the survival of black identity became powerful undercurrents of the Black Power Movement in the United States in the 1960s. But when Du Bois discussed these at the beginning of the twentieth century, he was considered an outspoken radical.

Du Bois often found himself at odds with African American leaders of his day. He frequently criticized Booker T. Washington for his stand on civil rights. Washington had been raised up to a position of national prominence by those in white society attracted to his minimalist view of social change. In his so-called "Atlanta Compromise" speech of 1895, he called for black people to neglect radical changes in voting and civil rights in exchange for technical training and jobs in the trades. Only upon economic advancement should these things be pursued. He opened the Tuskegee Institute in Alabama with financial help from northern industrialists. There he taught young African American men trades such as printing, tailoring, and plumbing, but he also prepared young people to enter into domestic service. Washington was acclaimed a race hero nationwide and was awarded honorary doctorates at Harvard and Dartmouth. Du Bois took issue with this position. He instead called for greater social activism in the area of civil rights. In response to Washington's belittlement of higher education for African Americans, Du Bois called for the "Talented Tenth," a group of 10 percent of the black population that would be highly educated and assume important positions of leadership in business and government. For Du Bois, Washington was too self-serving and limited in his vision of what the near future could hold.

From his position as an academic Du Bois was able to launch, or help to launch, a number of important political programs. The one for which he is probably most renown was the Niagara Movement organized in 1906. This was in response to Washington's call for good behavior, vocational training, and patience. Niagara was to pull together those who would help construct a civil rights agenda, lobby for the interests of African Americans, and establish an important political dialogue on civil rights. Because this group was prevented from meeting in the United States, they met on the Canadian side of Niagara Falls, New York. This organization became the precursor to the National Association for the Advancement of Colored People or the NAACP, established in 1909. Du Bois was named editor of the organization's regularly published magazine, *Crisis*.

After a trip to France in 1919 where he served as the NAACP's representative to the Paris Peace Conference, he organized the first Pan African Congress to bring attention to the plight of Africans around the world. It was Du Bois's position that for Africans to be free anywhere they had to be free everywhere. The conference was held in 1923, but the turnout was embarrassingly small. The same year, he traveled to Africa to further its cause. In 1927, Du Bois was invited to Russia. While there he noted the inroads the Russians were making in addressing some of the important social problems, including poverty.

Back in the United States, he became the target of FBI investigations. By 1933 he gave up on the importance of integration. This caused an ideological split between him and the mostly white hierarchy of the NAACP. He was asked to resign his position as editor of *Crisis*.

In the late 1930s he returned to academia. He continued writing and publishing. In 1940 he helped pull together the Fifth Pan African Congress. This was the most successful meeting by far. Guests included Kwame Nkruma, Jomo Kenyatta, and more. Du Bois was elected president of the Congress.

By the 1940s and 1950s, he was being hounded by the American intelligences services. The fact that he joined the American Communist Party and blasted American racism in the press did not help matters. After the bombing of Hiroshima and Nagasaki, he called for the outlawing of atomic weapons. Shortly thereafter, he was condemned by the United States Secretary of State as a Soviet propagandist. The Justice Department ordered him to register as a foreign agent under the new Foreign Agent Act, which was similar in some respects to the Patriot Act of today.

CONCLUSION

Du Bois's movement to the left was gradual. He became increasingly outspoken and frustrated with the lack of social progress being made in the United States by people of color. In 1961 he was invited by President Nkruma to Ghana where he was appointed as Secretariat for the *Encyclopedia Africana*. He eventually became a citizen of Ghana.

In 1963, when Martin Luther King led a march on Washington, Du Bois led a similar demonstration on the streets of Accra, the capital of Ghana, calling for rights for African peoples around the world. He died on August 27, 1963 at the age of ninety-five.

BIBLIOGRAPHY

Du Bois, W. E. B. 1989. *The Souls of Black Folk*. New York: Bantam.

———. 1968. *Autobiography of W. E. B. Du Bois: A Soliloquy on Viewing My Life From the Last Decade of its First Century*. New York: International Publishers.

Lewis, David Levering, ed. 1995. *W. E. B. Du Bois: A Reader*. New York: Henry Holt.

———. 1993. *W. E. B. Du Bois: Biography of a Race*. New York: Henry Holt.

13

Antonio Gramsci: Critique of Hegemonic Capitalism

Antonio Gramsci was both a radical political activist and a profound social theorist. As an important journalist, outspoken antifascist, and a founder of the Communist Party of Italy, his life was devoted to issues of human liberation and social justice. He spent the last ten years of his life in an Italian prison for his opposition to the fascist state.

Born in the village of Ales in the province of Cagliari in southern Sardinia (a Mediterranean island off the Italian coast) on January 22, 1891, Antonio Gramsci was the fourth of seven children. His father, Francesco Gramsci, was Registrar in the nearby town of Ghilarza; his mother, Giuseppina Marcais Gramsci, was an educated and cultured woman, a rarity for the social class her family occupied.

At the age of four, Gramsci suffered a fall that caused him a severe spinal injury. Aggravated by rickets, which he acquired at an earlier age, the accident produced a curvature of the spine and, according to his family, left him hunchbacked and dwarfed. He was humiliated and often ostracized by his playmates. Adding to his shame, his father was arrested two years later and sentenced to prison on charges of embezzlement and falsification of documents. This incident severely hampered the well-being of the family. Even though his mother took in work as a seamstress, it was hardly enough to support the children.

Gramsci's early education proved him to be a boy of enormous intellectual promise. However, his schools were inadequate. Poor facilities and teachers led him to compensate by becoming an avid reader. He loved stories about escape and adventure. By the age of seven he had become an avid reader of Robert Louis Stevenson. He did well in all of his schoolwork. However, at age eleven, upon graduating from grade school, he was obligated to work for two years to support his family.

In 1908 he was sent to live with his older brother, Gennaro, in the city of Cagliari where he attended high school, Dettori Liceo. Gennaro was a socialist activist and politically involved with the local labor union. Antonio did well in his studies, especially in Greek, Latin, Italian, history, and mathematics. An influential teacher, Raffa Gazia, taught him about socialism and class struggle and inspired his reading of radical intellectuals such as Benedetto Croce and his humanist philosophy. Gazia was the publisher of *L'Unione Sarda,* a radical newspaper for which Gramsci worked in the summer of 1910. It was essentially through his brother and Gazia that his radical ideals began to coalesce.

Winning a scholarship to the University of Turin, on the Italian mainland, in 1911, he left Sardinia to become a full-time university student. He was now nineteen. Turin was cold and inhospitable. Everything was enormously expensive compared to Cagliari and he struggled to make ends meet. Gramsci retreated into a world of books and ideas. Under the guidance and tutorage of Umburto Cosmo, a professor of Italian literature and Dante scholar, he played with the idea of becoming a professor of historical linguistics. It was with his philosophy professor, Annibale Pastore, that he studied Marxist theory.

Gramsci's love of literature and the art, most particularly theater, is essential to our understanding of his politics. Cultural revolution becomes the foundation for political change, according to Gramsci. Not only is he to become a man of keen political insight, but an important critic of contemporary culture.

In 1913, through the efforts of his college friend, Angelo Tasca, Gramsci joined the youth federation of the Socialist Party. He also began working as a professional journalist. Unable to afford tuition and desiring to devote his life to radical journalism, he quit the university in 1915. He became editor of *Il Grido del popolo,* a radical worker's paper, and a columnist for the Turin edition of *Avanti,* the Italian socialist newspaper. The pieces written for these publications helped broaden the focus of the socialist movement in Italy. These were not political diatribes, but works that attempted to open up a new cultural order. Predicated on his belief that the ruling class maintained its power through cultural consensus, he combined political critiques and debate with literature and theater review.

The early twentieth century saw the world in turmoil. Classes were becoming more and more polarized. World War I had broken out and insurgency movements were sprouting up everywhere. Italy, like Russia, found itself to be a cauldron of political unrest. Both countries struggled against the remnants of feudalism and were coming to terms with an emerging capitalistic system that did not fit well with the cultural sentiments of the people, most of whom were poor.

During World War I, Gramsci threw himself deeply into the movement and into the politics of world socialism. Unlike Georg Simmel, he opposed the War and the imperialism it seemed to represent. He carefully followed the revolutions in Russia. He outspokenly challenged the Socialist Party of Italy for its conservativism and gathered young radicals to form a Communist faction of the party. A new newspaper, *L'Ordine Nuovo,* was founded that exposed fascism as a threat unleashed on workers by the ruling class and focused on the possibility of revolution. In it Gramsci proposed the establishment of factory councils that would become the vanguard for a new political order, or a new worker's democracy. Despite the Socialist Party resistance, fifty thousand workers throughout Turin joined into such councils at their respective plants.

In the fall and summer of 1920 workers in Turin went on strike. But the Socialist Party failed to support them. Workers not only incurred mass firings, but also police beatings and the vicious assaults by what appeared to be the attack dogs of the ruling class elites, local bands of armed fascists. The rise of these groups served the interests of their capitalist sponsors. This was becoming a major concern not only to leftist intellectuals of the day, but to all who opposed the rise of a vicious totalitarianism.

Realizing that the Socialist Party was no longer to be depended on, in 1921 Gramsci and others formed the Italian Communist Party. Taking a page from Lenin, he proposed that the new party would work within the parliamentary system to expose the self-serving program of the Italian bourgeoisie. On the other hand, he called for a total armed defeat of the emerging fascism that threatened the lives of workers.

In 1922, through the efforts of those capitalists and landowners fearful of worker and peasant revolution, Mussolini was brought to power.

In May 1922, Gramsci was invited to Moscow as a delegate to the Comintern of the Third International. When he arrived, failing health forced him to spend six months in a convalescent home near the edge of the city. But as soon as his health was restored, he met with Lenin and discussed strategies for the defeat of fascism. He spent a year and a half in Moscow. While there, he met his wife-to-be Julia Schucht, a violinist and Communist Party member. Prevented from returning to Italy because of an arrest warrant issued for him, he settled into Vienna where he awaited word that he had been elected to the Italian Parliament's House of Deputies. As a result of this, he gained parliamentary immunity.

He returned to Italy in May 1924 and was elected secretary general of the Italian Communist Party. He threw himself into winning party members to his radical revolutionary ideals. Top items on his agenda were the defeat of fascism and the promotion of a mass revolt by peasants and workers. The real challenge was bringing together a very divided political left in an effort to bring down Mussolini.

The political climate around him was deteriorating. The Mussolini gained dictatorial powers and immediately rescinded most constitutional rights, including the right of parliamentary immunity that had protected Gramsci and other legislative communists up until that time. On November 8, 1926, Gramsci was arrested in Rome and charged with promoting the overthrow of the fascist state and Italian capitalism.

PRISON AND THE PRISON NOTEBOOKS

Gramsci was committed to solitary confinement at the Regina Coeli prison in Rome. Shortly thereafter he was transferred to the island of Ustica off the Sicilian coast where he was interned for six weeks with fellow Communist Party leader, Amadeo Bordiga. Together with Bordiga, Gramsci organized a school to educate and raise the political consciousness of prisoners. In January 1927, he was transferred to the San Vittore Military Prison in Milan. He remained there while Fascist officials gathered information against him for his trial. Finally, on June 4, 1928, Gramsci was sentenced to twenty years in prison by a military tribunal headed by a Fascist army general.

After spending a month at Regina Coeli where he was found to be suffering from chronic uremia, he was transferred to a special medical prison at Turi in Bari on the southern Italian coast. All the while, his health was further declining. Still, he was not only able to write over three thousand pages of manuscript, but with the help of his sister-in-law, was also able to smuggle these papers out of Italy to the Soviet Union. The work covered not only social theory, but also politics, literature, philosophy, education, and cultural theory. It was an amazing set of essays, which would become known as the *Prison Notebooks*. Even though it is impossible to cover here even a fraction of the broad ranging material that was of concern to Gramsci in his notebooks, it is important to gain some insights into his sociological thought.

Perhaps the most important consideration of Gramsci's sociology is his socialist humanism, which frequently conflicted with what he viewed as orthodox Marxist determinism. This is not to say that Gramsci rejected Marxism. In fact, he owed much to Karl Marx, his theory of class conflict, and his more humanistic thoughts. He found himself at odds with what he considered to be a very crude Marxist understanding of the rise of the bourgeoisie.

As noted earlier, Gramsci viewed the condition of Italy prior to the rise of fascism as preparing the way for the development of primitive capitalism. According to Gramsci, Marx failed to adequately assess the importance of culture to the rise of the ruling class. By controlling culture and its inherent values, people could shape social organization, including the political and economic machinery. This is what happened in Italy.

Gramsci uses the term hegemony to represent the dominance of one social class and its value system over another. Those in power rule not simply with an iron fist, but through the delicate and strategic engineering of a cultural consensus. In this case it was capitalism.

The position of hegemony represents not merely economic dominance with all other control emanating from it, but the ability of the capitalist elite to promote its particular way of seeing the world and imposing that worldview on others through cultural means. To those of the working class, this worldview becomes "natural" and "common sense." Gramsci sees hegemony as the "fortress" and the "earthworks" propping up the state.

The idea of common sense is an outcome of a mass-produced social consensus. It is never a given based on crude economic dominance and political power, but is won through ongoing struggle. Thus, Gramsci's argument is one that focuses on power as a result of winning "hearts and minds."

Drawing upon his experiences in Italy, he contends that the consent of the masses emerges from the prestige and confidence held by the hegemony. This too is manufactured. Without cultural and intellectual forces supporting it, no ruling class can stand. Hegemony is a product of intellectual and moral leadership. Gramsci saw the Church clerics and the intellectuals in southern Italy colluding with the emergent capitalist class and laying a foundation for fascism. The failure of the Italian working class to overthrow its oppressors in Turin in 1920 could be laid at the feet of intellectuals who accepted the ideological outlook of the capitalists. Most of those intellectuals tended to be administrators serving the interests of the existing hegemony. Gramsci asserts that the working class cannot win power without its own intellectual and cultural leadership and without offering up an alternative worldview—one that more accurately reflects the proletarian experience and value system. Such a perspective makes more sense to those it serves.

Overcoming the dominant ideology is a challenge, especially when the majority of the working class is willing to accept it. Even though reforms are deemed just and good, there is little questioning of the value system that underlies capitalism. Thus, education is necessary for change to occur.

It is education and cultural reform that constitute the foundation for any successful revolution. Although the system is already established to promote interests of the ruling class, Gramsci calls for the use of informal education to advance the interests of the revolution. He calls for a host of new working-class intellectuals committed to serving the interests of the community of which they are a part. The new educational system, he envisions, will prepare children to become critically thinking adults ready to rule or control those who do.

CONCLUSION

In 1933 Gramsci was again transferred to the Cusumano prison clinic in Formia, on the shore of the Mediterranean, in Italy's southern coast. His health was rapidly declining. There he remained until 1935 when he had another medical problem and was transferred to Quisisana Hospital in Rome. On the morning of April 27, 1937 he died of a massive cerebral hemorrhage.

In the true revolutionary spirit, prison became not an end for Antonio Gramsci, but an opportunity. A man of great character, he was both a scholar and an activist. His *Prison Notebooks* shed light not only on history, but also on the sociology of class struggle.

BIBLIOGRAPHY

Fiori, Giuseppe. 2000. *Antonio Gramsci: Life of A Revolutionary.* New York: Pluto Press.

Fogacs, David, ed. 2000. *The Gramsci Reader.* New York: NYU Press.

Gramsci, Antonio, and Boothman, Derek, ed. 1995. *Further Selections from the Prison Notebooks.* Minneapolis, MN: University of Minnestoa Press.

14

The Frankfurt School: Horkheimer and Adorno

Critical theory has been described by sociologist George Ritzer as "largely comprised of criticism of various aspects of social and intellectual life." Marx, in his work, is credited with having given shape and direction to much of what we refer to as critical theory. Still, most critical theorists find fault with what they often refer to as orthodox Marxist determinism—the idea that the economy directs all aspects of culture.

Historically, some of the most significant critical theory came from Weimar, Germany and specifically emerged from a social research institute affiliated with the University of Frankfurt in the 1920s. Founded on February 3, 1923 at the University of Frankfurt, the *Institut für Sozialforschung* (Institute for Social Research) was comprised of a dedicated cadre of left-wing intellectuals who hoped to bring a socialist enlightenment to the European heartland through a program of scholarly activities. Felix J. Weil, a student of politics, conceived the idea, which was endorsed by his father, Herman Weil, a prosperous grain merchant. Along with a number of his fellow students, including Max Horkheimer, Friedrich Pollock, Leo Lowenthal, and Charles Grunbürg, he embarked upon scholarly endeavors aimed at critical examination of contemporary society. Grounded in neo-Marxian thought, these researchers stressed the importance of history and philosophy for illuminating causes of social ills.

Even though each of these theorists shared a hope for a more socialistic world, their work was in no way utopian. The critical questions they raised, relative to capitalism, provided an avenue for social and cultural critiques of their own society. The Frankfurt school was a term often used interchangeably with the Institute. But there was extraordinary autonomy among the scholars who comprised it.

Max Horkheimer assumed the directorship of the Institute in 1931 and continued as its guiding force well into the 1950s. The institute funded the work of such renown intellectuals as Theodor Adorno, Herbert Marcuse, Erich Fromm, Paul Lazarfeld, Paul Messing, and, though not an insider, Walter Benjamin.

In 1933 the Institute was forced to leave Nazi-controlled Germany and relocate in Geneva, Switzerland. However, in 1935 the work of the Institute was relocated to New York's Columbia University where key intellectuals found a haven safe from strict censorship, Nazi persecution of Jews, and the internment of communists. Of course, they brought a large endowment with them. The unusual teaming up of the conservative Columbia University and a Marxist institute was beyond interesting. The then-president of Columbia Nicholas Murray Butler gave space to Horkheimer at 429 West 117th Street and agreed to a loose affiliation. Columbia faculty, by and large, were supportive. Soon Horkheimer, Pollock, and Marcuse were living in New York. Adorno stayed behind. Finally, at Horkheimer's behest, he joined his friends in New York in 1938.

UNIQUENESS OF THE FRANKFURT APPROACH

Although the theory that emerged from the Frankfurt school was particularly dark and leftist, in many ways it was an extension of the Marxian humanist tradition—a line of reasoning that placed the individual central to all else. Capitalism was viewed as a dehumanizing force and an engine of alienation. Horkheimer, Adorno, Marcuse, and others were not only inspired social theorists, but also significant philosophers, well schooled both in the classical tradition as well as in Kant and Hegel, and capable of integrating these ideas into a unique critique of modernity. They were also profound sociologists who frequently drew on the work of Max Weber. It was through the Frankfurt school that Freud, Nietzsche, Weber, and Marx were somehow joined together to provide a critically perceptive framework for better understanding modern social life.

Frankfurt theorists took issue with what they termed "the Enlightenment project" and what they saw as its overly confined notion of reason in the service of the advancement of civilization. They resented the segmentalization of the individual into thinking-feeling beings and rejected the emphasis on positivism and pragmatism in social research. They promoted a reflective criticism of society, culture, and the arts. Many looked at the psychological conditions wrought by the forces of modern capitalism. Some examined authoritarian personalities, narcissism, and sadomasochism as outcomes of these forces. They studied psychoanalysis and examined the irrationality of human beings. The work in which they engaged varied: music criticism, theater reviews, psychology of mass behavior. The Frankfurt theorists were as comfortable looking at the alienated worker as examining the political significance of a new opera.

Those who were part of this intellectual program were themselves seminal thinkers. Each contributed on an individual level to a new range of dialogue bridging the gap between European classicism and avant-garde experimentism. The politics of social life was not obvious in their work, but it was inherent in it.

HORKHEIMER AND ADORNO: THE DIALECTICAL DUO

One of the central figures of critical theory and a founding member of the Frankfurt school was Max Horkheimer. Born in Stuttgart in 1895, he was the only son of an upper-middle-class family. Moritz Horkheimer, his father, was a stern disciplinarian. He had worked his way up in the textile business to become a successful business owner. Although the family identified themselves as German, they maintained a Jewish household and the home was kept kosher.

It was anticipated that the young Horkheimer would some day take over his father's business, but this was not to happen. As a adolescent, he was enraged at his father's treatment of the factory workers and wanted no part of it. He emersed himself in political and literary work and contemporary Expressionistic art. Ibsen, Zola, and Kropotkin intrigued him. After World War I, Horkheimer studied at the University of Frankfurt where he became fascinated with social theory and took seminars with Karl Mannheim and Paul Tillich. He became intrigued with the subject of psychoanalysis and attended lectures at the Frankfurt Psychoanalytic Institute.

He studied both philosophy and psychology and went to the University of Freiburg where between 1920 and 1921 he studied with the famed social linguist Edmund Husserl and his assistant Martin Heidegger. After completing his dissertation on Kant, he became a *Privatdozent,* an unsalaried lecturer at Frankfurt, teaching the history of philosophy. His personal scholarship led him to find in Marx and Schopenhauer a high degree of complimentarity. Here was a philosophy of pathos and revolution that seemed ripe for marriage.

In 1930, he was appointed head of the Institute for Social Research and, simultaneously, made a professor of social philosophy—a new position that was created for him at the university. As director of the Institute, he gradually became coordinator of what came to be known as the Frankfurt school and used his university position and the Institute endowment to steer the institute's work away from empirical work toward more social philosophical endeavors. Under his leadership the Frankfurt school took on a particular caste—mostly Jewish assimilationist males from upper-middle-class backgrounds: Herbert Marcuse, Leo Lowenthal, Friedrich Pollock, Erich Fromm, and others. In the 1930s he produced a steady stream of work and coaxed others to do likewise.

Almost single-handedly Horkheimer rescued the Frankfurt school and many of its contributors from the wrath of Adolf Hitler.

Theodor Adorno, his close colleague, was born Theodor Ludwig Wiesengrund on September 11, 1903. He would change his name late in his career. His father Oskar Weisengrund was a wealthy merchant and his mother, Maria Calvelli-Adorno, was a woman of noble Genoese descent.

It was Adorno's mother who would have the greatest impact on him. She was a singer and a musician and, despite her Catholic background, was as much as a secularist as Adorno's father who was of Jewish descent. She introduced her son to the beauty of music and secured regular piano lessons for him. As a child he attended the Kaiser Wilhelm Gymnasium in Frankfurt and by the age of fifteen had already read Kant's *Critique of Pure Reason*. Throughout his early education, Adorno was sensitized through his readings to human pain and suffering. By the time he was enrolled in the Johann Wolfgang Goethe University, he had already published a paper on Expressionism and another on an opera written by his piano teacher, Bernhard Sekles. In college, he concentrated on course work in philosophy, psychology, sociology, and music. By the age of twenty-one, he had earned a doctorate in philosophy.

It was Hans Cornelius, an esteemed Kantian philosophy professor, who had supervised Horkheimer's work who profoundly influenced Adorno as well. He supervised both men's dissertations. It was in a Cornelius seminar on Husserl in 1922 that Horkheimer and Adorno met. Aside from coming from upper-middle-class backgrounds where art and intellectualism were stressed, they shared many of the same socialistic sympathies and ideals.

Leaving the university, Adorno went to study music and composition with the innovative Alban Berg in Vienna whose opera, *Wozzeck,* impressed him tremendously. It was as a student of Berg that Adorno became involved with a circle of ground-breaking musicians including Arnold Schoenberg.

In 1927, he returned to Frankfurt to continue his studies to prepare himself for university teaching. He was just twenty-four. Although he wrote several music compositions, his music never gained critical acceptance. He turned to writing criticism and between 1928 and 1932 edited a journal, *Anbruch,* on the new music coming out of the Vienna circle. During this period, however, he was investing more of his energies in working with Horkheimer and others at the Institute for Social Research. He became close friends with the renown Marxist Ernst Bloch and with Bertolt Brecht, Kurt Weill, and Walter Benjamin. His circle now encompassed artists, musicians, philosophers, and critics.

It was in the 1920s that Adorno began to integrate a newly discovered (for him) Hegelian approach to Marx in his writings. Much of this influence came from Horkheimer. At the same time, he became fascinated with the intellectual implications of psychoanalysis in examining the phenomena of social life. When he was in Vienna, he had gone to lectures given by Sigmund Freud and his followers.

All throughout this time Adorno was working with his mentor, Hans Cornelius, for a *habilitation,* or thesis, that would give him access to university teaching. But by the early 1930s, bands of fascists were beginning to exert their influence, and antisemitism was becoming a more menacing force. Cornelius, seeing the writing on the wall, took off for Finland just prior to Adorno's winning a teaching appointment. But by 1933, Hitler had come to power.

Although most who were affiliated with the Frankfurt school fled Germany, Adorno stayed on, hoping that the nightmare of Nazism would blow over. But it didn't. Having come from a Jewish family, and having been decidedly leftist in his politics, he became a target. Forced to give up his university position, he left Frankfurt for England where he found low-level work at Merton College, Oxford. His English was poor and he was alienated from much of the intellectual life of Britain. His radical perspective marginalized him there. Yet, he continued to write, but now under his new name—Theodor Adorno. All along his Frankfurt school colleagues who had moved to the United States asked him to join them. At Horkheimer's invitation he visited him at Columbia University in 1937. In 1938, he reluctantly accepted a part-time position working with Paul Lazarfeld on Princeton University's Radio Research Project.

THE FRANKFURT SCHOOL IN AMERICA

Bringing the Frankfurt school to America was a difficult decision. The Institute for Social Research at Columbia University was not really a marriage of choice, but one of necessity. Some Frankfurt school associates, such as Walter Benjamin and Adorno, were reluctant to move to the United States. Benjamin never made it. For him, it was a place of last resort.

The deep philosophical grounding and the radical Marxist orientation of these European intellectuals made them hesitate to come to a place characterized by shallow and pragmatic self-interest. At first glance, America, which was characterized by greater fear of communists than of fascists, was not a good fit. Yet, there was hope that in America the school would be allowed to survive. Still, it remained an anomaly throughout its existence in the United States. While focusing more on the dangers of Nazism and Stalinism, its members remained antagonistic to capitalism and the culture it produced. America seemed safe, far away from the insanity of war. And so they came, most not to stay.

With Adorno joining Horkheimer, Pollock, and Marcuse in New York, the Frankfurt school appeared to be in working order. With the continued financial support of Herman and Felix Weil, it seemed to be fiscally sound for at least a few years. Much of the funding of the Institute went to support doctoral research at Columbia. Ironically, some of Adorno's salary was paid through a grant given by the Rockefeller Foundation to support Paul Lazarsfeld's radio research project. The Institute continued to publish its journal, *Zeitschrif für Sozialforschung,* in German, which further helped to cement the group.

In 1941, due to declining health and a doctor's advice, Horkheimer moved to California, along with some of the work of the Institute. It was hoped that a change in climate would be therapeutic. But there can be little doubt that Columbia University was growing restless with the group. The Frankfurt school began focusing on studies of racial conflict, antisemitism, and authoritarian personalities. Members became more active in the American war effort, and a number of them worked with the Office of War Information in Washington.

Adorno eventually moved to California and between 1941 and 1944 he collaborated with Horkheimer on several projects.

THE DIALECTIC OF ENLIGHTENMENT

The Dialectic of Enlightenment was published right after World War II and toward the end of the Frankfurt school's career in America. Horkheimer had just written a book, *The Critique of Instrumental Reason,* arguing that critical reason and not revolution was the key to dramatically altering the human condition for the better. If the book appears to be fragmented and often disjointed, it is because it is based on notes taken during a conversation between Adorno and Horkheimer in Adorno's kitchen in New York several years prior to their writing of it.

The subject of this work is the failure of the European Enlightenment to recognize the centrality of humankind, and the Enlightenment's negative impact on the human condition.

Horkheimer and Adorno borrow from Max Weber to explain what they see as the Enlightenment's disenchantment of the earth and all things natural in order to maximize utility and profit from nature's exploitation. Like Marx, they view the alienation and commodification of nature, along with the commodification of people, in the name of progress to be socially and ethically troubling.

Accordingly, modernity seems to usher in new myths about the incorruptibility of science. It is through the scientific domination and exploitation of nature, Enlightenment thinkers propose, that civilization is measured. Adorno and Horkheimer see one of the primary purposes of science, under modern capitalism, as the prevention of people from identifying with nature and with one another. In advanced capitalist and fascist societies, the individual exists only for the purpose of production and consumption and nothing more.

Adorno and Horkheimer focus on what they refer to as the "culture industry." It is their contention that culture was something that emerged from individuals as they adapted to their environments and to each other. It was often a product of artistic impulse. Now it has become something that is mass produced for mass consumption. It is determined by those who own the means of production and communication and use these resources to impose it upon those who do not. But this imposition is welcomed by the consumers who cannot help be affected by print media, radio, television, and the like.

The industry produces a hierarchial range of products aimed at different categories of consumers. This is really a triumph of capital over culture. Using stock formulations for film, radio, television, and the like, the system conditions consumers to be passive vessels or containers of the new culture. According to the authors, everything is subservient to the need of industrial production, which, on occasion, will produce a novelty or allow for some experimentation that will quickly be reigned in for commercial purposes.

There is a general consensus on who manages the culture and what they can do to achieve their goal. Culture is populist in that it is geared to common people. Those on the receiving end of it are happy to take what they are given. In fact, people are quick to deride cultural experts and critics as elitists. They accept the aesthetics and morality imposed upon them "more seriously than do the rulers themselves." Nothing new or risky is attempted. High art and low art, serious art and light art are absorbed into a commercially textured totality.

Horkheimer and Adorno assert that the culture industry provides for everyone, demonstrating that all submit to it. Where some might not, there are alternatives that eventually become incorporated into the mainstream. For instance, the tattoo that was once a sign of individualism, marginalization, and rebellion has become a fashion statement. Advertising that is embedded (sometimes merely through unconscious placement of products) in television, radio, music, magazines, and cinema becomes a means of social control. Everything that does not bear its stamp is suspect. Thus, propaganda and advertising are considered inevitable and useful. Individualism is allowed as long as it is a function of the market. A person who rejects market values is tolerated, but is also marginalized.

There is a fatalism to all of this, an inherent understanding that consumers have only the ability to buy or not buy. Thus, the system triumphs as people feel compelled to buy things they are told that they want.

Adorno and Horkheimer also address the issue of antisemitism and the rise of fascism in Germany as another example of the Enlightenment's failure. Like with the culture industry, antisemitism is held in place by psychologically undermining individual critical thought. It works on the same principle of propaganda noted earlier. It is the purpose of fascism and state capitalism to undermine critical thought and to have the citizen take as truth that which is fed to them by the hegemonically controlled mass media. As with the culture industry, to be rejecting of this truth subjects people to marginalization, ridicule, and worse.

The authors assert that mass culture produces and promotes antisemitism and other forms of racism through the production of stereotypes and laying blame. Whether it be Jews, Arabs, or blacks, the forces of production work to deflect disfavor from those in power and redirect it to others.

FRANKFURT SCHOOL RETURNS HOME

Horkheimer and Adorno both returned to Germany in 1949. Horkheimer resumed his chair in social philosophy in Frankfurt. He helped reopen the Institute there in 1951 with some funding from the American High Commission and headed it for a while. Adorno returned to work at the Institute and eventually served as its head a few years later after Horkheimer's retirement. Marcuse, Fromm, Lowenthal, and others remained in the United States. All remained active scholars.

In 1950 Adorno published his most important sociological work, *The Authoritarian Personality*. Based on extensive interviews and family studies in the postwar period, he looked at Hitler's rise to power, in part, as an outcome of psychological forces at work in Germany at the time.

Horkheimer traveled to the United States frequently and became a guest lecturer at the University of Chicago between 1954 and 1959. After retiring in 1959, he lived in Montaguda, Italy until his death in 1973. He was seventy-eight years old when he died.

With the Institute reopened for business, a new generation of students, among these Jürgen Habermas, took their place in the line of intellectual genealogy. Adorno's tenure at the Institute spanned the politically turbulent 1960s. During one of his lectures in April 1969, three female members of a militant political group rushed to the podium where he was speaking. In a act of reproachfulness they bared their breasts and showered him with flowers and erotic embraces, humiliating him in front of the crowd. The radicals geered that "Adorno is dead!" Four months after the incident, at the age of sixty-six, he suffered a fatal heart attack.

BIBLIOGRAPHY

Benhabib, Seyla, et al., eds. 1993. *On Max Horkheimer*. Cambridge: MIT Press.

Horkheimer, Max, and Adorno, Theodor. 1996. *Dialectic of Enlightenment*. New York: Continuum Press.

Jay, Martin. 1996. *The Dialectical Imagination*. Berkeley, CA: University of California Press.

———. 1984. *Adorno*. Cambridge: Harvard University Press.

Ritzer, George. 1996. *Social Theory*. 4th ed. New York: McGraw-Hill.

Tar, Zoltan. 1985. *The Frankfurt School*. New York: Schocken Books.

15

Herbert Marcuse: Eros and Liberation

An icon of the 1960s and the so-called "father of the New Left," Herbert Marcuse had a major impact on mid and late twentieth-century sociology. Throughout his life he put himself in the limelight expostulating radical ideas for his time. Among his students were hippie leader Abby Hoffman and Angela Davis, a leader in the Black Liberation movement. Unlike many of his Frankfurt school colleagues, Marcuse believed in direct action and participated in political protests both in Germany and in the United States.

Marcuse was born on July 19, 1898 in Berlin, Germany to a wealthy family of assimilationist Jews. His father, Carl Marcuse, was a prosperous merchant. His mother, Gertrud Kreslawsky Marcuse, was the daughter of a wealthy businessman.

He attended the Mommsen Gymnasium in Berlin and began his advanced studies at the University of Berlin. When World War I broke out, he served in the infantry, but never saw combat. In 1919 he joined the Socialist Democratic Party and briefly participated in the German Revolution, which helped bring an end to the war. When the revolution failed, he returned to his studies at Berlin and in 1922 he received his doctorate in literature from the University of Freiberg.

Like his soon-to-be Frankfurt school colleagues, Herbert Marcuse was a Left-Hegelian. He believed in a Marxist materialist interpretation of Hegel. Marcuse had a strong interest in the humanistic side of Marxist theory, in phenomenology and in existentialism. Eventually, he developed a fascination with psychoanalytic thought, particularly the theories of Sigmund Freud.

Between 1922 and 1928 he worked as a bookseller in Berlin. He married Sophie Wertheim in 1924 and returned to Freiberg to continue his studies with Edmund Husserl and Martin Heidegger in 1929. Both of these men had a significant impact on his thinking. He wrote several pieces on Hegel and Kant for journals and in 1932 published a book on Hegel. His mentor at Freiberg was Martin Heidegger, an important existentialist with whom he was preparing to apply for a position as his assistant. However, as Heidegger moved further to the right, eventually becoming an active Nazi Party member, their relationship dissolved.

In 1933, just prior to Hitler coming into power, Marcuse left Freiberg and went to the University of Frankfurt where he secured work with the Institute for Social Research. Not only was he comfortable with the unorthodox Marxism evident at the Institute, but he also was captivated with their interdisciplinary approach to theory. Almost immediately, he became part of the Frankfurt school's inner circle. When they moved their offices to Geneva that year, he joined them. Eventually, he left Germany for the United States where he worked with the Institute when it was housed at Columbia University.

In 1940, Marcuse became a U.S. citizen and joined the Office of Strategic Security in Washington as a section director, ultimately becoming head of the European department there. Throughout the 1950s he assumed a number of teaching responsibilities. He taught at Columbia, Harvard, and Baradise and lectured at the Washington School of Psychiatry. In 1955, he published one of his most important works, *Eros and Civilization.*

EROS AND CIVILIZATION

In this work Marcuse develops a synthesis of Marx and Freud and discusses the feasibility of a nonrepressive society based upon some of their ideas. Influenced by Wilhelm Reich who had a solid impact on the work of other, more psychoanalytically oriented Frankfurt School theorists (such as Erich Fromm), Marcuse begins with Freud's repression hypothesis outlined in *Civilization and Its Discontents* (1929) and concludes that Western societies structured under capitalism have a surplus of repression. That is, capitalism in the West, tainted by Protestant asceticism, imposed unnecessary restrictions on sex that helped to convert these repressed libidinal energies into a production of excess profit. It is Marcuse's assertion that the internal conflict that drives the world is not one between the reality principle and *Eros* (the pleasure principle). Rather, it is alienated labor and *Eros.* It is Marcuse's belief that a socialist society could produce a civilization based not upon alienated labor, but on the functioning of the pleasure principle, or as he refers to it, "non-alienated libidinal work."

It is important to understand here that Marcuse attacks the contemporary notion of *Eros* and its primary association with genital sex. For him, as well as for Freud, *Eros* represented a totality of joining—a full connection of body and spirit. Under capitalism, sex becomes alienated from the entire body. Thus, the body is de-eroticized as it is put into the service of profit. He argues in his book for a polymorphous sensuality. He contends that the self needs to be reconnected to the sensate world.

The social repression of libidinal energy, including sex drives, divert this energy away from self-fulfillment and into the service of capital, and sometimes into the service of war. The greater the sexual repression, the more intense the violence. Freud's pessimism in *Civilization and Its Discontents* could be unfounded if society was willing and able to provide constructive avenues for release of this energy through nonalienating work.

There is evidence that this book, which gained considerable popularity in the United States, was an important intellectual inspiration for the countercultural revolution of the 1960s. The book, which was written in the staid 1950s, actually anticipated the coming wave of social change around the world and, in many ways, championed the motto "Make love not war!" This work, more than any other, helped to establish Marcuse as a leading figure in the movement for cultural change.

It was not only a call to break the shackles of a repressing and imposing culture epitomized by an increasingly regulated and regimented white-collar workforce, but it was also a call for the rediscovery of nature, within and without, as an avenue to liberation.

ONE DIMENSIONALITY

If *Eros and Civilization* was a book of great optimism and hope, *One-Dimensional Man* was a admonition.

Published in 1964, *One-Dimensional Man* is one of Marcuse's most important works. Here Marcuse attacks both institutionalized mass communication and capitalism for their betrayal of democratic principles and the abrogation of human freedom. He argues that in advanced industrial societies, false needs are created by systems of social manipulation and propaganda. These systems are aimed at forcing people into a system of production and consumption not really of their choosing. This system is held together by a web of mass media advertising and public manipulation that limits choice and restricts critical thought.

It is Marcuse's assertion that scientism and bureaucracy are displacing politics and ethics with a technocratic imperative. Such an imperative not only demands the sacrifice of human sensuality, but also requires an abandonment of basic humanity to the instrumental rationality of the marketplace. Furthermore, the drive for human emancipation is being undermined by this new order of one dimensionality. Technology is merely a tool used to bring this about.

Facts and values are manufactured to serve hegemonic ends, and people are willing to accept these at face value without so much as a challenge. This is because they very much want to believe in a centrality. Also, to venture outside the one-dimensional world creates for the masses a sense of isolation and aloneness. In this state of potential exile, the individual is vulnerable.

The one-dimensional world is a place of one-dimensional people. It is a place of "happy conscience" where everyone lives in the security of false beliefs. Here there is no critical awareness, no worry except for security that the patriarchal state will provide.

One-Dimensional Man was a warning.

SCHOLAR AND ACTIVIST

Marcuse prided himself on his social activism. Unlike his colleagues who returned to Europe and took a low profile in the political turbulence that was all around them, he was willing to promote his ideas and in doing so gained a large following. Large audiences would gather to hear him lecture.

Marcuse not only embraced the civil rights movement, but also the more radical black power movement and the movement for women's liberation. He spoke out against the war in Vietnam, and joined in peace marches and political rallies. He continued to publish articles and books and was called by the American press "the guru of the New Left." He traveled extensively discussing his idea, condemning campus violence as quickly as he'd condemn police brutality.

Unlike many of his Frankfurt school colleagues who returned to Germany after the war, Marcuse decided to stay in the United States. He did travel to Germany and lectured at Freie University in Berlin as well as the University of Frankfurt. In 1965, he was given a teaching position at the University of California at San Diego. It was there that he met Angela Davis, a student in his class. They became close friends and he worked with her on a number of projects.

In 1974 he participated in the celebrations marking the fiftieth anniversary of the Institute for Social Research. On his last trip to Germany in July 1979 he died. His book, *The Aesthetic Dimension,* was published posthumously.

BIBLIOGRAPHY

Kellner, Douglas. 1984. *Herbert Marcuse and the Crisis of Marxism.* Berkeley, CA: University of California Press.

Marcuse, Herbert. 1974. *Eros and Civilization.* Boston: Beacon Press.

———. 1964. *One-Dimensional Man.* Boston: Beacon Press.

16

Walter Benjamin: Art and Modernity

Although not a central figure in the Frankfurt school, Walter Benjamin inspired much of its thinking. His contributions to modern social theory have been extensive.

Born in Berlin on July 15, 1892, he was the oldest of three siblings. His father, Emile Benjamin, was an auctioneer and partner in a firm specializing in art and antiques. His mother, Pauline Elise Schoenflies Benjamin, was sixteen years younger than her husband and came from a relatively affluent Jewish home.

As a child, Walter Benjamin received his earliest education from a tutor brought into the home to teach reading, writing, and mathematics. At the age of nine, he was sent to the Kaiser Friedrich School, one of the most prestigious grade schools available to the middle class. He hated it. He hated the regimentation, the gloomy asceticism, and most other things about it. He was often sick and missed weeks of classes. His parents removed him from school in 1904 and sent him to the Haubinda boarding school where he became a student of one of the country's most important educational reformers, Gustav Wyneken. It was with Wyneken that Benjamin took his first courses in German literature and philosophy. After spending two years there, he returned to Kaiser Friedrich and prepared for his university career.

Benjamin was admitted to the University of Freiburg and majored in philosophy with a minor in psychology. One of his classmates there was Martin Heidegger (who couldn't have been much fun). He took courses in literature and the history of art and eventually transferred to the Royal Friedrich Wilhelm University in Berlin. In Berlin, he regularly attended lectures given by Georg Simmel who he deeply admired. At the University, he joined the Free Students' Union and became a member of the League for Free School Communities. He wrote for *Der Sprechsaal Am Empfang,* the youth magazine, and became part of the growing youth movement. In many ways, this was a countercultural movement pressing for social change and reforms on many levels. It was around this time that he became extremely interested in the progressive wing of the Zionist movement.

Benjamin was influenced by several people in this regard. Connections made in the youth movement eventually brought him into contact with the noted Jewish scholar of the Kabbalah Gershom Scholem, a young man who would become his lifelong friend, and Donna Kellner (Dora Pollak at the time), the woman he would eventually marry. Pollak's father was a professor of English in Vienna who once served as an advisor to Theodor Herzl, the renown student of Zionism. As Benjamin was brought closer to the inner circle of the Frankfurt school, however, he began losing his interest in Zionism.

During World War I, Benjamin was exempted from military service because of health reasons. Still, the war had taken a toll on many of his friends who, like himself, found the atrocities and carnage difficult to accept. One of his closest friends, Fritz Heinle, sunk into a deep depression and committed suicide. Many others, however, were caught up in the romance of war and the power of Imperial Germany. Among these was his former teacher and mentor Gustav Wyneken.

In the autumn of 1915, Benjamin left Berlin to continue his study of philosophy at Ludwig Maxmillian University in Munich. In some sense, this was an escape from bad memories. The city of Munich itself held no appeal for him, and he found little he could appreciate in his new teachers or in their subjects. But he did make several lifelong friends there.

In 1917 he married Donna Kellner who was a highly successful writer and translator. She was also an extremely talented musician. In the winter semester of that year, he enrolled at the University of Bern to further his studies and finish his doctorate. There he focused on philosophy and psychology. He became fascinated with Freud's work as a result of seminars taken with the philosopher, Paul Häberlin. These courses also directed him to pay more attention to the issue of perception, which played a role in many of his later literary projects. His thesis, however, was on the philosophical foundations of romantic art and criticism. However, his initial interest in the philosophy of Kant never left him. His thesis was eventually published as *The Concept of Art Criticism in German Romanticism.*

In the early 1920s, Benjamin began applying himself to works of literary criticism and translation. He was keenly interested in translating the works of French modernist Charles Baudelaire into German and had done meaningful work on *Les Fleurs du mal.* He wrote extensively on Goethe, and began to make plans for a literary journal. However, postwar inflation and economic turmoil prevented this from happening.

He put much effort in attempting to secure a university teaching post. Having failed to achieve a foothold in Bern and Heidelberg, he headed to Frankfurt in 1921 to pursue his *habilitation* (a thesis that would grant passage to a teaching post). It was at Frankfurt where he met Theodor Adorno with whom he would eventually develop a relationship based on mutual respect for one another's work.

In 1923, Benjamin traveled to Capri where he attempted to complete his thesis. In Italy, Benjamin made the acquaintance of Asja Lacis, a Russian director and actor also vacationing there. They had a brief affair. It was Lacis who is credited with influencing Benjamin to turn more seriously toward Marxism. It was through his acquaintance with Lacis that a visit to Moscow was arranged for him in the winter of 1926–1927. Subsequently, she introduced him to Bertolt Brecht, the radical German playwright. The two men became close friends.

But when he returned to the University of Frankfurt, Benjamin's *habilitation, Origin of German Tragedy,* was rejected. With such a defeat, an academic career was now most unlikely. He became a freelance writer. However, he kept his ties to the University of Frankfurt and maintained his association with Adorno. From Adorno's Institute he received funding for some of his work, and he began a translation of Proust's *Remembrances of Things Past.*

In 1927, Benjamin began work on his famous *Arcades Project,* or *Passagen Werk.* By this time he had been in Paris for several visits and was enthralled with its history and architectural beauty. His stay in 1927 was much longer. He began experimenting with marijuana, and in 1928 saw the publication of *Origins of German Tragedy* and *One Way Street*—a collection of mental images and aphorisms. He became fascinated with surrealism and delved deeply into the subject. He was now writing regularly for a variety of publications, including *Frankurter Zeitung* and *Die literarische Welt.* In 1930, Benjamin and Dora divorced.

THE NAZI RISE TO POWER

Like his friend Adorno, Benjamin was reluctant to leave Germany even with Hitler's rise to power in 1933. In April of that year he traveled to Spain and Italy and witnessed the ascendance of National Socialism from afar. Although reluctant to return home, he nevertheless did in November of that year. The fascists had increased their program of violence against working-class Jews. Newspapers seemed reluctant to record these atrocities.

The majority of Benjamin's friends began disappearing. Concentration camps were being erected. His brother Georg, much more of a devout leftist than himself, was arrested and eventually died in the Wulheide Reform Camp east of Berlin. The Nazis assumed control over newspapers and radio. The publication of his work ceased. In the middle of March 1933, Benjamin left Germany for Paris.

Attempting to find a market, let alone an audience, for his works in German was no small task. He began to devote more time to his work on the Parisian arcades, constructing a series of brief observations, a montage of architectural and cultural impressions. During his stay in Paris, he resumed contact with Adorno and Horkheimer and was invited to submit his work to their journal, *Zeitschrift für sozialforschung,* which was still being published. He used pseudonyms for much of what appeared in German publications.

ART IN THE AGE OF MECHANICAL REPRODUCTION

Like many critics, Benjamin explored and expressed his own ideas through his analysis of other people's work. Many of his writings of this period are fragments, most of which were very well crafted. But some of this appears unfinished, incomplete. Themes seem to rotate around poverty, exile, and loss—no doubt his own personal struggles. Some of his ideas even appear mystical.

If there is any one essay that linked Benjamin to the Frankfurt school and for which he gained considerable acclaim as an exiled writer living in Paris, it was his essay dealing with the sociology of contemporary art in which he proposes that the uniqueness of any work of art cannot be separated from its history.

Although works of art have always been reproducible, Benjamin asserts that mechanical reproduction represents something very new. With the rare exception of woodcuts, stampings, engravings, and castings, most works of art have been one of a kind. This held true even for the written word up until the advent of the printing press. With lithography, however, mechanical reproduction was revolutionized. Soon added to this was photography, film, music, and voice recordings. Given these innovations, art is freed from space and time. It is also freed from history and ritual. But it is tradition and ritual that have imbued works of art with special meaning and mystical content. In fact, the earliest works of art emerged in the service of ritual and religious practice. However, with the advent of art reproduction this no longer is the case. Most art comes at us through a vast variety of media in the form of reproductions that no longer necessitate that it be grounded in time and space.

Authenticity is diminished or even neglected through reproduction. Authenticity is not reproducible. Forgeries were always deemed inferior to the original. With photographs, however, the original is not necessarily the most authentic. Developing and processing of the same print could produce a variety of the same picture with an emphasis on different aesthetic elements. The same might hold true with recording where technical production enhances or distorts the quality of the product.

Benjamin speaks of the "authority" of a work of art in terms of tradition. That is, when art is removed from its content and when it is reproduced, it shatters the tradition associated with it. It is what he refers to as the "aura" of the work that is diminished; that is, the sense of distance from it declines and with this so does a sense of reverence for the work. The more familiar it is, the less power it has. In ancient times, certain statues or images were only available to the shaman or priest. Thus, aura for Benjamin means something magical or sacred.

Cinema is an example of distancing from the sacred. In film, for instance, the observer is required to identify with the camera. This diminishes the individuality of the observer and distances the observer from the object of observation. The viewer's perception is controlled by another through a machine—forced to view the world in a particular way. Film actors also feel a sense of distancing or alienation as they are required to act without an audience. Nevertheless, every "take" is planned and designed so that the control of what the observer sees rests in the hands of the filmmaker. Benjamin attempts to make the case that there is no aura for the actor in film.

> The aura which, on stage, emotes from Macbeth cannot be separated for the spectators from that of the actor. However, the singularity of the shot in the studio is that the camera is substituted for the public. Consequently, the aura that envelops the actor vanishes, and with it the aura of the figure he portrays.

There is a substitution, according to Benjamin's analysis, of an image invented for the actor's own, but not based on the work. Instead it is based on the need of the studio. He also predicts Andy Warhol's idea that anyone can be a work of art if he or she is captured on film. One must question if film actors, blown up to five times their actual size, connect in some different way to the film audience. Nevertheless, many agree with this notion of the decline of acting as an art as it was defined in theater. Anyone who knows how cinema is made understands that the job of acting is broken down into scenes and shorts, which make little sense out of context, but which are pieced together by the director.

Benjamin expresses the belief that film enhances our perception of things by broadening our sensibilities. Accordingly, a different view opens itself up to us through the camera than "opens to the naked eye." It even produces the viewer to "unconscious optics" as does psychoanalysis to unconscious impulses. Yet, Benjamin has a disdain for the masses that view film. The public becomes the critic, he asserts, but unlike the critic of art, there is no attention required.

CONCLUSION

Many of those who critique Benjamin see in him a desire to preserve an elitist aesthetic, one not accessible to proletarian audiences that he professes to admire. He saw that fascism, itself, emerged from the working-class rabble and he was quite suspicious of the masses. He believed that fascism gave them what they wanted—greater participation in the aesthetic life of Germany expressed through war. Despite this disillusionment, he continued to write up until the Nazi occupation of France. He surrounded himself with a close grouping of friends including Hannah Arendt and Georges Bataille.

Although he was invited to join his Frankfurt school colleagues when they relocated to New York, he stayed on in Paris hoping that the war would be brought to a swift conclusion. Often he was hungry and had to sell some of his personal books in order to purchase food. Still, he continued to work on the Arcades project.

With Hitler's army arriving in Paris in May 1940, two million people left the city, taking with them, often on their backs, their most prized possessions. Benjamin and his sister who had herself just escaped from an internment camp wound up in Lourdes and then Marseilles. Waiting for a special visa to arrive that would allow him entry into the United States, he grew impatient. The Nazis seemed to be everywhere.

On September 26, he set out on foot to cross the Pyrenees into Spain with a small group of friends. Although he loved the mountains, he was fatigued. He also had a heart condition. He took frequent rest stops. He was carrying his large briefcase that supposedly contained this work on the Parisian Arcades. The small group arrived in the town of Port Bou on the Spanish border. But just when they thought they had escaped the Nazis, orders had come down that invalidated their papers. The group stayed at a small hotel overnight where it was believed that Benjamin took his life with an overdose of drugs.

The tragic life of Walter Benjamin came to an end, but the work he was carrying became an important monument to his keen social and artistic perception. The work he left behind remains a tribute to his talents as a writer and cultural critic.

BIBLIOGRAPHY

Benjamin, Walter. 2002. *Arcades Project.* Cambridge, MA: Harvard University Press.

———. 1968. *Illuminations,* ed. by H. Arendt. New York: Schocken Books.

Brodersen, Momme, and Green, Malcolm. 1997. *Walter Benjamin: A Biography,* trans. by I. Ligers. New York: Verso.

17

Norbert Elias: The Civilizing Process

The work of Norbert Elias represents what some have called "figurative sociology"—a sociology that refrains from splitting and fragmenting the world for the purpose of studying it, a sociology that combines a macro-approach to understanding society with a micro one.

Norbert Elias was born in Breslau, Germany (which today is the city of Wroclaw, Poland) on June 22, 1897. His father, Herman Elias, was an assimilationist Jew, a manufacturer of clothing; his mother, Sophie, was a dedicated and loving parent. The family attended synagogue a few times each year and on special holidays. They lived in what was then the Polish section of the city, close to his mother's parents and grandparents.

Elias attended the Jonannes Gymnasium until he was fifteen years of age. He had several influential teachers there including instructors of math, French, and the humanities. He read Schiller and Goethe and was well prepared for university life.

Unlike his father, young Elias found himself opposing the First World War in 1915. However, at the age of eighteen, he enlisted and joined the signal corps and was sent to maintain telegraph lines on the western front. It was there that he saw the real carnage that was World War I.

In 1918 he returned home and, at his father's urging, became a medical student at the University of Breslau. While taking course work in medicine and observing gruesome operations and amputations, he dropped his courses in medicine and continued in sociology, psychology, and philosophy under Richard Hönigswald. He read Husserl, Heidegger, and Jaspers, and later went on to the University of Freiburg to study with Jaspers. During this time, however, Germany was experiencing a dire economic crisis including record-setting inflation. He took some time from his studies to help his parents financially. His father, who was then retired, was having problems making ends meet. Elias took a job as an export manager at a local foundry. He remained there until he could ensure the well-being of his parents. In 1924, he returned to his studies and received a doctorate in philosophy and psychology at the University of Breslau. The following year, he went on to study sociology at the University of Heidelberg.

Settling into Heidelberg, Elias was introduced to the Max Weber circle. Although Weber had taught at Heidelberg, he died in 1920. However, his brother Alfred occupied a chair in sociology there, and Max Weber's wife, Marianne, presided over a salon. It was at the University of Heidelberg where Elias was introduced to the in-depth study of Marx, Weber, and the newly emerging Karl Mannheim. Mannheim was a *privatdozent* at the time. He was paid for his teaching by the course. Elias took classes with him and Alfred Weber and became close to both men.

When Mannheim was called to chair the new sociology department at the University of Frankfurt in 1929, Elias was asked to go with him as his departmental assistant. Mannheim, whose first language was Hungarian, was a fine speaker in German; however, he frequently relied on Elias to help him with the language. Elias taught small seminar classes and assisted with doctoral dissertations. He worked side by side with Horkheimer, Adorno, and other Frankfurt school members while working on his *habilitation,* to prepare him for a teaching post, under Mannheim. In fact, the sociology department was housed in the basement of the building owned by the *Institut für Sozialforschung.*

In 1933, Hitler came to power and there was a mass exodus from Nazi Germany and the University of Frankfurt. Elias completed his Habilitation thesis, *The Court Society,* just as the army was moving onto campus. The rise of fascism would force him to abandon both Germany and his academic career there. After a brief stay in Paris, he moved to England.

THE CIVILIZING PROCESS

The Civilizing Process (*Über den Prozess de Zivilisation*) is a two-volume study of the ways in which European people increasingly came to suppress their emotions and establish an elaborate set of standards for social etiquette and decorum, and how, in line with this process, human violence accrued into the hands of a powerful few. Published in German in 1939, it was not released in English until more than thirty years later.

Beyond a mere study of manners, the work is a study of dominance and control—very much in the vein of the Frankfurt school and highly critical of Western civilization. Elias believed that the rise of nation-states had much to do with the imposition of strict codes of conduct. So-called advancements in culture were carried out at the expense of humanity. Thus, culture occupies a central position of importance in his analysis and is a main component of the civilizing process.

Elias recognized that the term *civilization* had powerful symbolic significance. In his examination of this term, he looks at its origins as well as its use as a propaganda tool for evaluating cultures—the civilized versus the uncivilized. However, he remains astutely aware that it is something that has enormous sociological content. It has become a metaphor for power. There can be no doubt that Elias intended to take Freud's *Civilization and Its Discontents* into a sociopolitical realm. Here civilization is not only associated with the repression of id-like instincts of aggression and violence, but it also is representative of the state's patriarchal monopoly over violence. This is played out in the external relationships between and among states, as well as the internal pacification of domestic populations to achieve order and stability serving the interests of those in power. It is played out in colonialism and the political game of dominance.

To understand how the world has come to this point of the "civilized" imposing their standards on the "uncivilized," he looks at the transition in emotional life from the Middle Ages onward. However, this particular period is only a snapshot of the historical process that has taken place since ancient times. He selects this era only because it is more historically accessible.

Elias looks at the French court society that he believes was a model for both the English and German court life. The bourgeoisie lived alongside the old aristocracy as teachers, advisors, and technical consultants. Peering into the social court practices, he maps out the historical development of manners. The aristocracy and courtly bourgeoisie shared the same sensibilities, read the same books. It was out of these two groups that a codified set of manners emerged.

Elias offers all sorts of evidence as support for his position, including books, paintings, murals, songs, and drawings. It is in his detailed section on manners that we gain a sense of how these rules of etiquette came about and became embedded into culture. In his book, he provides us with sections on table manners, defecation and urination, blowing one's nose, spitting, bedroom behavior, and other categories of conduct.

Many of the books on proper court behavior appear in the sixteenth century. Mostly directed to young boys, such as Desiderius's *De Civilitate Norum Purilium* published in 1530 or Baldessare Castiglione's *Cortigiano* published in 1528, these works continued to influence court elites in succeeding centuries. Originally directed to youngsters of the court, they ultimately were aimed at securing proper adult behavior.

With blowing one's nose, for instance, there had been few prohibitions in the early Middle Ages. People like Erasmus instructed that there were courteous and discourteous ways to accomplish this task. One courteous way was to use a handkerchief (something rare for those days) rather than blowing one's nose on the ground or into one's hand and wiping this on to one's clothing. Blowing one's nose onto the table cloth was discourteous. When one did use a handkerchief, one needed to turn one's head away from others and not later search the handkerchief for whatever came out of the nose.

These small actions of personal hygiene became associated with civility or cultural refinement. Certainly, these rules did not apply to peasants, and at first, they did not even apply to the bourgeoisie. This only evolved as the bourgeoisie assumed greater control of the state. Initially, these rules affected only a narrow grouping of nobility. But gradually, from the Renaissance onward, there was a trickling down of these standards of corporeal restraint and personal reserve. Rules began to proliferate. Eventually these became coded standards, what some sociologists refer to as folkways. How to approach a person of the same rank, or a higher or a lower rank was spelled out in detail. How to speak, what to say, and what not to say were described. Inhibition replaced uninhibitedness. The tame replaced the untamed.

As time progressed, the rules of civil behavior became internalized and while, at one time, a person of high rank might defecate shamelessly in public or spit on the ground, later on one would be humiliated if seen by another. Thus, the rules of society along with feelings of shame would be internalized. It was not social pressure that would enforce these rules, but rather self-imposed pressure. Shame could be felt without necessarily being observed.

Eventually, rules of behavior would become internalized—unconscious. Elias refers to this as a shift in balance from external constraint to self-constraint. There is, of course, a relationship between the civilizing process and what we commonly refer to as socialization. But in Elias's understanding of the historical dynamics, this gives his position a unique value. This is the essence of what he would later term *process sociology*—embedding the behavior in history.

In *The Civilizing Process,* Elias also shows that there were greater constraints placed upon violence. Certainly, the early Middle Ages were characterized by warfare between rival ruling bands. He discusses the joy and pleasure these groups gained from warfare and inflicting pain and injury on one another. Mutilation of captives was practiced with relish as was rape and pillage after battle. Eventually, these practices of warring factions were discouraged by states and controls were imposed upon some of them.

Everyday behavior in the early Middle Ages was quite brutal. Argument frequently led to bloodshed. It was not unusual for people to be pummeled for a wrong word, a queer look, or an accidental push. Violence was an everyday affair with revenge being practiced openly and with considerable delight. This continued simultaneously with codes of proper behavior for nobility. But with the rise of nation-states and bourgeois ascendance, things began to slowly change.

Throughout the Middle Ages great pleasure was taken in spectacles of burning, lynching, and public human torture as direct involvement in violence began to wane. Cruelty to animals was commonly practiced. In Paris Midsummer's Day was celebrated by lowering a net filled with cats into a large fire and listening to the cats scream as they burned to death, all for the amusement of the local crowd. Killing of humans became more and more controlled as voyerism displaced hands-on violence. Boxing matches and drawing and quartering were treated as blood sports. Elias, in fact, traces the history of sport to the substitution of controlled violence to the uncontrolled variety.

By the seventeenth century there is evidence of increased sensibilities to suffering. Executioners are masked; execution is generally sequestered as is torture. The unstable crowd, the volatile mob, needed to be reigned in. The nation-state needed order. States, therefore, assumed tight monopolistic control over violence.

In the second half of *The Civilizing Process,* Elias shows how this was carried out in the history of the transition from medieval to modern times. He speaks of power and civility in terms of a monopoly mechanism that concentrates both the power to tax and to commit violent acts into the hands of a state sovereign. Both were linked together because money was used for weaponry to support state-sponsored violence that was used, in turn, to collect revenues that were, in turn, used to develop larger armies. On and on it went.

Elias was interested in understanding the relationship between the social mechanisms or structures responsible for these changes and how they were played out among the people. This was his figurational approach to understanding society. Thus, change in the form and nature of the state had much to do with the development of the psyche. This, however, was no simple deterministic relationship. It was a process comprised of an intricate web of relationships between muscle and nerve—between structure and function.

Overall, Elias saw much of the civilizing process emanating from an intense concentration of power. Using what he refers to as "royal mechanism," he describes the process through which this historically occurred. How, for instance, did the French monarchy accrue inordinate power while those in its employ, as well as its subjects, worked to ensure its monopoly over violence? The growth of the nation-states came about with strict restriction and control over violence legitimized by the acquisition of power. How and when violence could be used was dictated by the state and delegated to its agents: police, military, and mechanisms of correction and control.

At the same time, the state apparatus gained considerable control over culture. Through this culture it could impose rules of proper conduct. The bourgeoisie and working classes could be manipulated by acquiring an internalized shame mechanism based on standards of civility. Through the erection of social institutions of social control, a program of pacification could be easily carried out.

Elias's ideas were grounded in the work of Weber and influenced by Mannheim's ideas on bourgeois intellectualism. It was Weber who saw the rise of the administrative state as resting on legitimization of authority, by which he meant an ultimate ability to use force to get things done. Like Weber who saw a gradual emergence of new forms of asceticism and disenchantment ushering in a rational world order, Elias proposed that emotional restriction and a heightened emphasis on reason were the basis of civilization. Like Mannheim, he saw bourgeois intellectuals helping to prop up this new world order.

EXILE AND LOSS

In a small rented room in London he threw himself into his work, spending most days at the library of the British Museum. While writing *The Civilizing Process,* Elias was visited in 1938 by his parents who he attempted to convince not to return to Germany; but they insisted on returning to Breslau. His father had been a patriotic German all of his life. During that year they worked with their son to get his book published by a German publishing house despite the rise of Nazism.

In 1940 he received a letter from his mother via the Red Cross. His father died in Breslau and she was in transit to Auschwitz. She is believed to have died in the concentration camp in 1940. After the publication of *The Civilizing Process,* he was hired as a research fellow at the London school of economics where he worked until the British authorities sent him and many other German refugees to an internment camp on the Isle of Man.

Eventually, he was able to leave there for Cambridge where he eked out a living by guest lecturing. His English was still quite poor. Nevertheless he became good friends with author and theologian C.P. Snow. He renewed his friendship with S.H. Foulkes whom he had known in Frankfurt before they were both forced to leave. Foulkes was a practicing psychoanalyst and well connected in analytic circles in London. He was a good friend with Anna Freud. Elias began working with him and being trained by him and attending lectures at the Tavistock Clinic. Eventually, Elias joined with him in forming the Group Analytic Society and led his own therapeutic groups.

In 1954, he was hired to teach sociology at the University of Leicester just outside of London. He was now fifty-seven years old and his academic career was just beginning. It wasn't until 1968, however, that *The Civilizing Process* was translated into English. He continued writing and published several more books including *What Is Sociology*, published in 1970, and *Sociology of Community* in 1974. He retired from Leicester and began lecturing around Europe and in Africa. With the assistance of Theodor Adorno, he was awarded the pension of Professor Emeritus at the University of Frankfurt. Adorno had convinced officials that Elias would have had an important tenured career at Frankfurt if it had not been for Hitler's rise to power.

In 1977, several years after Adorno's death, he was awarded the first Theodor W. Adorno Prize conferred by the City of Frankfurt. He was also recognized with honorary doctorates from various universities in Germany and France. In 1979, he went to New York University to give a series of lectures. He continued in a life of active scholarship until his death on August 1, 1990 in Amsterdam.

BIBLIOGRAPHY

Elias, Norbert. 1994. *The Civilizing Process*, trans. E. Jephcott. Oxford: Blackwell Publishers.

Fletcher, Jonathan. 1997. *Violence and Civilization: An Introduction to the Work of Norbert Elias*. Cambridge: Polity Press.

Mennell, Stephen. 1989. *Norbert Elias: Civilization and the Human Self-Image*. Oxford: Basil Blackwell.

18

Simone de Beauvoir: Otherness

Simone Lucie-Ernestine-Marie-Bertrand de Beauvoir was born into a respectable middle-class family in Paris on January 9, 1908. She was the eldest of two daughters. Her father was a successful lawyer and her mother, schooled in a convent, a strict Roman Catholic who attempted to raise her daughters according to the conservative social conventions of the day. Although Simone de Beauvoir was not a sociologist, per se, her contributions to social theory and social philosophy were expansive. De Beauvoir dedicated her life to radical ideas and progressive social causes. She would claim a place for herself among the most important French *literati* of the twentieth century and would become renown for her contributions to existential thought and women's studies. Her intense, long-term association with Jean-Paul Sartre as his most intimate acquaintance would influence her own work and his.

As a child de Beauvoir dreamt of becoming a famous author. She began writing at the age of eight and was very much influenced by women novelists including Louisa May Alcott and George Eliot. She retained this enthusiasm for writing her entire life. As a girl she seemed relatively happy and self-confident. She was eager to experience the world fully, and anxious to strike out on her own. In her youth she rejected both the Church and the belief in God. Along with this, she also rejected her bourgeois background.

After completing her course work at the local *lycée* and her secondary education at the *Cours Désir,* her parents sent her to suburban Catholic institutes in 1926 where she studied mathematics and literature. There, they had naively hoped, she might be turned back to the Church. Of course she stood her atheistic ground. At Saint Mary's Institute in Neuilly she met Robert Garric, a ardent Catholic who in addition to teaching founded an organization to help the poor and homeless. She was greatly impressed by Garric's dedication to a cause and viewed him as a man who created his own life, rather than settling into one that was created for him. His ethical stance prefigured her own existentialist ethics. Educationally, however, she was discontent.

In 1927, over mild parental protests, de Beauvoir entered the Sorbonne. There she studied Greek, philology, and philosophy. In 1929, she met a fellow student, Jean-Paul Sartre, who greatly impressed her. This year was to mark the beginning of a lifelong association. Both wound up taking the highly competitive test for the most prestigious academic degree offered in France—the *agrégation de philosophie.* Upon receiving their degrees in 1931 both were appointed to teaching positions in philosophy; Sartre went to a *lycée* in Le Havre and de Beauvoir to a school in Marseilles. Although they had discussed the idea of marriage, they rejected it and opted for a freer, more open relationship.

De Beauvoir rented a very simple room in Marseilles. In it she found a place to read and do her writing. She loved to hike and when not teaching would frequently venture off alone, knapsack on her back, to take in the beauty of the French countryside. She spent many of her evenings socializing in the bars and cafes of Marseilles. She was a voracious reader and consumed the works of Faulkner, Hemingway, Dos Passos, Heidegger, and others. After a year in Marseilles, she was transferred to Rouen—a town much closer to Le Havre and one made famous in Flaubert's *Madame Bovary.*

In her autobiography de Beauvoir makes clear that she had rejected the materialism associated with bourgeois existence. Her personal quest was for personal development by experiencing life in its many forms. She had no intention of finding a comfortable place in the world, but wanted to make a unique life for herself. Each experience would be new, each encounter with life would be met with exuberance. Both she and Sartre had a resolve to stay young forever. They rejected family life, Sunday crowds, properness of all sorts. They hated the provinces and the romantic humanism associated with the past.

De Beauvoir and Sartre spent the summers together hiking in Spain, Italy, and Greece. At home they frequented cafes and established an intellectual coterie of close acquaintances. When the Nazis came to power in 1933 and the war began raging around them, they gave little thought to a world outside of their small circle of friends. In their self-centeredness they failed to recognize themselves as having obligations to others. Thus, as de Beauvoir would later note, they displayed many of the qualities they detested in the privileged class they rejected.

In 1939 Sartre was re-conscripted into the military. Although he had served in the French army for eighteen months prior to having met de Beauvoir, he was reactivated and taken into the meteorological service where he helped to launch weather balloons—indeed an existential enterprise. He was captured by German troops in June 1940, the same month the Nazis took France. He served nine months as a prisoner, but in March 1941 he was granted a medical discharge. Soon thereafter he published *Being and Nothingness,* a work he had commenced writing while in the army and in the stalag. Although many scholars have contended that de Beauvoir contributed extensively to the ideas in this work, it is difficult to draw any definitive conclusions based on available evidence.

Still, in 1943 de Beauvoir published her first novel, *L'Einvitée* (*She Came to Stay*). In some ways this was a fictionalized account of the very real tension that emerged between herself and Sartre due to an extended visit of a young, former student of de Beauvoir—Olga Kosakiewicz. Kosakiewicz had a destabilizing effect on their relationship. Certainly, this work has an existential theme as do most of her works. Here de Beauvoir focuses on the Hegelian notion of predatory consciousness. This work was the first of many fictional pieces she would write while living in occupied France.

Although de Beauvoir sympathized with the French Resistance, she did not take part in it. She and Sartre lived in relative safety. They were for the most part absorbed with ideas and followed their creative impulses. De Beauvoir completed several important works in the early 1940s including two novels—*La Sang des autres* (*The Blood of Others*), and *Tous les hommes sont mortels* (*All Men Are Mortal*), and a lengthy essay in philosophy, *Pour une morale de l'ambiguité* (*The Ethics of Ambiguity*). *Pyrrhus et Cinéas* was published in 1944. This was a lengthy essay that popularized many of the concepts contained in *Being and Nothingness.* Again, it dealt with such issues as ethics, conscience, and choice.

THE SECOND SEX

After the Second World War, de Beauvoir's interest in politics increased. She had joined Sartre at *Les Tempes Modernes,* an intellectual journal dedicated to radical thought. It was here that many of her essays would first appear. Here is where she joined forces with other great writers and thinkers to map out a new vision for a war-torn world. *Les Mandarins* (*The Mandarins*), which was published in 1954, was her novel depicting the colorful and exciting lives of a small group of radical intellectuals and writers greeting the liberation of Paris in 1944. As with most of her other works of fiction, it was semi-autobiographical depicting her cherished social and intellectual adventures of that year. By the time *Les Mandarins* was published both Sartre and de Beauvoir had gained celebrity status of sorts and were invited to speak and give lectures throughout Europe and the United States.

In the late 1940s, de Beauvoir began working on the book that would stake her claim as a major contributor to both sociology and women's studies. This was her work dealing with gender and, specifically, womanhood. The work was entitled *Le Deuxiéme Sexe,* or *The Second Sex.* According to de Beauvoir, she originally wanted to write an autobiographical confession, but in discussing the idea with Sartre it came to her that a treatise on gender was more of what she had in mind. The world seemed to be a very masculine place to her and she frequently felt like an outcast. Even though she had always realized this, she began to discover the enormous role gender played in women's lives.

Le Deuxiéme Sexe (published in 1949) is in the tradition of great works in anthropological sociology. The book is quite ambitious and deals with the social, psychological, and economic distress encountered by women living in a society dominated by males. It makes extensive use of existential theory as well as anthropological research and constitutes one of the first comprehensive works in existential sociology. Nevertheless, it integrates classical social thought along with more phenomenological approaches to the subject.

As a work of existentialism, de Beauvoir begins with the assertion that both women and men are essential beings in the Hegelian sense. This means that each person is a subject attempting to make the world his or her own. However, men have made women into unessential beings, the *other.* De Beauvoir asserts that *otherness* is inherent in consciousness itself and is a basic category of human thought. Borrowing from Hegel and Sartre, she posits that all otherness engenders hostility and conflict. This was a point she had made more subtly in her first novel. Still, she asks why men make women into *other* and why women accept this designation. According to de Beauvoir, women see themselves not only as unessential, but also as existing primarily for men, not for themselves. Perhaps, some conclude, this has something to do with their nature. But as an existentialist, she asserts that there is no human nature—no femininity in the natural world. Existence always precedes essence, thus only in the process of living or being do people create their own essence. This leads Simone de Beauvoir to posit an essential foundational element of modern gender theory: "One is not born a woman, one becomes one." Thus, de Beauvoir asserts that gender is individually and socially created, and femininity merely a construction.

But why do women submit to this imposed *otherness*? Can there be something inherent in being female that leads to this? For de Beauvoir the answer rests in the woman's body—particularly its functions of menstruation and childbirth. Whether she wills it or not, a woman is forced into serving the species by replacing it. This is of course a matter of biology. Women have been condemned by their bodies to serve men. Thus, the only way of transcending this position is to act against it. Because the existential measure of being human is the degree to which one transcends one's existence or biological nature, women must react against nature. Short of this, women can *assume* their assigned roles rather than accept them. Thus, she does not reject motherhood out of hand, but she implies that choice is an essential ingredient in making one human. It is important to note that de Beauvoir was a very strong advocate for choice and birth control long before it became politically fashionable. In her second novel, *Le Sang des autres (The Blood of Others)*, she has a lengthy discussion of abortion and the importance for making one's own choices in one's life. It was her contention that biology need not condemn a woman to fulfilling some natural maternal impulse. She, herself, had made the decision early in her life not to have children.

De Beauvoir makes extensive use of Friedrich Engel's *The Origin of Family, Private Property and the State* to show how private property and capitalism relegated women to the task of reproduction of labor. However, she criticizes what she views as his economic determinism and romantic notions of primitive matriarchy. She asserts that public and social authority always belonged to men. Women's power only existed, as defined by men, to serve their own needs throughout history. This is due, in part, to the universal imperialism inherent in human consciousness.

Existentialism asserts that each person is an individual; it is everyone's initial inclination to think of the self as independent and autonomous. Throughout history, men's physical strength gave them power not only over nature, but over women. Women who lacked muscular power were prevented from dominating nature, and, therefore, relegated to a mere extension of it. They became objects of domination.

In a section of her book dealing with myths of femininity, de Beauvoir reviews a variety of images men have ascribed to women and women have accepted. She suggests that even though men must reject *being* and embrace *becoming*—projecting themselves into some unknown future, they require security and love. To this end they construct women as *other*—an embodiment of passivity and gentleness—an image of their own deep-seated desires for themselves. However, because the male perceiving consciousness must view itself as good, the other must also become its opposite; the other must represent evil.

Next, de Beauvoir takes up the issue of gender socialization—the process through which people become women. By giving examples of early childhood conditioning in Western cultures and in tribal ones, she notes that around the world girls learn early that they are *other*—that they are objects of manipulation and control. Adolescence in the West is particularly difficult, she asserts, because girls must come to terms with giving up their innate need for autonomy. She looks at the various roles women are expected to play: mother, wife, sister, prostitute, and the powerlessness inherent in all of them. Attacking the myth of men as heros and providers, she decries representations of women in literature. These images prepare women for their unwanted fate.

Most significantly, she claims, women are refused violent contact with the world. They are kept busy in passive roles engaged in activities that seem unimportant and unfulfilling. They are frequently condemned to narcissistic existences, or asked to identify completely with more dominant males. De Beauvoir shows how women have occupied secondary positions throughout history, much like that of other oppressed minorities. She calls upon men and women to join together to reverse this enslavement.

THE COMING OF AGE

In the late 1950s and early 1960s de Beauvoir was writing and traveling extensively—mostly with Sartre. Anticommunist sentiments were sweeping much of Europe and had become a centerpiece of the Truman and Eisenhower administrations in the United States. The House on Un-American Activities Committee and men like Senator Joseph McCarthy developed lists of communist sympathizers and helped to blacklist leftist intellectuals from their work in America. The United States propped up dictatorships throughout South America and Africa to protect American corporations in their exploitation of natural resources and labor and to prevent agrarian reform. The viciousness of the French crackdown on Algerian dissidents and the tortures of family members of anticolonial guerillas by the military led to massive protests by leftist dissenters and people of conscience and to an eventual restructuring of the new postwar government. De Beauvoir reacted to these events with condemnations of both French and U.S. colonialism. She and Sartre spoke out eloquently and frequently against the military actions in Algeria, and later, expressed strong opposition to the role of both France and the United States in Vietnam. They joined in with student dissidents in the 1960s and 1970s giving their strong support to the street protests. They spoke out in the news media and at public rallies for the many who were not given a voice in the societies in which they lived.

De Beauvoir took a leading role as a spokesperson for the dignity and rights of women, but also for the rights of the aged. In 1970, at age fifty-two, she published her second major sociological work—*La Vieillesse* (*The Coming of Age*). This work received critical praise in the popular media and raised people's sensitivity to the marginalization and disempowerment of elderly people in modern societies. In this work de Beauvoir examines the biological, historical, and ethnographic elements of aging and looks at the social and economic condition of the elderly in modern societies. Society, she contends, looks upon the elderly as some sort of "shameful secret." In the contemporary world, she argued, the aged are relegated to poor health, poverty, loneliness, and despair. They are socially exiled—segregated from the young, so not to contaminate them.

She places her study in an existential context, just as she had done with her study of women. The elderly are also *other,* alienated from those who are allowed to take full advantage of the world in which they live. They represent everything the young are not—they have no future, yet they symbolize everything the young will soon be. For this reason they are despised. De Beauvoir reconnected with her long-time anthropologist friend Claude Lévi-Strauss and received permission to use the ethnographic materials he and his colleagues had collected for the Human Relations Area Files of the *Laboratorie d' anthropologie sociale.* In *La Vieillesse,* she asserts that biology is central to determining who is old and who is young, who is denied and who is privileged. Thus, the body stands to represent the condition of aging. One strives to overcome biology, but in the case of the aging, this is indeed an impossible task. Still, it is what the body *represents* that makes it so central to the aging process. Each culture, therefore, creates myths of the aged and develops cultural archetypes: the venerable sage, the old fool, the witch, the god.

De Beauvoir in no way romanticizes the treatment of the elderly in other societies. Even among the apes, she contends, the oldest males are attacked and banished by younger, more aggressive apes. In many tribal societies, the elderly are put to death, are expected to commit suicide, or are abandoned as they become weaker with advancing years. Nevertheless, there is reverence for the elderly in other societies, but this is primarily for reasons of convenience. Where the old are seen as conveyors of important secrets, rites, and even magical powers, they tend to be very few in number and their existence nonthreatening to the welfare of the group. When age becomes associated with possession of property and wealth, there is always privilege associated with it.

She concludes, however, that the differential treatment of the elderly has mostly to do with the division of power relations and exploitation of one group by another. Age becomes a convenience for this purpose. Under capitalism, particularly, where we have larger numbers of the elderly than ever before in history, they are among the poorest of society. Their social position, their health, and their lives can only be sustained if they possess material resources. Because of age, they are denied access to those things, including work, that can sustain them. But even here there is a problem as society comes to associate with the aged a loss of strength, a diminution of intellect, and a failure to contribute to the economy.

De Beauvoir assumes a Marxian tone in her analysis. The age at which one begins to physically decline has always depended on one's social class, she claims. The most exploited worker tends to decline most rapidly due to the years of physical and psychic abuse. Thus, the surplus value takes its toll on the laborer who is usually relegated without work to an existence verging on poverty. The loneliness, poor health, and poor mental condition of such people must be viewed as products of the economic system, not age per se.

The solution to aging is not a poor parody of one's former youth, but a pursuit of goals that give existence meaning. People need to connect to the world. They need to devote themselves to creative work, to political, social and intellectual projects. "One's life has value," she claims, "as long as one attributes value to the life of others, by means of love, friendship, indignation, compassion."

CONCLUSION

Simone de Beauvoir's life was impassioned. As a young girl she noted that she wanted to take in the entire world—taste it, consume it. She did just this. In her autobiography she speaks of her youthful awareness of death and the finite nature of existence. She struggled her entire life to resist its end. But when her longtime friend and lover, Jean-Paul Sartre, died in the *Hôpital Broussais* on April 14, 1982, a piece of her died with him.

Still, she continued to write, travel, and give lectures. She resumed her work on *Les Temps Modernes,* but it wasn't quite the same without Sartre and the old inventive coterie. She produced several more books and an autobiography. When it was over, she died quietly of pulmonary edema at *Hôpital Cochin* on April 14, 1986. Her cremated remains were buried next to those of Sartre.

BIBLIOGRAPHY

Bair, Deirdre. 1990. *Simone de Beauvoir: A Biography.* New York: Summit Books.

Cottrell, Robert D. 1976. *Simone de Beauvoir.* New York: Frederick Unger Publishing.

de Beauvoir, Simone. 1989. *The Second Sex,* trans. by H. Parshley. New York: Vintage Books.

———. 1972. *The Coming of Age,* trans. by P. O'Brian. New York: G. P. Putnam.

19

Hannah Arendt: Banality of Reason

Although Hannah Arendt was not primarily known as a sociologist, her contribution to social theory was indeed significant. Considered by many as a major social thinker of the twentieth century, she provided groundbreaking work that enabled a better understanding of modern life and the nature of human relationships that comprise it. Even though much of her theory is both radical and disturbing, it is also viewed by many as conservative if not reactionary. Like many social theorists of the last century, she remains somewhat of an enigma.

Hannah Arendt was born on October 14, 1906 in Hanover, Germany and was the only child of Paul Arendt and Martha Cohn Arendt. Both of her parents were middle-class people of Russian-Jewish descent. They had their roots in Koenigsberg, the capital city of East Prussia at the time and an important center of Jewish intellectual life.

Paul Arendt was well educated and had traveled extensively in his youth. He and Martha both came from families of professionals—doctors, educators, and lawyers. Both had become socialists in their teens and held leftist political views most of their lives. Although they were secular Jews, they were mindful of their marginal status and made sure that Hannah learned to recognize signs of racism surrounding her. Their home was filled with books and learning.

As a young child, Hannah Arendt was taken on visits to see her grandparents in Koenigsberg. Relatives and friends often visited her parents in Hanover. Their modest frame house was a social gathering place. It was fueled with laughter and storytelling.

In 1910, Paul Arendt was forced to give up his job as an electrical engineer. He had contracted syphilis in his youth and even though he had been treated for its signs at that time, it was thought to have gone into remission. Now its symptoms were reoccurring with devastating consequences. In this same year, the family moved back to Koenigsberg to be closer to his parents. By 1911, the disease was in its third stage. Associated lesions developed and then ataxia and paresis—a combination of physical paralysis and insanity. He was institutionalized in a psychiatric hospital in Koenigsberg later that year. Hannah was only four. She saw her father frequently until he could no longer recognize her. Just as she was developing a closer relationship with her grandfather, Max Arendt, he died in March 1913. Her father died in October. World War I was now on the horizon.

In August of 1914, the Russian army was closing in on Koenigsberg. Jews feared for the worst. Martha and Hannah found refuge in Berlin. That same year Martha Arendt enrolled her daughter into a girl's school outside of that city. However, by the following spring it was obvious that Koenigsberg was not a target; they returned to their home.

Despite many bouts with childhood illness, Hannah did well in school and appeared to keep a cheerful disposition through all of the turmoil. This concerned her mother who considered this to be peculiar behavior. But in 1920, Martha remarried giving Hannah a stepfather, Martin Beerwald, and two older stepsisters. Hannah Arendt was now fourteen. Although there was some adolescent acting out, she settled into the life of a serious student, performing brilliantly in school. By the time she was sixteen she had read most of the classics and was particularly influenced by Goethe, Kant, and Kierkegaard. She won a scholarship to the University of Marburg in 1924 where she met and fell in love with Martin Heidegger, her professor. He was soon to become a renown existential philosopher.

COMING OF AGE

Hannah Arendt came of age between the two world wars. Her romantic involvement with Heidegger was to end before he became deeply involved with the National Socialist movement and its related antisemitism. She later studied with the famous phenomenologist philosopher, Edmund Husserl, at the University of Freiburg and from there went to Heidelberg to study with another existentialist, Karl Jaspers. It was under Jasper's supervision that she wrote her dissertation on Saint Augustine's concept of love (*Der Liebesbegriff bei Augustin*).

In 1929 Arendt met Gunther Stern, a writer and leftist intellectual. They soon married, taking up residence in Berlin. Stern was a political radical and had worked with left-wing artists and dramatists. He was friends with Bertolt Brecht. Arendt and Stern lived a bohemian lifestyle, sharing time with friends and discussing the politics of both Zionism and communism.

After the Reichstag fire in February 1933, which German authorities blamed on leftists, Stern was compelled to leave Berlin for Paris. Arendt stayed behind. Later that year, she was arrested by the Gestapo for doing unauthorized research on antisemitism for a book she was working on. Not only was Arendt taken to jail, but so was her mother. After eight days of imprisonment they were released by a sympathetic official and quickly left Germany for Paris. There she rejoined Stern.

In Paris their relationship gradually dissolved. Arendt fell in love with Heinrich Blucher, a close friend of the famous intellectual Walter Benjamin. He was a self-educated gentile, an activist, with ties to the local communist political organization. They eventually married. The political situation in France, however, was worsening. Even before Arendt and Blucher could get the necessary visas to leave, they were interned for brief periods in separate camps.

In 1939, the Germans occupied Paris. Arendt's mother joined the couple. With her financial assistance and the right connections, the three of them were able to gain passage to New York in the spring of 1941. They found a small Manhattan apartment; Arendt found a job working for a German language newspaper, her mother did piecework, and Blucher found work in a factory in New Jersey. Eventually, Arendt found a part-time job teaching modern European history at Brooklyn College while working as research director for the Conference on Jewish Relations. Between 1946 and 1948, she wrote pieces for a number of political and intellectual journals including the *Nation* and the *Partisan Review*. In 1951, while teaching and working as an editor for Schocken Books, she published her first critically acclaimed work, *The Origins of Totalitarianism.*

POWER AND ITS ABUSE

The Origins of Totalitarianism dealt with Arendt's understanding of the basic causes of the emergence of Nazism and Stalinism in post–World War I Europe. Although it is impossible to summarize the book here, it is important to recognize that this project laid the groundwork for much of her emerging social thought.

For Hannah Arendt, modern life was not only characterized by a loss of God, but it was also representative of the loss of traditional identity. Instability and disorder came in the wake of modernization. But so did opportunity. Modernity and its accompanying pluralism enabled people to make choices and develop their own identities. However, this was met with fear and resistance. Arendt saw the development not of a highly pluralistic society with inordinate freedom, but of the emergence of mass society with a preference for order and security. A society of mass culture, mass employment (or mass unemployment), and mass consumption. This was a society in which people became superfluous and atomistic, a place characterized by a loss of human connectedness. Such conditions produced feelings of estrangement and isolation—and feelings of powerlessness. Totalitarianism was an answer to these conditions. It was a mechanism of centralized authority and unified control—it obliterated the possibility of pluralism and substituted a false sense of totalism.

Unlike previous forms of centralized power, Arendt believed that totalitarianism was rooted in this reaction to modernity. It was a quest to find solid ground and definitive answers where there were none. Over time, community gave way to the mob. Out of this there arose voices commanding others to follow in an orgy of hate and murder. Their words resonated with heroic romanticism from a previous era.

Even though totalitarianism was most pronounced in Germany, it was by no means exclusively Germanic. It had been part of the reactionary landscape for some time. Cultural romanticism, antisemitism, revenge, imperialism and unrestrained capitalism helped to create both Hitler and Stalin. Arendt documented how deeply embedded racism was in nineteenth-century Europe; how colonialism, imperialism, and capitalism provided models for dehumanization and mass cruelty. Death camps were a radical extension of these dreams for genocide, technological control, and domination.

The totalitarianism of which Arendt spoke was one of the most gruesome variants of despotism—one that had been held at bay by the Enlightenment. However, the ideals of the Enlightenment could not hold. In her work she paid particular attention to the plight of the Jews, to the Holocaust, and to the Jewish diaspora. She was able to weave together literature, politics, history, and philosophy. She captured the horrors of the Holocaust and was able to articulate an impressive understanding of the course of events that changed the century.

Sociologically speaking, much of Arendt's work was a subtle variation of Max Weber and the Frankfurt school. The former stressed mass society and the importance of modern bureaucracy as an instrument of impersonal control; the latter dealt with the relationship between domination and modernity.

ARENDT'S SOCIOLOGY OF BANALITY

While writing *Origins of Totalitarianism,* Arendt's mother died. Her mother was traveling to London to see her stepdaughter when she developed a severe asthmatic attack on board the ship. She died in London on July 27, 1948. Both Arendt and Heinrich Blucher were saddened but in many ways relieved. There had been considerable tension in the household. Blucher now delved into his own metaphysical scholarship, which won him an academic appointment at Bard College. He taught there for a number of years.

When the book was released in 1951, a number of reviewers faulted Arendt for not being as critical of communism as she was of fascism. Of course, the early 1950s was a time for a great deal of communist paranoia in the United States. It was the era of the House Un-American Activities Committee in Congress and the time of Senator Joseph McCarthy's hearings, which aimed to expose and indict for treason anyone who had ever had anything to do with communists or whoever held communistic ideals, which included things like putting an end to capitalism and private property and establishing of a system of universal equality. Even though Arendt was highly critical of communism and even Marxism, she still became a target for what was considered by some as her un-Americanism.

Arendt had pointed out in her writings that she saw many of the same totalitarian signs in American society, including a surrender of personal involvement in political life, a focus on material achievement at the expense of community, and a growing need to conform. Although she took on American citizenship, she did not give up on her ideals of human equality and an end to political and economic exploitation.

Arendt's own struggle with values was reflected in her position on Zionism. For most of her life she had been a strong supporter of the development of a Jewish state. However, with passing time she believed that a homogenous religious state would be a disaster for the Jews. Only in a combined venture with the Palestinians could Israel ever find a place of acceptance in the Arab world. She believed that this was essential, and this position won her many enemies.

In 1952 she was awarded a Guggenheim Foundation Fellowship to work on her new book, which became known as *The Human Condition.* Nowhere else in her work is Arendt's critique of modernity made more explicit. Although intended as an anti-Marxist treatise, it became something else as she hunted for the political significance of the human condition. This book explores the loss of political life or of *vita activa.* According to Arendt, it is in this loss that we find the deepest tragedy of modern existence.

Hannah Arendt delves into the meaning of political or public existence, and she finds it in the Greek *polis,* which she identifies as the essence of communal life. It is only here in the polis, or community, that one can be free and not be subject to the commands of another. Only in the public realm could true individuality exist. The private realm of family was a place for the mentally disturbed, the slave, the woman, and the child. Arendt associates the private sphere with the banality of society. Society becomes, for her, a collective of families "economically organized into the facsimile of one." All societies are comprised of high degrees of inequality, just like the family. With the rise of society there came a collective of private interests guided by tyrants, just like in the privacy of the home. This was radically different from the community, represented by the polis, where each was equal.

For Arendt, and many other theorists from whom she borrowed, virtue can only emerge from community—from the polis. The glory of the individual and the importance of human morality can only emerge from the public realm of equals and never from what she calls society. Like the classical sociologists who make the distinction between community and society, Arendt warns that society breeds bureaucracy, conformity, impersonality, and inequality on a massive scale. Although tradition once ruled private interests and law applied only to the public concerns, the law itself degenerates into a tool to protect and control private interests.

Some reviewers compare *The Human Condition* to de Tocqueville's classic study, *Democracy in America.* Much of the book was a critical review of American life and culture. It described loss of political idealism.

Even though she produced other important works under this grant, including *On Revolution* and *Between Past and Future,* her most popular work was taken from her journalistic reporting and reflections on the trial of Adolf Eichmann in Jerusalem in 1963. Her book, a series of articles for the *New Yorker* magazine, was later published as *Eichmann in Jerusalem: A Report on the Banality of Evil* (1963).

No one can overestimate the degree of controversy surrounding this project. Eichmann had been an S.S. officer for the Nazi Army and responsible for helping to send nearly six million Jews to their deaths. He was captured in Argentina and brought back to Israel for a trial. Although he freely admitted his role in the coordination of the roundup of Jews who were sent to their deaths, he did not appear to be the innately evil monster people expected. He seemed small and timid as he took the stand. He was not boastful, but he appeared proud of having efficiently "served his country."

Hannah Arendt saw Eichmann as the modern man, one whose sense of right and wrong was willingly placed into the hands of superiors. He was an automaton—efficient and capable of doing his job without questioning authority. The horror for Arendt and others was that he appeared to be so normal. Even though there might have been sadism here, it seemed balanced by his gentlemanly manner. He seemed unmoved by photos of camp victims, of piles of human corpses; he was quiet and still through most of the interrogation and rarely raised his voice. He was a soldier, just following orders, he would say, a cog in the machine. "If I didn't do it, someone else would have."

The horror for Arendt was that Eichmann was the modern man. The world was made up of people just like him working in large bureaucracies. His behavior was characterized by bureaucratic reasoning. This was not a particularly German characteristic. The world was made up of people who could just as easily lose themselves in a system of despotic terror—people who were no longer human in any ethical sense. She saw in Eichmann and in others what she called a banality of evil. Although Arendt supported the death penalty for Eichmann, her reports angered many who believed that she appeared too sympathetic to the man. How could such a monster be banal?

CONCLUSION

In the 1960s Hannah Arendt was busy teaching and writing. It was the decade of the Kennedy assassinations, the civil rights movement, the black power struggle, and the war in Vietnam. It was the time of black church bombings in the United States, the election of Richard Nixon, and the assassinations of Dr. Martin Luther King and Malcom X. Arendt found herself opposing many progressive causes and embracing others.

She traveled to Europe frequently to visit Jaspers. She lectured briefly at Berkeley and at the University of Chicago. She taught at Princeton where she was the first woman to be appointed full professor. Later, she took a position with the New School for Social Research in New York. In 1967 both her husband and Karl Jaspers died. She continued her scholarship and turned further toward philosophy. She died of heart failure in December 1975.

The "banality of evil" legacy she left behind was to influence the work of many, ranging from the famous social psychologist Stanley Milgram to the postmodern sociologist Zygmunt Bauman.

BIBLIOGRAPHY

Arendt, Hannah. 2000. *The Portable Hannah Arendt*, ed. by Peter Baehr. NewYork: Penguin Putnam.

———. 1967. *The Origins of Totalitarianism.* London: Allen and Unwin.

———. 1963. *Eichmann in Jerusalem: A Report on the Banality of Evil.* London: Faber and Faber.

———. 1958. *The Human Condition.* Chicago: University of Chicago Press.

Bradshaw, Leah. 1989. *Acting and Thinking: The Political Thought of Hannah Arendt.* Toronto: University of Toronto Press.

Canovan, Margaret. 1992. *Hannah Arendt: A Reinterpretation of Her Political Thought.* Cambridge: The University of Cambridge Press.

Hansen, Philip. 1993. *Hannah Arendt: Politics, History and Citizenship.* Stanford, CA: Stanford University Press.

McGowan, John. 1998. *Hannah Arendt: An Introduction.* Minneapolis, MN: University of Minnesota Press.

Pitkin, Hanna Fenichel. 1998. *The Attack of the Blob: Hannah Arendt's Concept of the Social.* Chicago: University of Chicago Press.

Wolin, Richard. 2001. *Heidegger's Children: Hannah Arendt, Karl Löwith, Hans Joas, and Herbert Marcuse.* Princeton, NJ: Princeton University Press.

Young-Bruehl, Elizabeth. 1982. *Hannah Arendt: For Love of the World.* New Haven: Yale University Press.

20

Claude Levi-Strauss: Structural Anthropology

A seminal figure in the development of structuralist social theory was the French anthropologist, Claude Levi-Strauss—not to be confused with the Bavarian New Yorker, Levi Strauss, who made a fortune in the manufacture of blue jeans in the 1800s.

Claude Levi-Strauss was born in Brussels on November 28, 1908. His father, Raymond Levi-Strauss, was an artist and painter who had come to Brussels from Paris to do a series of portraits. His mother, Emma Lévy Levi-Strauss, had come from a well-educated, middle-class Jewish family.

Soon after Claude's birth, the family moved back to Paris and lived for a while in Versailles. There, young Claude came under the intellectual influence of his grandfather, a rabbi, and his uncles who were also artists. He attended primary school and later secondary school where he received his baccalaureate at the *Lycée Janson-de-Sailly*. In 1927, he was admitted into the Paris Faculty of Law and into the philosophy program at the Sorbonne. At the university, he came under the influence of Marxist theory and wrote his master's thesis on historical materialism. Throughout his studies in law and philosophy, his interests began shifting to anthropology or, as it was called then, ethnology. At the same time, his interest in psychoanalysis was deepening.

In 1928 he prepared for his *agrégation* in philosophy alongside of Maurice Merleau-Ponty and Simone de Beauvoir, both of whom he got to know personally. In 1931, he was awarded the *agrégation* with honors, which entitled him to teach in the French school system. The following year, he began teaching at *Mont-de-Marsan lycée* in the southwest of France. He married Dina Dreyfus who shared his passion for anthropology. In 1933 he was assigned to a lycée in Laon in the northeastern section of France, but he was already beginning to tire of teaching. He had read Robert Lowie's *Primitive Society* and wanted to travel and to explore.

Levi-Strauss's life was to be radically altered on an autumn morning in 1934. It was then that he received a call from Célestin Bouglé, director of the *École Normal Supérieur*. Bouglé had served as Levi-Strauss's master's thesis advisor in philosophy at the Sorbonne and knew of his strong interest in anthropology. A new position had opened up at the University of São Paulo in Brazil to teach sociology. Georges Dumas, a psychiatrist who was also a former teacher of Levi-Strauss and who was heading the French educational mission to Brazil, hired him.

On a February morning in 1935, Levi-Strauss embarked for Brazil from Marseilles via Barcelona, Cadiz, Algiers, Casablanca, and Dakar. He landed in the city of Santos. He was twenty-seven years old. He took up his position as a sociology professor with his colleagues in São Paulo and taught there until 1938. However, when his first teaching term was over, instead of returning to Paris, he accepted an offer to stay on to study Brazil's tribal peoples. He and his wife were engaged by the Paris *Musée de l'Homme* and the city of São Paulo to help with an expedition into the interior of the Brazilian countryside in the Mato Grosso. This was his very first venture into ethnology—something for which he was never formally trained. This became the basis of his study of the Caduveo and Bororo Indians. The entire jungle experience for Levi-Strauss was mystical and emotionally overpowering. "I felt like I was reliving the adventures of the first sixteenth-century explorers," he was later to remark.

In 1936, Levi-Strauss and his wife, Dina, returned to Paris with their collection of artifacts from the expedition and presented them to the *Musée de l'Homme*. It was in this year that he published his first ethnographic study of the Bororo, which happened to be read by two important anthropologists, Alfred Métraux and Robert Lowie, in New York. It gave Levi-Strauss some visibility in the field. Another expedition was conducted in 1937, this time into the territories between Culabá and Rio Madeira regions—one of the least documented areas of Brazil at the time. The venture was daunting and more physically and psychologically demanding than his last trip. It was difficult getting supplies through the jungle and illness was frequent. The venture lasted months. But it was there that they eventually came upon the existence of the Tupi-Kawahib tribe. Although most of the expedition was forced to turn back, Levi-Strauss spent several weeks alone with the tribal people. The work was life-changing. Upon his return to Paris, he and his wife separated. The trip was to become the basis of a work that he would write in early 1950, *Tristes Tropiques;* he would also draw upon some of this field work for his doctoral dissertation, *Elementary Structures of Kinship.*

When Levi-Strauss was drafted into the French army in 1939, Hitler was marching through Europe. The French military was no match for the Nazi machine. Levi-Strauss's unit was forced to withdraw, with the advancement of the Germans, to the Bordeaux region and southward to the Spanish border. Even after the French troops were demobilized and his unit was disbanded, he remained in France and secured a teaching position in a *lycée* in Montpellier. However, with the Nazis in control of France, the Vichy government enacted anti-Semitic rules that forced him from his position.

In 1941, Levi-Strauss was contacted by faculty at the New School for Social Research in New York. Alfred Métraux and Robert Lowie, who were there and had been impressed with his Brazilian studies, worked to secure him a teaching position. Although difficult, Levi-Strauss found passage out of France in February 1941. In New York, he settled into a studio apartment in Greenwich Village. He immediately came under the influence of Franz Boaz, who had just retired from Columbia, Margaret Mead, Ruth Benedict, Robert Lowie, and Al Kroeber. He became fascinated with the study of structural linguistics at this time and was strongly influenced by the work of Roman Jakobson in structural linguistics.

He worked as a speaker with the U.S. Office of War Information and developed friendships with other exiles including Max Ernst, Marcel Duchamp, Andre Bréton, and others. At the New School for Social Research, he taught a course on the sociology of Latin America and also taught ethnography at the New York *École Libre des Hautes Études.*

RETURN TO FRANCE

By 1945, the war in Europe was coming to a close. Levi-Strauss was hired by the *Direction des Relations Culturelles* to help advise people in France who wanted to come to the United States. At the same time, he was named as the director of the cultural center attached to the French embassy in Washington. His circle of friends and acquaintances was widening because of this and now included Albert Camus, Jean-Paul Sartre, and Maurice Merleau-Ponty. In this same year, he divorced Dina Dryfus and married Rose-Marie Ullmo. In 1948, Levi-Strauss completed his doctoral thesis at the Sorbonne.

LEVI-STRAUSS AND STRUCTURALISM

In an attempt to better understand the cultures he studied, Levi-Strauss employed a method he referred to as structuralism. According to him, structuralism is the search for "unsuspected harmonies." It was his claim that Marx and Freud had advanced the structuralist method of analysis by attempting to understand surface reality through reference to deeper structural levels. This is to say that Marx believed that the economic system and the rules that guided it often determined how people behaved and what the culture was like. Freud did much the same with the psyche. It was the rules governing the psyche, particularly the unconscious, that determined likely outcomes.

An important part of Levi-Strauss's work is its effort to find universal rules that underlie everyday activities and customs. Setting out to develop a structuralist approach, Levi-Strauss borrowed much of his method from structural linguistics, which had been advanced by Ferdinand de Saussure—a Swiss social scientist who died at the beginning of the twentieth century. Saussure's major work was contained in *Cours de linguistique,* a collection of his lecture notes published by his students a few years after his death. It sets forth basic principles of what he called semiology—often referred to now as semiotics. Semiology is the study of signs.

In examining language Saussure asserted that words have little or no meaning if we take them out of context. In fact, they can mean very different things according to how they've been arranged. It is really how these words are put together that constitutes meaning. Thus, the whole is greater than the sum of its parts. The study of semiology or semiotics looked at how meaning was constituted, but more than this, how there were rules in all languages (such as grammar) that determined how they could be structured. Thus, the rules, not the words themselves, constructed meaning. If we look hard enough, we will be able to discover those rules that are universal and inherent in our minds. That is, as Noam Chomsky noted, we are all born with what constitutes hard-wiring for learning language—for putting words together. This is what makes it possible once we know one language to learn another—not that the rules of grammar are always the same, but that there are always rules of grammar and they frequently are structured in similar ways.

Saussure's linguistic inquiry analyzed the social and collective dimensions of language. He was interested in the infrastructure of language. He believed that the rules governing the use of it functioned on an unconscious level. He spoke of binary oppositions as present in all languages, for example, hot versus cold, sweet versus sour, cooked versus raw, and so on. This notion seemed quite revolutionary. His ideas not only gained hold on the imagination of linguists, but also had a profound impact on philosophy, art, literature, and the social sciences, especially psychology, sociology, and anthropology. In their unyielding search for truth, social scientists wanted to go to the core of things—those rules that underlaid patterns of culture.

If Saussure was right, if structures existed that predisposed certain outcomes, we should be able to find them in the rules governing cultures. That is, even though we know cultures are different, they are actually more similar than they are different. There are aspects of culture that are universal: language, myth, kinship patterns, music, art—many, many things—though not identical are certainly similar. Myths, particularly, said Levi-Strauss, seem to be very similar, have similar components, and tell similar stories when we look at them in various cultures. Creation myths might be an example of this.

Claude Levi-Strauss's imagination was captured by what has become known as the "linguistic turn." For him, cultures can be viewed as systems of communication. Models could be constructed based upon those in structural linguistics drawing upon tools available in twentieth-century information theory, cybernetics, and mathematics to discover and prove laws governing behavior.

People are led to obey laws they do not themselves invent; however, it is a natural mechanism of the mind that conditions how we learn. Inherent structures also determine how we behave and what type of culture we have. In fact, Levi-Strauss would go down in history for helping to de-center the human being and question the actor's all-powerful significance in the process of the creation of culture. In structuralism, the rules guiding behavior become more important than the individual's choices that are guided by them. Thus, he saw the ultimate goal of the human sciences as not to "constitute man" but to "dissolve him." Structuralism in the social sciences becomes forever linked to antihumanism.

However, it would be misguided to lay all of this at the feet of Levi-Strauss. He was only one social scientist who sought to discover the essence of culture as residing outside of human activities. Sociologists, such as Roland Barthes and Jean Baudrillard, who drew upon principles of semiotics to assess culture were likewise influenced by Saussure. Barthes, himself, was revolutionary in that he set forth an agenda of finding these rules in text, images, and the readers rather than in the minds of authors. His concept of myth was much broader than that of Levi-Strauss. He looked at myths in everyday life, looked deeply into the imagery of popular culture, and looked at how myths worked in modern life to maintain sets of norms as "natural." Barthes, even more than Levi-Strauss, helped move structuralism toward poststructuralism and postmodernism, noting what he called "the death of the author," opening up the way for Jacques Derrida.

THE SCIENCE OF STRUCTURALISM

In 1958, Levi-Strauss published a collection of essays, *Anthropologie Structurale,* which were the focus of his new method. The book was to have a significant impact on the behavioral sciences. In this work he noted four elements central to structuralism. First, structural analysis examines the unconscious infrastructure of cultural phenomena. Second, it looks at the elements of infrastructure as relational, not independent. Next, structuralism must be seen as concerned with the system and not the individual. Finally, it proposes laws that underlie organizing patterns of phenomena.

Levi-Strauss notes that structuralism is part of cognitive science that gives insights into the mechanisms of the brain. The human must be seen as a product of these mechanisms, constructed through a process of learning.

Levi-Strauss advanced the new discipline of structural anthropology, which he viewed as an extension of semiology, established by Saussure. Every human culture was seen as having organization and structure similar to language. It is the task of structural anthropology to discover the semiotic and, therefore, find the cognitive structures deeply embedded beneath the surfaces of social activity. All such structures are layered and not readily available for examination. However, all of the rules of which these structures are comprised are logical and discernable.

STRUCTURALISM AND SOCIAL CHANGE

Claude Levi-Strauss was elected to the *Collége de France* to serve as chair of social anthropology in 1959. It was a position created just for him.

In the coming years, he continued to publish. Between 1964 and 1971 he published four volumes of his study of myths called *Mythologiques.* In this work he analyzes myths from all over the world finding vast similarities in their structure.

By the 1960s structuralism and semiotics was sweeping France as the latest intellectual craze. Although much of it relied heavily on hermeneutics, it significantly challenged the subjectivism put forth by existentialists like Jean-Paul Sartre. In fact, debates between Sartre and Levi-Strauss took place at the Sorbonne and were open to the public. Some of these were published in the journal, *Critique.*

Levi-Strauss continued to publish and remained teaching at the *Collége de France* up until 1982 when he retired. He was seventy-six years old. He continued to receive accolades from important universities throughout the 1980s, receiving an honorary doctorate from Harvard in 1986.

His work remains the central to an understanding of the changes that have taken place in social theory over the past few decades.

BIBLIOGRAPHY

Champagne, Ronald. 1987. *Claude Levi-Strauss.* Boston: Twayne Publishers.

Hénaff, Marcel. 1998. *Claude Lévi-Strauss and the Making of Structural Anthropology,* trans. by Mary Baker. Minneapolis, MN: University of Minnesota Press.

Levi-Strauss, Claude. 1963. *Structural Anthropology,* trans. by C. Jacobson. New York: Basic Books.

Paz, Octavio. 1970. *Claude Levi-Strauss: An Introduction,* trans. by J. S. Bernstein and M. Bernstein. Ithaca, NY: Cornell University Press.

21

Frantz Fanon: Race and Postcolonialism

One of the most vital contributors to social revolutionary thought and, most particularly, to the area of postcolonial theory was Frantz Fanon. It was Fanon who became a voice of the oppressed; it was he who presented the issues of race and colonialism in a global context. Fanon who drew important connections between racism, culture, and capitalism.

Frantz Fanon was born on July 20, 1925 in Fort-de-France, Martinique. One of eight children in a relatively upper-middle-class family, his father was a customs official and his mother worked as a shopkeeper. The family occupied a spacious apartment in the center of the city. They had domestic help in their home, subscribed to values of the black French *évolué* (the Europeanized privileged class), sent their children to private schools or *lycées,* and spoke only French.

The island of Martinique, a French colony in the Caribbean, originally received its name from the Carib Indians who called it "Mandinina," or Island of Flowers. It was colonized by France in the beginning of the seventeenth century when the French introduced slavery. With the exception of it coming under Nazi rule during World War II, it has remained under a form of French political control until this day. In 1946, however, its status of a colony was changed to that of a *department of France.* The character of Martinique, its colonialism, and its racial and class distinctions were to play an important role in helping Fanon formulate some of his more important ideas.

Frantz Fanon entered *Lycée Schoelcher,* one of the only private secondary schools open to black students on the island. There, he proved himself to be a brilliant student. He was particularly attracted to the study of philosophy. He eventually came under the influence of his teacher Aimé Césaire, an internationally renowned poet and leftist political intellectual, who had developed the concept of negritude. Negritude signaled the importance of blackness in developing a conscience of liberation from colonial oppression. Although Fanon did not fully embrace Césaire's ideas, he greatly admired the man and his political radicalism.

The surrender of France to the Germans during World War II shook the world and led to the Nazi occupation of Martinique. Soon thereafter Fanon left school and escaped to nearby Dominica. There, he trained for and joined with the Free French Forces. He was sent to Morocco in 1943 and served alongside white North African colonists, Frenchmen, and other black Antilleans. In North Africa he learned of the viciousness of racism from soldiers he served with as well as from the people he helped to liberate from the Nazis. This was far different than what he experienced in Martinique. He began to see race as a global issue of major importance.

Although he was decorated as a war hero, in the end he was disillusioned with war and the sacrifices he made for it. He felt that the blood he and other black soldiers had shed was in vain. After two years of service he returned to Martinique. The war was over, but he came home with serious doubts about his allegiance to France. His former teacher, Aimé Césaire, was running as the Communist Party candidate for mayor of Forte-de-France. Fanon worked to see him elected. He continued in and completed his studies at the *lycée* and applied for a veterans' scholarship to study medicine abroad. In 1947 he traveled to France to study dentistry. After a short stint in dental school in Paris, he left to study psychiatric medicine in Lyon.

Lyon was a city in turmoil—it was a hotbed of political unrest and racial tension. Fanon founded and edited a student newsletter called *Tom-Tom,* aimed at black students. He continued reading philosophy and wrote three short plays. He became interested in the existentialism of Jean-Paul Sartre. After completing his studies and a brief trip home, he returned to France to take a residency at Saint Albade-Lozere hospital. Upon passing his hospital examinations, he was qualified as a chief-of-service and was able to assume a directorship in any French or French colonial hospital that had an opening. Although he wanted a post in Africa, specifically in Senegal, in 1953 he selected a position in the Blida-Joinville psychiatric hospital in Algeria. This was the only opening available to him in Africa at the time. The period of his service there was to be marked by intense professional and political unrest.

Fanon immediately changed the practices at the hospital. It was his belief that the hospital needed to become more humanistic in its treatment of mental patients. The Blida-Joinville hospital housed nearly two thousand patients with only six medical doctors on staff. It was the largest hospital in Algeria stretching over acres of land and built originally as a showpiece of French colonialism. Nurses were responsible for all aspects of patient care and too often were quite brutal. Patients were frequently straitjacketed and kept in chains. Often they were beaten. Doctors and interns neglected the nurses as well as the patients. In turning procedures around, Fanon upset many hospital administrators by integrating his wards. Up until his arrival Europeans and Muslems were segregated from one another. Straitjackets and chains were removed and various therapies, including medication treatments, were integrated into regular hospital routines. He even established a soccer team of staff and patients and arranged matches with neighboring townspeople.

During the Algerian War of Liberation, which began in November 1954, Fanon worked secretly to supply Algerian rebels with medical supplies. He continued to work to support the efforts of the National Liberation Front (NLF) by both training Algerian nurses and by treating victims of colonial French torture at the hospital. He saw in his practice not only those who had been tortured during the war, but many of those French officials who had administered the torture. From that point on, his life was dedicated to the Algerian cause and to fighting colonialism around the world. Following the hospital's termination of striking Moslem workers in 1956, Fanon resigned his position, citing France's systematic brutalization and dehumanization of the Arab population in their own land.

BLACK SKIN, WHITE MASKS

It was during his training for his medical career and in his early years as a doctor that Fanon found time to write *Black Skin, White Masks.* This book deals with racism and group identity. This is perhaps his most sociologically ambitious project. In it he posits the notion that the distinct racial classifications of white and black have helped to create a very real form of mental illness. Black identity, as a product of the colonial experience, is one of self-subjugation and alienation. Fanon uses the notion of masking to make several important points. First, he draws upon the power of the mask as it was developed in Western and Central Africa and followed its later use by slaves as a form of concealment and social criticism in Carnival, Mardi Gras, and Boxing Day throughout the Caribbean and Americas. For Fanon the mask comes to represent black people taking on the role of being white, acting white, in order to survive.

It is Fanon's contention that black men living in a white-dominated society unconsciously desire to be white. This desire is forced upon them by the societies in which they live. Such societies have established white standards for beauty and goodness and have inculcated feelings of inferiority in those who are nonwhite. In being denied their history, culture, and language, those of African descent needed to confront existential feelings of substandardness. He claims, the black man who masters French most thoroughly will be deemed proportionately whiter than whose who have not. Although this mastery of the white language might increase a man's acceptance by whites, it alienates him from the roots of his own culture. These are the Martinicians—those who appear to take on the culture of whiteness. Language becomes an important instrument of power. It is used by whites to control and belittle blacks.

Where Freud held that most psychological problems have their roots in family, Fanon posits that for black people, their psychological difficulties are more connected to the black encounter with the white society. For many whites the black man becomes no more or no less than his skin color; Fanon refers to this as the "racial epidermal schema." This breaks the black man into three parts: a body, a race, and a history. The man of African descent is objectified and dehumanized in this way—he is made into otherness. In examining Césaire's notion of negritude as a defense agaist this process of dehumanization, Fanon considers and rejects the idea that blackness can be celebrated through its unique connection to rhythm, emotion, nature, magic, sexuality, and the like if these could be made to be viewed as positive black gifts worthy of celebration. He poses that the danger here is associating black culture with the irrational and regressive. For Fanon, race becomes a factor often more critical than social class.

Fanon rejects many of the universalist assumptions inherent in psychoanalysis. Many of these, such as the Oedipus complex, seem to him to have no basis in the cultures of the French Antilles, for instance. Generally, his discussions of sexuality appear to be homophobic and misogynistic. When he deals with sexuality, it is always from a heterosexual male perspective. For instance, he insists that homosexuality hardly exists in the Antilles and seems to view such sexuality as pathological. In analyzing sexual relationships between blacks and whites he also finds them to be an expression of pathology. Throughout his book he draws upon novels to describe interracial relationships. He appears to have a double standard when it comes to black women with white men and black men with white women. Black women appear to be victims of a need to become white. For him this is nauseating and sad. But for a black man to be attracted to a white woman is a self-affirming act in a racist society.

One of Fanon's more important propositions in *Black Skin, White Masks* is in his reaction to Octave Mannoni's book *Prospero and Calaban,* which was published in 1950. In that book Mannoni, who was a psychiatrist in the French colony of Madagascar, uses Shakespeare's *The Tempest* as a model for his own interpretation of colonialization. Although Fanon rejects much of his interpretation out of hand, he finds himself in agreement with Mannoni's belief that this play prefigured Hegel's master-slave parable in contrasting the relationship between the colonizer and the colonized. It is Mannoni's contention that Prospero in his self-doubt about his ability to rule Milan withdraws to an island where he can have complete authority and rules over Calaban, an aboriginal savage over whom he exercises complete control. It is Prospero's seemingly irrational fear that Calaban might rape his daughter. In Mannoni's interpretation Calaban, like all colonized people, is more concerned with losing Prospero's respect than being ruled over by him. Fanon rejects this so-called Prospero complex and instead posits the notion that under colonialism the oppressed remain oppressed. They are never given the recognition as anything but inferior workers to be used for gain, even after receiving a measure of political autonomy. There is never a mutual recognition of the need for each other. It is Fanon's contention that to gain such recognition one must win it. The colonized must rise up and violently overthrow the colonizer. Only in this way can self-respect ever be realized. Only in this way can true liberation materialize.

FANON'S REVOLUTIONARY EFFORTS

After a short period in France, Fanon returned to North Africa and joined the FLN where he edited the group's newspaper *El Moudjahid* and continued in his practice of psychiatry in Tunis. He not only wrote fiery articles condemning French imperialism, he also worked with the rebels to establish supply lines through the Sahara and was injured in the process when the jeep in which he was riding hit a land mine. He was hospitalized in Rome for his injuries and during the night an attempt was made on his life—assassins fired a machine gun into the bed he was thought to be lying in. By this time Fanon had become the target of the French Intelligence. A car that was to take him to the Roman airport was bombed shortly after this and he narrowly missed being killed, although he suffered extensive spinal injuries. Two children on the street nearby died in the explosion. His life was now in constant jeopardy.

In 1960 Fanon was appointed Ambassador to Ghana by the Algerian Provisional Government. He lived in Tunis and wrote extensively during this time. He dedicated himself to both the Algerian cause and to Pan-Africanism and worked hard to promote his anti-imperialist message. Although he desired to return to the Caribbean, Martinique was still part of the French empire and he was a marked man there. He instead requested that he become an Algerian representative to Cuba, but this plan was put on hold when it was discovered that he was suffering from leukemia. Even though stricken with cancer, Fanon wrote his classic work *The Wretched of the Earth,* which was in part derived from his experiences of working in Algeria. It combined political, social, and psychoanalytic perspectives. He drew extensively on the work of Marx, Sartre, and Lacan and in ten months had written one of the most important books of the twentieth century dealing with issues of postcolonialism.

WRETCHED OF THE EARTH

Wretched of the Earth deals with Fanon's insights into the workings of colonialism and the emergence of decolonialization or postcolonialism. Sociologically speaking, Fanon views hegemonic colonial powers as having worked to destroy native cultures both physically and psychologically through the categorical use of race and class. Colonialism not only physically disarms the colonized but also robs them of their cultural identity and heritage. It is Fanon's contention that bloody revolution and not colonialist condescending dispensation of rights is the only path to true decolonialization.

Fanon views bloodshed as necessary to liberation and contends that revolutionary violence is the inevitable consequence of colonialism, which was itself established and perpetuated through brute force. Through economic violence or police violence, the colonized are controlled by hidden and sometimes not so hidden acts of terror against them. As this violence becomes excessive, it pushes the population to react against it. At the individual level the violent revolt becomes a cleansing force freeing the colonized from feelings of despair and inferiority. There is a cathartic effect generating a sense of empowerment when the individual finally become a revolutionary. Violence also promotes group cohesion. People work together to free themselves from outside oppression. He asserts that in successful revolutions there can never be compromise.

Fanon views colonialism as an extension of Western capitalism in a vast globalizing network. Each colonizer's policies reflect their particular role in the world marketplace. Therefore, wars of liberation must discard the old ways of the colonizers. They must do away with their systems of stratification in particular. To just change those who are in power from the colonizer to the colonized will perpetuate the old ways. The whole system must be revolutionized. Thus, Fanon advocates socialism as a practical and ethical solution; he calls for decentralization of political control and an end to racism. It is Fanon's contention that racism is the badge of entitlement underlying colonialism and much of global capitalism.

Throughout the book Fanon attempts to guide would-be revolutionaries. He draws heavily from Marx and attempts to stretch his ideas to meet the conditions confronted by colonized peoples in their struggles for liberation. One of the important obstacles to revolutionary change, he contends, is the colonized admiration for Western culture and its emphasis on Euro-American individualism. Fanon views this as dangerous and counterrevolutionary. For him the Third World united through a common relationship to a colonial past offers the greatest potential for world change and social justice.

TOWARD THE END

Fanon asked Jean-Paul Sartre to write the preface to *Wretched of the Earth,* which he did. The two men convened in Rome for a seventy-two hour meeting in which they discussed all sorts of ideas. Soon after that meeting Fanon's leukemia became more virulent and he was forced to go to the Soviet Union for treatment. While physicians there did all that they could do, they convinced him that his only other hope would be to seek medical attention at the National Institute of Health in Maryland where there was the best medical treatment available for this particular cancer. Fanon hated the United States for its racism and policies of exploitation directed against the poor around the world. He also feared that he would continue to be the target of French Intelligence. Still he traveled as a last resort to Washington, D.C. under the "protection" of the Central Intelligence Agency. But upon his arrival in the United States, he was detained by CIA agents and held in a hotel for ten days without treatment where he was grilled for information. By the time he was hospitalized in Bethesda it was too late. After a massive blood transfusion he contracted pneumonia and died on December 6, 1961. He was thirty-six years old.

Fanon's body was flown to Tunisia from which it was then smuggled into Algeria. He was buried in an FLN cemetery there. Three months later Algeria became independent from France.

CONCLUSION

Even though Frantz Fanon's life was cut short, he lived his years fully and productively. His life was a tribute to what Marx refers to as *praxis*—learning through doing, through changing the world. His intellectualism was fueled by his revolutionary fervor and intolerance of injustice. Not only would he influence thought about colonial revolution throughout the globe, but he would become an inspiration to insurgency movements everywhere. He exerted a powerful influence on the black power movement in the United States.

Fanon's work is indeed relevant today because it speaks directly to the postcolonial experience. As an individual trained in the understanding of human behavior, Fanon gives us important insights into the psyches and cultures of oppressed peoples everywhere and the power of race and culture in people's lives. Only through a closer, more intense reading of some of his very complex ideas can we find the true power and breadth of his thought.

BIBLIOGRAPHY

Caute, David. 1970. *Frantz Fanon.* New York: The Viking Press.

Fanon, Frantz. 1968. *The Wretched of the Earth.* New York: Grove Press.

———. 1967. *Black Skin, White Masks.* New York: Grove Press.

Geismar, Peter. 1971. *Fanon: A Biography.* New York: Dial Press.

Gordon, Lewis R.; Sharpley-Whiting, T. Denean; and White, Renée T., eds. 1996. *Fanon: A Critical Reader.* Oxford: Blackwell Publishers.

Wyrick, Deborah. 1998. *Fanon For Beginners.* New York: Writers and Readers Publishers.

22

Structuralism and Beyond: Derrida, Lacan, and Foucault

Although there are divisions of sociological thought, the last half of the twentieth century was often characterized by distinction between structuralism and poststructuralism.

Structuralism is not primarily a sociological concept, but it is a term relevant to many fields. Its liberal use often makes it difficult to define. Generally, it is a term associated with areas of linguistics, philosophy, literature, and the social sciences. It is often explained as a method of analysis based on the assumption (in linguistic theory) that phenomena do not occur in isolation, but rather occur in relation to each other. That is, things (including words and concepts) need to be assessed in terms of how they relate to one another and it is in these structured relationships (not in words alone) that we find meaning.

Structuralism is associated with what has been called a "linguistic turn" in social theory. It is a turn or trend that began in the 1960s especially in the social sciences with the work of anthropologist Claude Levi-Strauss. Levi-Strauss developed a method, borrowing from the field of sociolinguistics, to study cultures. Generally speaking, he believed that it was possible to understand culture by examining the functions and relations of the smallest constituent elements of the specific culture to be studied. He borrowed extensively from the work of linguist Ferdinand de Saussure. Saussure proposed that language could be seen as a social institution with its own structure, which stood independent of its user (he called this *langue*), but might also be viewed as that which is used by any particular communication in everyday speech (something he termed *parole*). *Langue,* or institutionalized language, is a collective system that has its own grammatical structure, rules for syntax, and the like. For Saussure, the rules for grammar and structure were contained in the unconscious and, therefore, remain more stable than *parole,* or how people use words to communicate on an everyday basis.

Levi-Strauss argued that culture was like language. In order to understand how cultures change in any significant ways, it is necessary to understand their structure, which, like the structure of language, is hidden from view. Just as Saussure was interested in the infrastructure of language, Levi-Strauss was interested in the infrastructure of culture. He proposed that deep structures were contained in the unconscious and could be discovered. He also believed that it would also be possible to discern the laws governing them. For Levi-Strauss such structures appear to underlie all actions. One of the basic structures of his "discovery" was the oppositional arrangement of concepts and words such as cooked versus raw, violence versus peace. This notion of contrast was seen by him as changeless and universal. Likewise, he examined contrasting arrangements in kinship patterns. He saw an underlying code contained in such patterns that say something more about the culture than simply how the individual fulfills a specific kinship role. In this way, the researcher might be seen as an analyzer attempting to decipher a code or set of codes that are interdependent and interrelated.

A vast array of cultural components ranging from language to rituals can be examined in this fashion. Things like the measure of time and space, types of categories of foods, and a whole host of other cultural elements are open to examination. All of these structures shape how we confront the world and interact with it. However, much of this analysis is what Saussure called synchronic—ahistorical, not looked at in any historical context.

The structuralism of Levi-Strauss was akin to, but in many way different from, the structuralism of Emile Durkheim who looked at those social structures responsible for behavior. Here, in this new structuralism, these elements of structure rest not outside the individual, but are chiefly developed within the person. Understanding structure is not oriented toward understanding human group behavior; rather, it is oriented to seeing the individual as a container of structural patterns. The human being is merely a network or web of relationships of structures that determine outcomes. Thus, under such structuralism there is no subject, only structure. The actor is superfluous. Structuralists attacked existentialism and neo-Marxism as too humanistic—utilizing outmoded methods for understanding the social world.

Although evident in this structuralism is lineage to the work of such sociologists as Emile Durkheim who sought out the unwritten rules that governed human social behavior, we can also see in this work the close acquaintance to the projects of Talcott Parsons and Erving Goffman who moved the center of sociological interest away from the actor and toward the structures that seemed to govern the actor's behavior. Structuralism, therefore, frequently is seen as a drive toward dehumanizing sociology by denying the centrality of the person and insisting upon the determinism of the structure.

POSTSTRUCTURALISM

Poststructuralism was in some ways a breakaway faction of structuralism. Still in keeping with the linguistic turn, many thinkers such as Jacques Derrida, rejected most of Saussure's ideas on linguistics save one—words in themselves have no meaning; it is the context in which they appear that gives them this. In a sense, the existentialist notion of absurdity and the meaningless of life is transformed here into an emphasis on the meaninglessness of language. Unlike the structuralists, poststructuralists for the most part assert that it is the active participant who constructs meaning.

Instead of some search for hidden rules and structures, the poststructuralist looks at ways in which meaning is constructed—how people interpret the world through what they think, say, and do. This is a shift in focus from the signified to the signifier. It is much less concerned with deep structures and more concerned with the construction of meaning. Unlike the structuralists, these theorists see no stability in the world and no objective reality at play. They often attack the focus on structural rules such as binary oppositions proposed by Levi-Strauss. The whole notion of structure is challenged.

The project of the poststructuralists is not to discover some underlying objective truths that shape reality, but rather to examine the instability of language and signs. They challenge the notion of a unified system of identity or truth. Totalizing theory is rejected, as are positivism and causality that underlie structuralism. Social constructionism becomes central to much of poststructuralism. Here facts are seen as interpretations and the world is seen as full of conflicting ones. Language needs to be challenged as something that imprisons us, not a conveyor of some ultimate truth. Thus, language is viewed as an assortment of metaphors, metonymies, and anthropomorphisms.

Exactly when poststructuralism began and who started it or what it actually is are questions that have many answers. It is certainly a perspective that is broadly encompassing and very ill-defined. In fact, the line between poststructuralism and postmodernism a very porous one. Sometimes it is even difficult to distinguish structuralist theories from poststructuralist ones.

For the purposes of a short introduction to this area, three theorists have been selected to represent poststructuralism.

JACQUES DERRIDA

It is most accurate to classify the work of Jacques Derrida as poststructuralist as opposed to other possibilities.

Jacques Derrida was born on July 15, 1930 into a prosperous Sephardic Jewish family in El-Biar near French Algeria. Although not trained as a sociologist, his ideas have had a profound impact on the social sciences as well as the humanities.

In 1940, he was expelled from public school as a result of an anti-Semitic purge undertaken by the Vichy authorities while France was under Nazi occupation. However, the following year, he was allowed to return to his classes. As a youngster he was active in soccer and wanted to play ball professionally. His performance as a student was unexceptional. However, he was an avid reader. As a teenager, he was impressed with the work of Jean-Paul Sartre, Albert Camus, and Friedrich Nietzsche.

In 1952, he began his studies in philosophy at the *École Normale Superieure* in Paris; during this time he met and married his wife Marguerite Aucouturier, a practicing psychoanalyst. In 1955 he took and failed the oral portion of the philosophy *aggregation,* an examination that would have qualified him for a tenured high school teaching position. The following year he received a grant to travel to the United States where he served as a special auditor at Harvard University. Between 1957 and 1959, he served in the French military. Part of his responsibilities included teaching French and English to the children of soldiers stationed in Koléa near Algiers. Upon the completion of his military obligation, he began writing, presenting papers at professional conferences, and teaching at a *lycée* in Le Mans. In 1960, he suffered from severe depression and spent several months with his in-laws in Prague.

Upon his recovery, Derrida began teaching philosophy at the Sorbonne between 1960 and 1964, and in 1965 he returned to *École Normal Superieure* where he taught the history of philosophy and continued his own research. In 1966, he was invited to a conference at Johns Hopkins University where he announced the death of French structuralism in a paper he presented, entitled "Structure, Sign and Play in the Discourse of the Human Sciences." It was here where he revealed much of what would be termed deconstructionism. This work would launch a revolutionary turn in linguistic scholarship.

Deconstructionism

Derrida's contribution to the linguistic turn began in the late 1960s lasting through the mid-1970s with the publication of some of his most important works, including *Grammatology* published in 1967. In some of this work he lays out a new method of analysis unlike that proposed by

Saussure and Levi-Strauss; it is an approach he has called deconstructionism. Derrida begins by condemning Levi-Strauss for his romance with nature and natural relations and for his quest for some mystical structure and center. He also provides a powerful critique of Levi-Strauss's binary opposites as an example of essential truths.

For Derrida, binary oppositions represent an ideological dead end, not a avenue to truth. Like most ideologies they draw rigid boundaries around what is acceptable and what is not: man/woman, rich/poor, intelligent/stupid. It is Derrida's assertion that in such oppositions one member of the pair is always privileged. The term to the right: woman, poor, stupid are devalued and marginalized. In back of these oppositions is the desire to hold the term at the left in esteem or centrality. There is a hierarchy of importance in language that is ideological. Deconstruction seeks to subvert the central term. Deconstruction is a practice of decentering the hierarchy, enabling the reader to liberate meaning from these terms that might not have been intended. In so doing, language is liberated from essentialist meaning and becomes a free-play of words and meanings.

Generally speaking, deconstructionism rejects the search in metaphysics for unity of essence that will yield some ultimate truth. In its place it proposes the relativity of truth and of knowing, thus rejecting what most philosophy has led us to in the West until now.

In deconstructionism, there is an attempt to undermine the belief that language has an essential integrity associated with truth. For Derrida there is never one meaning attached to words. Language and meaning are constantly shifting. Language is frequently riddled with paradox and logical aporias. It is often too vague to convey an objective meaning. It is Derrida's task to expose the fallacies of universal meaning contained in writing and speaking. He borrows from the sociologist, Roland Barthes' notion of the "death of the author," who suggested that in modern society meaning is subjectively constructed.

For Derrida, all of life is text. This is part of what he means when he says that "there is nothing outside the text." According to the ideals of logocentrism, which posits the author as God, Derrida says that with deconstruction we are all authors, all gods. By working to undermine what is written (figuratively), we create a world of new meaning. But we have to come to terms with the power that rests within each of us. Knowing we have such power is only the first stage; action is revolutionary. However, Derrida has not moved beyond knowledge. For Derrida, there is no God, no center, no truth, no answer; there is only the meaning we give to the word—through language. But we have the power to use language to will ultimate liberation from meanings that attempt to bind us.

It is his contention that texts are traditionally believed to convey a specific or particular meaning, but in reality they do not. Thus, where it is assumed that language is capable of expressing ideas of the author without changing them, this is typically not the case. What the author intends to convey is subject to a variety of interpretations.

Derrida's style of reading undermines basic assumptions about clarity of objective meaning. Also, drawing upon psychoanalytic theory, he asserts that the author's intention in selection of words cannot be uncritically accepted. There are many unconscious influences that lead one to select one word over another, one tense in preference to another that might have greater significance than consciously intended. The reader becomes an instrument for giving the text meaning, which might be significantly different from what the author consciously intended.

The idea of hermeneutics enters readily into this system of meaning assignment. In Derrida's system, the signifier does not yield up a signified meaning directly—it is funneled through another. The signifiers and the signified are constantly in a state of disarray. So, if you wanted to know the meaning of a signifier, should you find a word in a dictionary, it will only give you more signifiers and those in turn need to be looked up and so on. Unlike Saussure and other structuralists who saw the signifier as describing the signified, Derrida believes that this is impossible. No true relationship exists between the signifier and anything signified. There is never an exact match.

Actually, signs hold no meaning in themselves. Meaning is scattered and dispersed along a chain of signifiers and cannot be "nailed down." This is a radical concept and one can readily see the implications this has for culture, generally.

Derrida at Home

By the late 1970s and early 1980s Derrida was applying deconstruction to art, psychology, and literature. He traveled extensively conducting annual seminars at Yale, Cornell, the New School for Social Research, and the University of California at Irvine.

Deconstructionism revolutionized the way many intellectuals and theorists saw the world. However, it also came under attack from political critics both left and right who viewed it as undermining previously held notions of social integration.

Derrida became a central, though controversial, intellectual figure at the close of the twentieth century. He currently serves as the director of studies at *École des Hautes Etudies in Sciences Sociale* in Paris.

JACQUES LACAN

Jacques-Marie-Émile Lacan was born in Paris on April 13, 1901. He was France's most celebrated psychotherapist.

Growing up as the first-born son in a middle-class family of conservative Catholics, he was educated in Jesuit schools until the receipt of his baccalaureate. He studied medicine at Stanislas College and went into a clinical residency at Sainte Anne's Hospital where he worked with women in the Special Infirmary Division. It was there that he came into contact with the renowned psychiatrist Clerambault who supervised his training. In 1932, he successfully completed his doctoral thesis on paranoid psychosis. In 1934, he began to train as a psychoanalyst with the prestigious *Le Societe Psychanalytique de Paris.*

Career as a Therapist

Just as Lacan began to settle into his career as a therapist and published his first studies, the Nazis marched on Paris. Lacan immediately suspended most of his scholarly and professional activities. *Le Societe Psychoanalytique de Paris* closed its doors. He worked quietly during the occupation at Val de Grace, a military hospital.

During this period he enjoyed an active social life and became acquainted with Georges Bataille, Salvador Dalí, and other celebrities who were living in Paris. He even served as Pablo Picasso's personal physician for a short time. Still, he did not resume his professional activities as a psychoanalyst until 1946 when *Le Societe Psychanalytique* reopened its doors and he became supervisor of training there. By this time he was forty-six years old.

In the late 1940s and early 1950s he organized seminars, presented papers, and began to make a name for himself in the psychoanalytic community. In his work he integrated the classical contributions of Freud with structuralist thoughts of Levi-Strauss. He began re-reading Freud in terms of modern linguistic theory and significantly transformed psychoanalysis in the process.

With the exception of the Frankfurt school, Lacan's theories moved psychoanalytic theory that much closer to sociology in the sense that his work attempted to break down the false distinctions between self and society created by language. For Lacan, language was the means through which the self became separated and alienated from others. Without language, there could be no subject. Borrowing from Hegel, he posits that language separated the social from the natural world. Even though each individual gains identity through it, each also becomes separated from others because of it. In his view, language fragmented the world as well as the self.

Like Derrida, Lacan views language as too rigid and incapable of accurate expression of affect. Words convey multiple meanings and can often be used to convey things they were never intended to convey. He proposes that the unconscious plays an important role in how we use language. Jokes, dreams, slips of the tongue are often ways in which hidden meaning is revealed. It is Lacan's belief that language creates the unconscious and that dreams are, in fact, representations of unconscious discourse, expressing things that are hidden from clear view. But like language, dreams are governed by linguistic mechanisms, especially metaphor and metonymy. Lacan rejects the Freudian concept of the cohesive ego, and although he affirms that the unconscious holds all meaning, he does not believe that it can ever be an object of knowledge. For Lacan, the unconscious is neither instinctual nor primordial. Each time we attempt to grasp the unconscious we lose it. It is fleeting, ephemeral.

The Looking Glass

Given the fragmented nature of modern society, Lacan believes that the individual is equally fragmented. Unlike those therapists who seek to humanistically reassemble the shattered remnants of self, Lacan sees this as a futile project. Because the self is a mere reflection of language and language is inherently non-cohesive, people cannot be otherwise. Still, he understands that there is a deep, internal craving for wholeness, not only of the self, but also a drive for a oneness with the universe.

At the very beginning of life, everyone has a sense that they are integrated into an undifferentiated whole. The world has no clear categories or divisions. This is a state of bliss, what he refers to as *l'imaginaire*. It is only as we mature that the world comes apart. It becomes fragmented—broken down into unrelated pieces—mother's arm, an elbow, a breast.

It is at what Lacan refers to as the "mirror stage" that we first delude ourselves in the belief that we are whole selves. This is a pre-Oedipal stage of human development in which the infant (between six and eighteen months) first recognizes its own reflection in a mirror. Incidentally, this is the same time when language develops. Upon viewing this image, the child is filled with joy that there is a unified self, separated from the rest of the world, yet integrated as a complete self. The self is seen as a object in and of itself, separated from the world, from others. But this too is a myth. Still, the child is accompanied by an adult caregiver who also looks into the mirror alongside the child and assures the child that this mirror image belongs to him or her and that the other image, that of the caregiver or parent, is the image of an "other." Thus, the child is indoctrinated into a delusional belief, a narcissistic falsehood, of self and other. Seeing the self in the mirror, the child simultaneously imagines an individuality that is at home in capitalistic society—at home in its shallowness and egocentrism. However, the self is but one of many objects that make up a world of objects. For Lacan, this notion of a fixed self or unified self undermines creativity and spontaneity of many separate selves with many separate aspects.

It is about the same time that a self emerges that the child develops language. For Lacan, language is a source of alienation and separation. Once the child begins to label things, he or she is separated from them. Language forces the person to give up on the sense of oneness with the universe. The world is objectified, objects labeled for their use to us. We are forever removed from the bliss of oneness because of language and so this oneness is relegated to the place without language—the unconscious.

Lacan links the process of individualization to the Oedipus complex of Freud. However, he calls this separation and not castration by *le nom du pere* or in the name of the father. Of course, this is a double entendre, meaning both God the father as well as the familial father or the son's sexual rival for his mother's love. The child's desire for sex with his mother is a desire to return to the womb, to return to the blissful place of origin when one was connected to everything. However, the father's word "no" is that which prevents this. It is language used to control the child. Thus, the child's move from a blissful state of *l'imaginare* where one is connected to the universe to what Lacan calls *la symbolic*—the stage of language—alienates and individuates. Once the child takes on the language, not so much the superego as proposed by Freud, he or she is socialized and can no longer even fathom a unity of all with all. Language forever alienates the individual from the universe and the self. If one were to return to this unity, the self would cease to exist.

For Lacan, this alienation is the root of all neurosis. It is a lack we cannot name. This is the poignancy in his theory, the longing not for love or sex but for an erotic connection with the universe. This lack is also central to the reason for the development of language in the first place—naming what is not immediately available to us, just as lack is central to Freud's Oedipus complex. The void that is left us—this lack—is Lacan's metaphor for castration. It is a removal of something we lose forever in developing as people. The phallus is representative of what we have lost.

Lacan's Impact

Lacan's work gained prominence in France and elsewhere after World War II. As a clinical practitioner, he became notorious for his brief clinical sessions—some of which lasted only five minutes. He was condemned by his colleagues for this and found it necessary to resign the presidency of *Le Societe Psychanalytique de Paris* in 1953. However, he began his own psychoanalytic society with a number of colleagues that same year, *Le Societe Francaise de Psychoanalyse.*

He remained working at Sainte Anne's Hospital until 1963 and continued to develop a large following by promoting a series of lectures at his newly formed institute. Claude Levi-Strauss served as a guest lecturer. The *Societe* published its own journal, which became an outlet for many of his ideas. He began training therapists and developed his own school for this purpose.

He gained considerable notoriety for his highly unorthodox methods of training analysts and conducting analysis. Yet, he became a figure of international acclaim. He traveled around the world giving lectures on his methods.

In 1975 he came to the United States to lecture at Columbia and Yale universities. Those who use his methods refer to themselves as Lacanians.

He died in Paris on September 9, 1981. He was eighty years old.

MICHEL FOUCAULT

If there was one poststructuralist who has become representative of late twentieth-century avant garde thought, it was Michel Foucault.

Foucault was born in Poitiers, France on October 15, 1926. His father, Paul Foucault, was a prominent surgeon and professor of anatomy and his mother, Anne Malapert Foucault, was the daughter of a surgeon, who was also a professor. The family was Catholic and financially well off.

As a child, Foucault attended a Jesuit school, Saint Stanislas, the school also attended by Jacques Lacan. He later entered *Lycée Henri IV* in Paris and was admitted to the *École Normale Superieuer* as the fourth highest ranked student. There, he studied philosophy with the renowned philosopher and linguist Maurice Merleau-Ponty. He was extremely depressed as a student and had trouble relating to his classmates. He attempted suicide more than once. It was a time when he was also coming to terms with his homosexuality.

Academically, Foucault excelled in school. In 1948 he received his license in philosophy and in 1952 passed his *agrégation* allowing him to teach philosophy in the French school system. In 1949, he received a license in psychology and in 1952 was awarded a diploma in psychopathology. In the mid-1950s, Foucault traveled throughout Europe teaching French first at the University of Lille in Uppsala, Sweden, later at the University of Warsaw, and finally at the University of Hamburg. His doctoral dissertation, *Madness and Civilization,* was published in 1961. He returned to France in 1966 to head the philosophy department at the University of Clermont-Ferrard.

Foucault was radical in his political and social thought. In the early 1950s, he joined the Communist Party. He and his lover Daniel Defert became very active in the French protest movements of the 1960s. In 1966, Foucault went to Tunisia with Defert and did some teaching there while on leave from Clermont-Ferrard. Upon returning to France, his second book, *The Order of Things,* became an important best-seller, giving him greater renown. He was offered a position at the University of Paris, which he accepted.

His Work

Foucault's intellectual radicalism was his trademark. As a trained philosopher, he was greatly influenced by modern German philosophers and was most profoundly affected by the work of Nietzsche. There were very strong currents of antihumanism in his work.

Of all the poststructuralists, it was Foucault who was most interested in the institutions that constituted social and cultural life. He also believed that there were unconscious structures and rules that governed all history, all economics, and all social practices.

His early work is very much a history of important social institutions in the West: the history of madness, the history of the clinic, the history of the prison. Yet, these are no simple histories; they are what Foucault prefers to call genealogies. This work is clearly poststructuralist, having a host of linguistic inputs, contours, and references. It is Foucault's intent in each of these works to explore how knowledge is acquired through ideas and modes of discourse, including recordkeeping. Above all, he is interested in finding both written and unwritten rules for the formation of knowledge by looking at events that have been written about or recorded in some way. He wants to find the elements that give shape to discourse. He refers to this as the archaeology of knowledge. It is Foucault's belief that disciplines like history or sociology are themselves forms of discourse that not only seek to discover what is, but also construct the world, and by doing so determine how we live in it.

Although early structuralists like Levi-Strauss and, to some extent, poststructuralists like Derrida looked at discourse as meanings imposed by the signifiers and the signified, Foucault looks at discourse as a system of exclusion and control. For him discourse is really the establishment of boundaries determining what can be said and thought and how one can or cannot behave. For example, madness is a type of discourse determining what behavior and speech is acceptable.

Unlike Derrida who looked at the falsity of binary oppositions and therefore uncovered the meaningless of words, Foucault looks at how these oppositions began. He is interested in the notion of truth and how truth is, in a Nietzschean sense, associated with the power to impose one's will on another. For both Nietzsche and Foucault there is no legitimate truth, only power.

It is his study of madness in which he aims to discover exactly how control over discourse is exercised and by what authority. Here he examines a point in time, the Renaissance, when madness and reason were not dichotomized and when there was no binary opposition separating the sane from the insane. His study led him to discover how between 1650 and 1800 there was a division established in discourse. Reason became the dominant power, trumping unreason. Anything that was not sane or reasonable was madness or nonreason. In his search for the basis of power and control, he finds it in medicine, but particularly in psychiatry.

At one time there was no distinction between the sane and the mad. The mad were integrated into society. The asylum emerged as a place that housed the destitute, the unemployed, and the thief. Special housing would be built for the mad to be overseen by reasonable people. In fact, the field of psychology, and later psychiatry, were developed so that they could draw some of these boundaries and exercise control.

Foucault advances the idea that with the Enlightenment the world saw tighter restrictions and categorizations of discourses and behaviors. These tighter restrictions seemed to reflect the imposition of power of one group over another. Like Max Weber and members of the Frankfurt school, Foucault is critical of the Enlightenment and the type of reason it promoted. Like Nietzsche, he sees post-Enlightenment reason as aimed at strict control and regulation of all discourse, including behavior, and the repression of unregulated affect.

Just as the insane are sequestered and moved behind walls for the purpose of isolation, observation, and control, so are deviants of all sorts. Beggars, criminals, the ill, and homosexuals are all categorized. He suggests that the methodologies of classification, categorization, isolation, and observation of these various types are rooted in the practice of medicine. By labeling and naming there is greater control or potential for control. In fact, Foucault becomes very interested in how discourse of social categories regulates and regiments modern societies. His later work is often seen to be a focus on the archeology of power, an examination of how knowledge classifies discourse, including behavior, for the purpose of controlling it. What can be said and what can't be said is the subject of those who seek to control others.

Foucault's studies are no mere explorations of sociological phenomena; they are detailed descriptions of how knowledge has been used to shape the world of human relationships—how it has become a base of power and control through a system of classification, observation, and, finally, manipulation. The mental institution and the prison are guided by the same scientific principles as the medical hospital, the school, the military, and the factory. In each of these we can see similar discursive elements aimed at observation and control. This is part of what he refers to as "carceral culture," a culture wherein we are imprisoned by both discourse and the institutions that support it.

Like Nietzsche and Freud, Foucault is concerned with the self-imposition of these methods of regulation and control—the internalization of the superego. In doing so, he moves away from a locus of power outside of the self opening him up to criticism by those who see this control imposed by forces external to the individual.

Legacy of Foucault

Foucault's work is intellectually expansive and intriguing. It examines the ways in which we have come to be dominated and explores the elements that condition this. However, for some critics, much of his discussion of power appears as a form of reification—breathing life into symbolic and institutional constructs. There is no search for the specific sources of control other than in discourse, which has a life of its own. There are few questions raised about those who benefit from these configurations, and we must, therefore, assume that we desire this control. People become simply products of discourse lost in an array of other words. Foucault's rejection of humanism leaves no hope for transcending this predicament.

Nevertheless, Foucault's work was in many ways revolutionary. Not only was his approach to the subject matter radically new and innovative, but his subject matter was intriguing: the marginalized, the oppressed, the abandoned. However, unlike Derrida and Lacan whose personal lives appeared tame by comparison, Foucault lived his life in the fast lane. He spent much of his nonworking hours obsessed by fleeting sexual relationships with young strangers and became heavily involved in the sadomasochistic scene in San Francisco. He frequented public baths there during the height of the AIDS epidemic and experimented with a variety of drugs. Yet, during this time he was still able to write a brilliant history of human sexuality. He died of AIDS at the age of fifty-seven on June 25, 1984.

BIBLIOGRAPHY

Campagne, Roland. 1995. *Derrida.* New York: Maxwell McMillan.

Derrida, Jacques. 1982. *Margins of Philosophy.* Chicago: University of Chicago Press.

———. 1976. *Of Grammatology.* Baltimore: Johns Hopkins University Press.

Eribon, Didier. 1991. *Michel Foucault.* Cambridge: Harvard University Press.

Foucault, Michel. 1977. *Discipline and Punish.* New York: Random House.

———. 1965. *Madness and Civilization.* New York: Random House.

Lacan, Jacques. 1981. *Language of the Self.* Baltimore: Johns Hopkins Press.

———. 1977. *Écrits: A Selection.* New York: Norton.

Marini, Marcelle. 1992. *Jacques Lacan: The French Context.* New Brunswick, NJ: Rutgers University Press.

Noris, Christopher. 1987. *Derrida.* Cambridge: Harvard University Press.

Roudinesco, Elisabeth. 1997. *Jacques Lacan.* New York: Columbia University Press.

Sarup, Madan. 1989. *Post-Structuralism and Postmodernism.* Athens, GA: University of Georgia Press.

Schumway, David. 1989. *Michel Foucault.* Boston: Twayne Publishers.

23

Talcott Parsons: The Systems Society

Talcott Parsons was a seminal figure in American sociology. His book, *The Structure of Social Action,* published in 1937, was responsible for moving American sociology away from its reformist roots and toward a more rarified view of the social world.

Talcott Parsons was born on December 13, 1903 in Colorado Springs, Colorado. The son of a Congregational minister, Edward Smith Parsons, and a suffragette, Mary Augusta Ingersoll Parsons, he was the youngest of five siblings. His home life was one of Protestant Puritan and reformist traditions. Edward Smith Parsons, his father, came from a prominent American family, a member of which had served as the U.S. Commissioner for Indian Affairs under President Ulysses S. Grant. Edward Parsons had a degree in divinity and was a supporter and participant in the social gospel movement. He was also a renown scholar, taught English at Colorado College where he became dean, and published several papers on John Milton. In 1919, when his son Talcott was fourteen, he became president of Marietta College in Ohio. He also influenced his son to pursue a university career. Mary Parsons, his mother, had descended from a prestigious family in Massachusetts and was the great-great granddaughter of the renown theologian, Jonathan Edwards.

Educated in New York's Horace Mann High School, upon graduation Talcott Parsons attended Amherst College. There he majored in biology, but became interested in the economics of Vilfredo Pareto and in European sociology. Upon graduation from Amherst in 1924, he attended the

London School of Economics. It was there that he took courses with the famed functionalist anthropologist, Bronislaw Malinowski. He also met Helen Walker, the woman who he would marry.

Parsons continued his graduate studies at the University of Heidelberg where he encountered the ideas of Max Weber and became fascinated with social theory. Weber had taught at Heidelberg, but died a few years before Parsons's arrival there. Nevertheless, Parsons joined a salon presided over by Marianne Weber, Max Weber's wife, who continued in the intellectual tradition of her husband. Parsons received his doctorate from Heidelberg in 1927.

More than any other scholar, it was Parsons who introduced Weber to America by translating his masterpiece, *The Protestant Ethic and the Spirit of Capitalism,* into English. One cannot help but see the important influence this brilliant German scholar had on Parsons.

Parsons returned to the United States after his studies and received an appointment as an instructor of economics at Amherst. The next year, he received a faculty appointment at Harvard University, which seemed well suited for a young man of his particular background and breeding. At Harvard, he began teaching economics, but soon transferred to the new sociology department there. In 1937 Parsons published *The Structure of Social Action,* which was to secure for him a special place in the annals of sociology.

PARSONS'S CONTRIBUTION

One of the essential problems with the book, *The Structure of Social Action,* was that few people understood it, even some of the most prominent sociologists of the day. The work appeared to be atypically American. It was neither empirical research nor ethnographic, which were the most common forms of American sociology at that time. The work was highly abstract, even abstruse.

Parsons wanted to take the classical theory he learned in Europe and extend it. Unlike most American sociologists, he was interested in constructing "grand theory" in an attempt to integrate all social science into one theoretical framework—an enormous and, in all likelihood, an impossible undertaking. His orientation was that of a functionalist. Although he extensively cited ideas of Pareto, Durkheim, and Weber in his review of theorists leading to his own ideas, he conspicuously omitted the theories of Karl Marx.

As a functionalist, it was his position that order and stability were essential to the well-being of any society. Because society could be viewed as a system of interrelated parts, he was interested in discovering how these interrelations worked to maintain such an orderly system. To this end he poses what he refers to as the essential sociological problem. In his mind this is the Hobbesian question: If the very nature of humankind is violence, why is it that society is not characterized as a war of all against all? (It is obvious from this that he accepts the Hobbesian premise of people being innately violent.) He finds his answer to this question in the work of Comte, Spencer, and Durkheim. He adds himself to this tradition of thought.

In the functionalist tradition, Parsons asserts that societies are made up of social structures and substructures that are intricately related to one another. Each of these individual structures serves functions for the other. He sees this collectivity as constituting a system. Each of these social structures performs at least four basic functions in order to maintain the orderly social system. These are: adaptation to the environment and its needs, attainment of goals that it has defined, integration and regulation of interrelationships of components, and pattern maintenance or latency, meaning that it must promote the existing cultural pattern through individual motivation.

Parsons's contribution is his attempt to move classical theory away from what was deemed to be too structuralist and toward what is now called action theory. In doing this, he dismisses the idea that structures of society alone determine outcomes. Instead, he proposes that human behavior is volunteeristic and that people act with free will and their actions are voluntary, intentional, and often symbolic—based upon interpretation of events. All behavior is seen as conditioned if not engendered by norms and values and directed toward goals. He makes clear that norms and values do not necessarily determine action. The most important social process in determining action is communication and interpretation of meaning.

Unlike Durkheim who proposed that systems are held together by collective conscience or a shared sense of the world coupled with common values, Parsons substitutes the Freudian superego or individual conscience. In this model, society socializes individuals who internalize the norms and values of society. In fact, a cornerstone of his theory is that values are institutionalized on a social plane and absorbed into the psyche on an individual plane. This, to him, explains the great degree of social stability he sees around him. However, he sees the individual as having a range of choice as to how he or she interacts with the world and assumes a place within it.

Parsons asserts that personal interaction is based upon what he calls pattern variables. This is where much confusion about his theory emerges. Nevertheless, the bottom line here is that individuals are not driven by goals and particular values to make choices, but are led by personal desire to maximize gratification. Values, however, do play an important role. In each individual and every social system what is viewed as gratification can be very different. Much of this is based upon what he refers to as need dispositions. That is, that which drives the actor to accept or reject objects or goals or leads one to seek them out.

Parsons constructs an elaborate system of what he calls pattern variables and identifies four fundamental dilemmas confronting all actors. These include particularism versus universalism, wherein actors must decide whether or not to treat the other according to some universally applied criteria emanating from general norms, or to treat the other in accordance with criteria unique to that person. Thus, a person might be viewed according to specific criteria established by the norms of society, or be accepted for whom he or she is, regardless of social norms. Performance versus quality is another. Objects can be valued by actors for how they perform a function or for their own sake. Another pattern, affective versus affective neutrality means an actor engages with an object (or the world for that matter) according to his or her feelings or works to maintain neutral feelings. Ascription versus achievement is when one judges others according to who they are rather than what they achieved. Finally, in diffuseness versus specificity actors either engage in a total relationship or choose one focused on a specific activity.

From the above, we can see how values might enter into this model; but we also come to recognize that inherent in this theory is Parsons's idea that all interaction is interpreted through symbolic understanding. By this he means that people do not directly relate to others but perceive and interpret before they relate. One makes a determination to be affective or nonaffective, for instance, based on any number of factors. It is the actor, himself or herself, who imbues the world with meaning and determines which values to apply.

According to Parsons, the patterned categories of interaction represent an exhaustive range of choices in human interaction. Societies and actors could be categories according to these patterns. Thus, American society might be categorized, empirically, as universal, affectively neutral, specific, and performance oriented.

The variety of categories proliferates in Parsons's theory as he attempts to cover every externality. His system image of society relies heavily on biological modeling and imagery. The entire theoretical package eventually becomes unwieldy. He does his best to avoid conflict even to the point of distorting Freud and setting aside the heart of his theory, the id and the innate drives, specifically the libido.

Parsons sees all action as directed, some have said by an invisible hand, to maintaining an orderly social system. For him, change occurs in an orderly way and there is much in his writings to support the idea of linear progress as societies move from nondifferentiation in their division of labor to intense differentiation. He echos the ideas of Durkheim who saw societies moving from a primitive state to a modern one. For Parsons, like Durkheim, science is responsible for such change.

PARSONS AT HARVARD

The ideas expressed by Parsons had a particular resonance with the times in which he wrote. Certainly, any sophisticated theory that could avoid coming to terms with Marx was significantly important to a nation that feared the growth of communism around the world and resented intellectual volleys against capitalism. Indeed, Harvard became the most important university in the nation for social theory, mainly because of Parsons. Although much of this had to do with his ability to direct academic attention to less proletarian activity, his work appeared to have relevance to the attempts made to keep the United States from being undermined by a growing cadre of leftist intellectuals. Sociology needed to become more mainstream in order to be more fully accepted. Here was a very sophisticate theory that did not really lend itself to class concerns.

In 1944 Parsons became chair of the sociology department at Harvard and two years later established the Department of Social Relations, which combined most of the social sciences into one department. In 1949 he was elected president of the American Sociological Association and throughout the 1950s and 1960s, with the publication of other important works such as *The Social System,* published in 1951, he became the central figure in American sociology.

Parsons was lauded for his discovery of the growing middle class after World War II, proving Marx's notion of two classes wrong. Of course, he needed to gloss over how Marx defined class. Still, there was a significant amount of support for his conservative view of the world; it seemed to resonate with the 1950s and early 1960s. But Parsons was no reactionary. He had stood up against fascism in Europe and was equally concerned about issues of civil rights in the United States.

PARSONS'S ECLIPSE

The curious world of Talcott Parsons was where society was a system, comprised of interactive subsystems adhering to a certain set of unwritten rules. Chief of these was that all components of the system worked to maintain order and homeostasis. No living, breathing system could exist without serving functions. It was also the description of the rules for the interrelationship of systems function and action that he gained a reputation as an important social theorist.

There could be no question that his systems approach to society was important. It found great acceptance in the 1940s and 1950s and even into the 1960s in the United States. It appeared to depoliticize human interaction. But history played no significant role in it. It was an important and significant alternative to the behavioristic models being advanced in psychology by people like B. F. Skinner.

But by the late 1960s the United States, and much of the world, was witnessing a significant cultural revolution. Pockets of resistance sprang up and confronted entrenched systems of power. The civil rights movement, the black power movement, the women's movement, the antiwar movements, the environmental movement, the workers' and human rights movements, and the movement for gay and lesbian equality shook the very foundation of society. Not only was the United States Army abroad, involved in a war that most Americans were rejecting as unjust and horrific, but there were now soldiers on college campuses aiming their rifles at protesters, attempting to maintain order in cities and shooting at rioters in the streets. The nation did not appear to be operating as one well-oiled machine where everything and everyone had a specific place working to maintain order. The face of society was changing.

The well-mannered and soft-spoken Talcott Parsons was to take a backseat to more radical theorists of social change.

BIBLIOGRAPHY

Gerhandt, Unta. 2002. *Talcott Parsons: An Intellectual Biography*. Cambridge: Cambridge University Press.

Parsons, Talcott. 1951. *The Social System*. New York: The Free Press.

———. 1949. *The Structure of Social Action*. New York: McGraw-Hill.

Rocher, Guy. 1975. *Talcott Parsons and American Sociology*. New York: Barnes & Noble.

24

Erving Goffman: The Drama of Self

One of the most innovative contributors to sociology in the latter part of the twentieth century was Erving Goffman. His books were not only of interest to sociologists, but also had a considerable audience throughout the behavioral sciences and among the general public. Goffman's work was rooted in ethnographic studies and dealt with issues of great human interest: identity, marginalization, and communication. Yet, his sense of what it meant to be human was frequently controversial.

Erving Goffman was born in the town of Manville in Alberta, Canada on June 11, 1922. He was the son of Max and Ann Goffman who had been part of a wave of Jewish Ukrainians who migrated to Canada at the end of the nineteenth and into the early twentieth century. He had a younger sister, Frances.

Goffman attended St. John's Technical High School and went on to study chemistry at the University of Manitoba in the fall of 1939. Between 1943 and 1944 he work at the National Film Board of Canada in Ottawa. He left the University of Manitoba to pursue his studies at the University of Toronto and completed his degree there in 1945, winning a scholarship to the University of Chicago. While there, Goffman studied sociology and social anthropology and took several courses with Herbert Blummer and Everett Hughes. In 1949, he received a master's, and wrote a thesis on radio soap operas.

He moved to the desolate Shetland Islands off the coast of Scotland in 1949 and lived there for over a year collecting ethnographic materials that became the basis for much of his dissertation as well as his book, *The Presentation of Self in Everyday Life.* He traveled to Paris in 1951 where he stayed several months before returning to Chicago, teaching and working on his doctorate. In 1952 he met Angelica Choate, who was studying psychology. They married in 1953 and soon had their only child, a son, Tom.

The family moved to Washington where Goffman became an assistant director at St. Elizabeth's Hospital. He used his position to observe behavior of mental patients. It was there that he gathered material for his book, *Asylums.*

THE PRESENTATION OF SELF IN EVERYDAY LIFE

If there was one book for which he would gain fame and notoriety, it was his first major effort. This was *The Presentation of Self in Everyday Life,* which was published by the University of Edinburgh Press in 1956. The book remains one of the most innovative approaches to understanding the construction and nature of the social self.

The framework of the book, which is aimed at better understanding human interaction, is based on the metaphor of theatrical performance. It is the premise of the book that in presenting the self to others, each individual attempts to control and construct the impressions they have on others. The book attempts to explain and describe the techniques used to achieve this goal. Goffman develops an array of terms for the tools he believes people use for this purpose. He calls his overall approach dramaturgy.

According to Goffman, each participant in the game of social relations is an actor engaged in a performance. The nature of each performance is shaped by the audience and the environment that help elicit impressions. It is the goal of the actor to give the audience what it seems to want. To illustrate how this works, he draws on different human experiences to explain some of the workings of this system.

For Goffman, behavior with others is not merely intended to get things done, it is meant to convey meaning about the self. It is possible to examine this activity which helps construct as self in terms of front-stage and back-stage behavior.

Front stage is where people are most likely to maintain decorum, to be polite, and to promote a particular image. This is where they are seen by others. There is always a conscious effort made in this arena to project proper character traits. Here the duties of role expectation are played out and fulfilled. Even though some of this is done through verbal communication, there is much in the way of symbolic communication going on here: the use of body language, facial expressions, and even the use of props. An attempt is made in the front stage to provide a consistent public image.

It is Goffman's assertion that much of what goes on up front is a dramatic program aimed at what he calls impression management. By this he means communication of information through performance in an attempt to control what others might think of the actor. What is being presented, however, is not real. It is a show. It is an idealized vision consistent with the expectations of society. Often there is mystery involved wherein attributes of the actor seem to be hidden or secret. This is done to keep up audience interest. However, Goffman notes, the only mystery is that there is no mystery.

The most successful performances are often staged by teams rather than individuals. A good example of this could be a husband and wife team out to dinner with friends. Members of the team cooperate in their performance in order to convey a proper image before the audience. Like individuals, teams perform in front regions but rehearse in back regions. According to Goffman, there is a "guarded passageway" between front stage and back stage. Those of a team sharing a common back stage usually share strong social bonds, because they need to trust each other with back-stage secrets as they go up front to perform. Disagreements are carried on back stage.

For Goffman, theater becomes the perfect metaphor. It is a place where people take on and then discard roles. There is magic here as well as suspended disbelief. Actors need to be in tune with the audience. They need to know just how much they can get away with. Front stages are carefully guarded, whereas back stages give the actor an opportunity to let his or her guard down. Still, the back stage could possibly be a front in another context. Each audience is different and there must be an understanding of the varying demands of various audiences.

Goffman appears to understand that reality is constructed through a complex set of social arrangements. The individual is not one self but rather a constellation of selves working before a host of audiences. Throughout *Presentation of Self,* Goffman seems to perceive the individual as nothing more than a cog responsible for the maintenance of the social world by playing his or her part. If fact, he refers to the self as a "peg" upon which "something of a collaborative manufacture will be hung for a time." The ways for maintaining the image of the self do not reside in the peg, but rather in the social establishments and demands surrounding the peg. In looking at Goffman, many come to the conclusion that he does not believe in an authentic self, and, if he ideally did, sees no hope for ever achieving one.

Still, this is a truly significant model. Goffman's contribution might raise the ire of many, but is just one more important theory attempting to explain the fragmentation that has come about with the process of modernization.

Through the efforts of Herbert Blummer, Goffman was awarded a position of visiting assistant professor at the University of California at Berkeley in 1958. By 1962, his book had already won several awards.

Goffman became full professor, and he was on his way to becoming one of the most prominent sociologists in the United States.

THE OUTSIDER AND THE STIGMATIZED

Goffman's work in dramaturgy deals with how everyday life is guided by unwritten rules of impression management. However, early in his career Goffman began to concern himself with those who remained outside these particular rules. In his book *Asylums* (1961) and in his later work on social stigma, he expresses interest in the identity of those who are deviant and marginalized. For instance, in his work on the mental hospital, he discusses the ways in which the total institution changes the very nature of human interaction.

For Goffman, the total institution is a place for imposing change on the patient or inmate from a point outside of the individual. Unlike the everyday life (described in his first book), where individuals work to sustain a particular identity and where one's fellow participants in the drama work to collaborate in this enterprise, the inmate in the asylum is segregated from those who could be supportive and must interact with staff who require a different form of interaction. Inmates are constantly subject to an array of degradations, humiliations, and personal debasements and a removal of those supports that previously assisted them in their projects. Goffman notes that this is the way society acts in the name of God, or justice, or cure to transform the sinful, the criminal, or the ill.

Goffman records the self's resistance to its transformations and degradations and illustrates what he calls "secondary adjustments" when inmates challenge the staff of these institutions and assert their own sense of self through exercising some forbidden control over their environment. In *Stigma,* Goffman deals with how stigmatized individuals work to maintain their own unique identities and the obstacles they confront in a society that discredits them. For Goffman, stigma is not merely physical deformity, but can be almost any type of perceived flaw in personality or character. Not having an MBA for a managerial job could be considered stigma. He discusses the various ways by which an individual acts to manage or hide stigma such as concealment, covering, or disclosure. In some ways, this work is an extension of Goffman's thesis in *Presentation of Self.*

PERSONAL CHANGE AND TRAGEDY

Goffman's work gained him an international reputation. *The Presentation of Self in Everyday Life* was translated into at least ten languages. It appeared to strike a harmonic chord with social life around the world.

In 1964, after the publication of his important work, *Behavior in Public Places,* his wife, Angelica, committed suicide. She was 35. Living off the royalties from his books and substantial investment returns, Goffman took some time to find himself.

In 1966 he spent a sabbatical year at the Harvard Center for International Affairs working with the famous game theorist, Thomas Shelling. In 1967, he published *Interaction Ritual* in which he applied game theory techniques to his own research. In fact, throughout his writing Goffman had a keen interest in this approach. He used game theory in his stock market investments and, in fact, had spent a considerable amount of time playing blackjack in Las Vegas. He had even worked there for awhile as a dealer and a pit boss.

In 1968 Goffman returned to teaching. However, he did not return to Berkeley. He was offered a sociology position at the University of Pennsylvania, which he accepted. Goffman continued to write and further develop his ideas. Although he produced some of his most important work early in his career, much of what he did now seemed to be a further elaboration of his earlier thoughts.

Frame Analysis, published in 1974, was his most ambitious effort. Here Goffman attempts to examine how people compartmentalize experience in life and how they even compartmentalize aspects of the self. Although basically a set of intricately woven essays, the book uses Gregory Bateson's notion of "the frame" to structure an analytic paradigm for the investigation of social interaction.

It is Goffman's assertion that whenever people experience something, they tend to categorize or frame the experience. Each situation is assigned a context that has its own rules. He begins by looking at two essential or primary frameworks. The first is what he refers to as a natural frame and the second is the social frame.

The natural framework identifies and categorizes phenomena as being physical or natural events with nothing social instigating them. Weather could be an example of this. Thus, a warm sunny day can frame certain behavior (such as going to the beach) whereas a bitterly cold or overcast day might not. The social framework is based on past experience in which the subject places the phenomenon in a social category that emerges from these experiences. An example of this might be going to a doctor for a yearly physical. Inherent in this category is a element of planned action directed by someone at someone else with an aim of directing or controlling the other. Social frameworks are always built upon natural ones, or at least overlap with them. Actually, there are multiple frames and many overlays.

How people come to share these frames, understand, use, and control them is of the utmost importance to Goffman. He launches into a taxonomy in which he details an array of frameworks. Key to Goffman is who gets to control the frame. But, of course, power is in the speaker or the listener. There is little effort here to explore the power that lies outside of this setting. He develops his own terminology for the functions he observes.

Goffman's task here seems not merely to explain the concept of framing, but to establish a methodology for examining and interpreting human interaction and its conveyed meaning. There is much game theory here and a reconsideration of some of his earlier work. Although the project is indeed an ambitious one, it often misses its mark and degenerates into a lexicon of jargon, at times spinning in some mysterious direction, away from the casual reader.

CONCLUSION

Erving Goffman's life came to an end in 1982 when he was stricken with cancer. It was the year he was elected to serve as president of the American Sociological Association. In fact, when he was hospitalized and preparing his presidential address, he must have known it would not be given.

Goffman is considered to be an anomaly by many. This was a man of great creativity and a keen interest in how people made sense of the world and of themselves. Like Simmel and other great thinkers, he dealt with the phenomenology of everyday life in order to discern how the social world worked. Unlike Simmel, his approach was more interpersonal. His work constitutes a cohesive body of theory and research that raises many important questions about the social interaction, particularly, why we behave as we do. To this end, his life was dedicated to discovering that answer.

BIBLIOGRAPHY

Burns, Tom. 1992. *Erving Goffman.* New York: Routledge.

Goffman, Erving. 1974. *Frame Analysis: An Essay on the Organization of Experience.* Garden City, NY: Doubleday.

———. 1967. *Interaction Ritual: Esays on Face-to-Face Behavior.* Garden City, NY: Doubleday.

———. 1963. *Stigma: Notes on the Management of Spoiled Identity.* Englewood Cliffs, NJ: Prentice-Hall.

———. 1961. *Asylums: Essays on the Social Situation of Mental Institutions.* Garden City, NY: Doubleday.

———. 1959. *The Presentation of Self in Everyday Life.* Garden City, NY: Doubleday.

Manning, Philip. 1992. *Erving Goffman and Modern Sociology.* Stanford, CA: Stanford University Press.

25

Feminist Social Theory: Chodorow, Butler, and hooks

Unlike critical theory, structuralism, poststructuralism, and postmodernism, the feminist paradigm in social theory is broad enough to include all of these perspectives and more.

In a very important sense feminist theory is not a stand-alone category of theory. It is not one that is exclusive of others. In fact, what distinguishes most feminist theory from other perspectives is its attempt to dissolve boundaries and categories that have historically characterized the social sciences, the natural sciences, and the humanities.

Feminist theory does not owe any particular allegiance to sociology. It is obvious, even from this book, that over the course of social theory's historical development the field has been dominated by males to the very exclusion of women's voices and views. This, indeed, can be said about other fields. It is an embarrassing exclusion when we think of social theory as concerned with explaining the social world.

Feminist social theory is distinguished from other types of feminist theory not simply by the methods it might use or the issues upon which it might focus. Although all feminist theory is a movement away from the phallocentric perspective, its methods can include the tools of psychoanalysis, literary criticism, philosophy, sociology, anthropology, and more. It often attempts to break down these distinctions by employing a range of methods. Thus, the body can be examined not only biologically, but can be read as discourse or interpreted psychoanalytically.

Although many date the development of feminist social theory back to the early Western movements for women's suffrage and the work of people such as Mary Wollstonecraft, many more locate its origins in the cultural and sexual revolutions of the 1960s and 1970s, particularly the Women's Liberation Movement in the United States and Europe.

Feminist social theory is not a single perspective, but many perspectives and has been fertile ground for the development of new paradigms, new epistemologies. Politically and ideologically, it can occupy a variety of positions. Topically, it can focus on a wide array of concerns ranging from gender socialization to pornography and rape.

Feminist social theory often finds affiliation with poststructural and postmodern theories, often rejecting the grand narratives that describe society, and the inherent essentialism of classical social thought. However, much of it maintains a radical socialist set of assumptions and values.

For purposes here, feminist social theory will be examined in its modern context. By this it is meant that its origins will be traced to a concern with gender and the role of women in society that began to evolve in the 1970s. The experience of women becomes essential to this project. Although the focus in such theory often begins with inequities inherent in the system of stratification and power relations, it evolves into a questioning of the notion of gender itself.

Even though one small chapter on feminist theory cannot do justice to the diversity and level of production to emerge from feminist social thinkers, it can be considered a beginning.

NANCY CHODOROW

Nancy Chodorow often refers to herself as a humanist feminist. This classification is held in contempt by those feminists who reject humanism as a tool of male oppression and domination. For Chodorow, however, it means simply a person-centered approach as opposed to a structuralist one.

Chodorow was born on January 20, 1944 in New York City. Her father, Marvin Chodorow, was a professor of theoretical physics; her mother was Leah Turitz Chodorow. After attending schools in New York, she studied anthropology at Radcliff College with Beatrice and John Whiting and graduated in 1966. She went on to study sociology at Brandise University with Philip Slater, who was renown for his psychoanalytic approach to social theory. While working on her doctorate there, she taught in the Women's Studies Program at Wellesley College and finished her degree in 1975. She completed her psychoanalytic training at the San Francisco Psychoanalytic Institute.

Between 1975 and 1986, Chodorow taught at the University of California at Santa Cruz. In 1977, she met and married Michael Reich, a professor of economics, with whom she had two children. She currently teaches at the University of California at Berkeley and has a private clinical practice.

The Reproduction of Mothering

Chodorow became a central figure in constructing feminist psychoanalytic theory with the publication of her first book, *The Reproduction of Mothering*, in 1979. Here she provides a reinterpretation of Freud, drawing upon the work of object relations theorists.

The central concern in this work is the process of socialization that both boys and girls undergo, and particularly the way they learn to take on gender roles and develop personal identity. As a sociologist, she is interested here in the manner in which the process of mothering is enacted, constructed, and maintained. Like most sociologists, she rejects the notion of biological determinism, dismissing such ideas as mothering instincts among women. For her, motherhood is more than childbearing and giving birth to infants. It can be socially defined as the process of physical and emotional care for children. Thus, although birthing is important, a biological birth mother need not be capable of mothering in this sense. Actually, she need never be a mother to the child to whom she's given birth, in any social sense. Why then, she asks, are women assigned this mothering role in society when men can be equally good at this work?

In fact, she contends that caring and nurturing of others has become associated with the role of woman in society. This is despite the fact that there is a wealth of research literature revealing that both men and women react similarly to infant cues and expressions of need and have similar potential for infant and child care. Women not only mother their children, but they often are required to mother their husbands. As they grow older, they even mother their mothers and fathers. Women take on the major responsibilities for child care, care of infants, toddlers, even the care of older children, often compared to the token participation of men if not their near exclusion.

Many feminists have argued that women are conditioned to be mothers and are expected, from early childhood, to serve in a caregiving capacity. Chodorow also challenges this assignment of role to women and, in fact, sees it as socially harmful. Delving into psychoanalytic theory she attempts to reexamine this construction through the process of socialization.

For Chodorow and Freud, both boys and girls are born into an undifferentiated world—there is no ego, no self, only a sense of oneness with the world and one's mother. This feeling will later be emulated, Freud posits, through the drive for reconnection (through sex) as the ego-centered self attempts to reunite with the world and recapture this oneness.

Of course, the desire to reunite with one's mother must be denied. Freud speaks of this, for boys, as the Oedipus complex. There are incest taboos at work here as the father's threatening pressure creates in the boy castration anxiety. The boy is forced to seek substitutes for his mother in partners of the opposite sex. He must also internalize his father as his personal superego. The boy must deny any personal identity with his mother in order to forge masculinity, which is defined as a rejection of femininity within himself. He must also deny himself the personal intimacy with the woman he loves. He needs to push away and is in turn pushed away.

However, the little girl is encouraged to remain both physically and emotionally close to her mother. She is not forced away from her as the boy is. In fact, her problem is the opposite of the boy's. Mothers hold on to their daughters often narcissistically believing them to be extensions of themselves. Chodorow refers to this as narcissistic object attachment. The girl typically finds separation and differentiation from her mother as difficult. She is frequently emotionally hindered in her development of autonomy—important in capitalistic society. Therefore, the girl suffers from weak ego boundaries and a fear of merging with others.

Mothers see their sons as different from themselves. Chodorow refers to this as "anaclitic object attachment." They help lead them to reject emotional dependence and intimacy. On the other hand, girls are often discouraged from being physically and emotionally close with their fathers, especially as they begin to mature. Fathers become more distant from their daughters and, therefore, girls are discouraged from identifying with them. Unlike the boy, the girl is deprived of a way to free herself from her mother by being cut off from a path of independent identity—namely, her father. Chodorow translates Freud's concept of penis envy into the daughter's desire for autonomy that is denied to her. Issues of identity and agency plague girls and women.

For Chodorow, and many other feminist psychoanalytic theorists, the female personality is "under separated" unlike the boy's personality, which is "over separated." There are no sharp and sudden divisions for the girl who is never forced into giving up her mother. Where boys and men become distant, emotionally detached, and domineering, girls and women tend more toward intimacy, empathy, and overall human connectedness. These characteristics become the hallmarks of femininity and the basis of social structural patterns. They become central to mothering.

Male domination emerges from idealization of fathers and the absence of male primary attachment. For boys and girls alike, fathers are often outsiders and remain shadowy figures long after the passing of the Oedipus complex. They come to represent the nonfamilial, something to which only boys can aspire. Thus, core male personality structure is inherently different from that of the female. However, both are relationally constructed through the process of socialization.

Chodorow argues that these patterns not only promote exclusive female mothering, but also produce an ideology of male domination and devaluation of women. Exclusive female mothering is responsible for most of this. As it exists, she contends, mothering becomes a system for the reproduction of gender inequality.

The only way this can be overcome is to incorporate men into the mothering system. Males and females alike must care for and nurture children. Only through shared parenting can both sexes develop emotional intimacy and autonomy.

Conclusion

Chodorow shows in her work the sociological significance of gendering and the role of mothering in the oppression of both women and men. Her unique sociological perspective, sheds much light on the dangers inherent in typical parenting patterns that become the basis of unhappiness and social inequality. Although there have been many changes since the first publication of *The Reproduction of Mothering* in 1979, men still remain at the margins of child care. Much of this condition stems from the system of gender stratification in the workplace where men continue to make considerably more money than women, having greater access to high-paying jobs, and being paid more for the same work. Chodorow argues that the social structure of society, with built-in inequalities, promotes the reproduction of these important gendering conditions.

JUDITH BUTLER

Born in Cleveland, Ohio in 1956, Judith Butler has become a major contributor to both feminist social theory and queer theory.

She attended Bennington College, but received her bachelor's from Yale, and was awarded a doctorate there in 1984. She taught briefly at Wesleyan University and later at Johns Hopkins. She now serves as the Maxine Elliot Professor in the departments of Rhetoric and Comparative Literature at the University of California at Berkeley.

The Trouble with Gender

Butler's most important works were *Gender Troubles,* published in 1990, and *Bodies that Matter,* published in 1993. She has since gone on to write several other important works. In her writings, Butler challenges not only mainstream feminist theory, but the entire notion of gender and womanhood. She poses many important questions including: What does it mean to be female in modern society? Who is included in this category? Who decides who belongs there?

In most early feminist theory, woman is seen as a universal concept. Butler denies such universality. In both feminist theory and psychoanalytic theory woman refers to an intrinsic biological essence. She challenges this assumption as well. For Butler woman is more discontinuous than comprehensive. Woman, she insists, is not a category with ontological integrity. Woman must be thought of in terms of fragments. Thus, feminism, itself, cannot be unitary.

She takes Freud's classical psychoanalytic theory to task for favoring a linear narrative regarding the developments in familial life—its origins, the care of children therein, sexual evolution, and the familial dynamics in the development of gender. She contends that the family, gender, and sex are fragmented and discontinuous. She believes that gender and sexuality emerge from fragmented experiences and are, themselves, fragmented constructions. She sees the Freudian narrative as short-sighted, failing to take account of the dynamic variety of early socializing influences. In denying the multiplicity of gender and sexual identity, Freud contends that there are only two choices: one either identifies with a particular sex or one desires that sex. In his understanding, it is not possible to identify with the sex one desires. So, if you are a woman desiring other women, you must identify with men.

Taking a radical social constructionist approach, Butler not only proposes that gender is a creation of social forces at work in society, but that sexuality is also such a product—a social construction and not a biological given. Gender as well as sexuality are performed and policed in line with the dictates of power. The body, itself, is a cultural product. She denies the standard divisions used by sociologists that claim sex to be vested by nature and gender by culture. Such a view, she insists, fails to recognize that the "sexed body" is a cultural, political, and economic product.

Butler understands gender identity to emerge from our internalized fantasies of whom we identify with. If we identify with our mother, we are not really identifying with whom our mother actually is. We internalize, in our unconscious, who we want her to be and identify with that fantasy of mother. Gender identity does not rest on a cohesive picture of mother, but a group of images of what we imagine her to be. Our identity is fragmented, a set of internalized fantasies. It is an illusion.

It is Butler's contention that gender itself is a type of performance, often improvised. It is this theatricality that helps give shape to our identity. Her notion of "doing gender" is similar in many respects to Goffman's dramaturgy. Both she and Goffman depict the individual as not having a whole integrated self, but constructing what is needed at any particular time by the fragments modern life presents to us. Here, perception is key to shaping a stylized, gendered self. Gender is frequently done by imitating or copying cultural representations of masculinity and femininity absorbed both from family and other agents of socialization, including mass media. At the same time, gender identity is also developed through external prohibitions that people internalize.

Likewise for sexuality: anatomy does not dictate sexuality, the psyche does. The inner psyche is imprinted on the body. Nevertheless, sexuality is also influenced by enforced cultural codes—straight, gay, bisexual, and transsexual. These are more or less caricatures presented in the culture for mass consumption. Of course, as Foucault suggested, labeling is often a means used to classify in order to control. To give a name to something is to control it, to force it to yield to power.

For Butler, creative performance provides a means of liberation from these strict assignments. Even though all gender is a form of drag, those extreme drag queens who push the limits reveal to us the untruth of gender and sexuality and the myth of gender/sexuality cohesion. In the hands of some, drag is a liberating act, both revealing and attacking strict standards for behavior and gender structure.

Performance becomes a powerful means through which both sexuality and identity can be individually constructed and a means of liberating gender from the overdetermined categories constructed for our consumption. Transgressive performances, particularly drag, have the potential to undermine the heterosexual construction of society.

Conclusion

Butler continues to be in the vanguard of those challenging the notion of gender cohesion. She has also challenged traditionally held positions in the feminist movement by raising radical questions concerning not only how one defines female, but also how one constructs human sexuality.

BELL HOOKS

One of the most creative approaches to feminism comes from bell hooks who has dealt with issues of gender, race, class, and popular culture as complementary social constructs. Born on September 25, 1952 as Gloria Jean Watkins, hooks has become a leading public intellectual. Much of her career has been dedicated to exposing and eradicating both racism and sexism.

She was born into a working-class family in Hopkinsville, Kentucky—a segregated community. Her father, Veodis Watkins, whom she has described as rigid and patriarchal, worked as a custodian for the postal system. Her mother, Rosa Bell Watkins, cared for the children and kept house. She had six siblings, one brother and five sisters.

hooks's home life was filled with reading poetry and storytelling. She was influenced by the work of Langston Hughes and Gwendolyn Brooks. She wrote poetry, herself, as a child. Some of this was published in her church's bulletin. She was close to her extended family, particularly her maternal grandfather, and took the name of her great-great grandmother

(Bell Hooks) who was a Native American. She also claims to have taken this name to "celebrate feminine legacies."

After attending local public schools, hooks graduated from Crispus Attucks High School in 1968, and went on to study English at Stanford University on a scholarship. After completing her undergraduate education, she went on to complete a master's degree at the University of Wisconsin and then taught English and Ethnic Studies at the University of Southern California. She completed her doctorate at the University of California at Santa Cruz in 1983 writing her dissertation on the African American writer, Toni Morrison.

She wrote several important works including a few volumes of poetry. Her first venture into the field of feminism was her book, *Ain't I a Woman*. The title for this she borrowed from the title of a speech given by nineteenth-century black feminist, Sojourner Truth. She was to follow this with several more volumes on feminist theory.

Whose Feminism?

In *Ain't I a Woman* hooks argues against the tactics and strategies of both the feminist movement and the black liberation movement that tended to disregard African American women. She takes to task black leadership for internalizing American patriarchal values. She attacks mainstream feminism's reliance on white, middle-class spokeswomen to the neglect of important, if not central, waves of poor women and women of color in the movement. She is highly critical of the mainstream media for failing to recognize the complexity of the feminist movement.

She contends that although all feminism is a struggle to end sexist oppression, there is no one feminism. Feminism is affected by one's social class and race. Poor people's definition of feminism is different from that of those in the middle class. Often, black feminism is different than white feminism in terms of priorities. Of course, there are universal concerns of oppression.

In her work hooks draws attention to what she sees as contempt for feminism in the black community and the support for conventional gender roles and benevolent patriarchy. This she sees as a holdover from slavery. She contends that black males suffer the most vicious attacks of white supremacy and racism and are denied full participation in white-dominated culture. But despite this, they cling to the belief in the patriarchal family as a means of addressing the hurt inflicted by racism and class injustice. This belief emerges from white patriarchal society that can more easily accept black male domination over family life than the revolutionary consequences that would emerge from an end to racism, sexism, and class exploitation. Many black families, she contends, subscribe to this notion that patriarchy is a more feasible alternative to more radical change.

hooks posits that media, when it focuses on black males, does so to their detriment—often portraying them as criminals and marginal people. Political talk shows are often projecting conservative black male images—men who discuss the necessity of men assuming greater economic responsibility and family leadership and who reject feminism as undermining this goal.

For hooks, gender equality will be the only force that will allow a true revolution in the black community—one that will raise the awareness and potential development of all. However, feminism still has not gained a secure foothold; black feminist thought has not had an adequate impact on the way people lead their lives. Feminism is discredited in many black households and black females are viewed as privileged, even though they are more disadvantaged than men and white women. She views a festering antifeminist backlash as having a major impact on black women. Black females fear rejection and male rage and often join the forces of patriarchal rule.

Popular Culture

An important cultural critic, hooks has spent considerable time analyzing the cultural content of plays, films, novels, television, as well as music. She has been able to apply critical feminist theory to a unique assessment of popular culture.

In her critique of "gangsta rap," for instance, she turns the tables on the white-dominated media that attempt to demonize young black men. It is her assertion that this brand of music is an expression of the white male majority, namely sexism, misogyny, and patriarchy. These outpourings of misogyny are not an expression of male deviance so much as an articulation of the attitudes portrayed and supported by the white supremacist capitalist patriarchy for the purpose of maintaining social order. She contends that misogyny is a field that must be labored in and maintained both to sustain patriarchy, but also to serve as an ideological antifeminist backlash. What better group to labor on this plantation than young black men?

Although hooks understands that there is a need for a rigorous feminist critique of the misogyny expressed in this music, it needs to be contextualized and seen in relation to the wider society. Rape and violence against women projected in gangsta rap videos and in lyrics of songs remind her of *Birth of a Nation*—the racist propaganda film by W. D. Griffith that attempted to convince the white population that they had better be concerned about the dynamics of black savagery. In actuality, these images reflect the values of the white patriarchal society that dominates media. This music has gained enormous popularity among white males who are the primary market for it. Even though hooks is unwilling to place total blame on the young black performers who labor in the field (some of whom have become millionaires), she contends that each individual is responsible for his or her own words and actions and that there can be no excuse for misogyny. However, she condemns white cultural critics for ignoring the larger picture.

Much rap celebrates the greed of the materialist capitalistic world in which you eliminate competition by whatever means are necessary. It is a crude expression of capitalistic logic. The belief promoted by critics of this type of rap is that these young black men live in a self-created, self-contained cultural vacuum and that young black males are not influenced by the same media (magazines, films, and television shows) as young white men. This is racist to be sure and it is the overt attribution of these values to one group while ignoring them in another. Many who attack such music, including conservative ministers, ignore their own misogyny. They desire censorship, not recognition of the place from which this genre has come.

Conclusion

As an outspoken defender of black feminism, bell hooks has written extensively on the subject. Her work tends to be more accessible to the general reader than other feminist social theory, and it frequently makes important connections and deals with topics others ignore. She currently serves as Distinguished Professor of Literature at the College of the City University of New York.

BIBLIOGRAPHY

Butler, Judith. 1999. *Gender Trouble: Feminism and the Subversion of Identity*. New York: Routledge.

———. 1993. *Bodies That Matter*. New York: Routledge.

Chodorow, Nancy. 1979. *The Reproduction of Mothering*. Berkeley, CA: University of California Press.

hooks, bell. 1984. *Feminist Theory: From Margin to Center*. Boston: South End Press.

———. 1981. *Ain't I A Woman: Black Women and Feminism*. Boston: South End Press.

Salih, Sara. 2002. *Judith Butler*. New York: Routledge.

26

Postmodernism: Baudrillard, Haraway, and Bauman

Postmodernism is not a theoretical perspective. It is a category that encompasses theoretical perspectives as well as other elements of contemporary culture. Therefore, some types of art, music, television, politics, clothing, religion, shopping malls, office buildings, and food (to name only a few) can be classified as postmodern.

What makes something postmodern as opposed to modern is still debated in scholarly papers, but what becomes obvious to the social theorist is that postmodernism is a category reserved for the contemporary focus on the relativity of truth, the dismissal of wholism, the renunciation of humanism, and the rejection of grand narratives. For theorists like Ihab Hassan, there are oppositional parallels between modern and postmodern. He names some of these in his book, *Theory, Culture and Society* (1985). These are just a sampling of the elements from his extensively quoted chart:

Modern	Postmodern
form	antiform
purpose	play
hierarchy	anarchy
centering	dispersal
presence	absence
paranoia	schizophrenia
metaphysics	irony

Hassan does not insist that these are opposites. Actually, most postmodernists reject the notion of binary oppositions. Rather, the chart is intended to suggest that a large variety of cultural characteristics that once helped to describe modern society no longer serve us. The set of characteristics to the right are frequently used to describe postmodernism. But there are more. Kitsch or parody, ephemeralness, the emphasis on language, the collapse of time and space, are all characteristics of postmodernity. Postmodern theorists call into question the need for comprehensiveness, reject Enlightenment reason, and tend to be ahistorical.

One of the most important exponents of postmodernism, the French theorist Jean-François Lyotard posited that postmodern societies could be defined by their "incredulity toward grand narratives"—large-scale encompassing explanations of social and natural phenomena. Although socialized as a Marxist, he rejects Marxism because he believes that its desire to create a homogeneous society can only be achieved through coercion. Others have followed this reasoning.

JEAN BAUDRILLARD

Jean Baudrillard has been one of the most outspoken and celebrated exponents of postmodern discourse. Born in Reims, France in 1929, he was the first in his family to attend a university. His parents were civil servants and his grandparents were peasant farmers.

Although much of his early university training was in linguistics with a focus on German languages, Baudrillard studied for his doctorate in sociology with the renown Marxist theorist Henri Lefebvre. He was very much influenced by the structuralism that was sweeping France in those years and became familiar with the work of Claude Levi-Strauss and later studied with the renowned sociologist and semiologist Roland Barthes.

In the 1960s he dedicated himself to integrating Marxian analysis, psychoanalysis, and semiology into a unique brand of social theory. He embarked upon university teaching in Paris at a new university at Nanterre. He was active in the May 1968 student protests that shook the French establishment and was very much in sympathy with the revolutionary new left movement. His scholarship, however, began to take him in other directions.

His interest in structuralism led him to question some of the essential principles of Marxism. He contended that much of *Das Kapital* had little relevance to the situation of the world in which he lived. Structuralism had exploded the myth of grand narratives. Yet Baudrillard's early theoretical work was not a complete rejection of his early politics, it was a refinement of them. Catching the "linguistic wave," he threw himself into the sea of semiotics.

The Culture of Commodities

Baudrillard found himself in agreement with those structuralists who contended that words in and of themselves had no intrinsic meaning. They were arbitrary symbols assigned meaning. It was context that gave them meaning. Roland Barthes's work in semiotics, examining fashion, sports, politics, media, music, and advertising as part of the language system influenced him significantly. Barthes had looked at things like fashion ads and saw that each image, each piece of clothing, each model was impregnated with meaning. These images were as much a part of the communication system as written text. In some cases, they spoke more powerfully than words.

Baudrillard saw the relevance of this to Marxism and what Marx had referred to as the fetish of commodities. Needless to say, Roland Barthes was already influenced by Marx in this regard. In Baudrillard's early work, which included *The System of Objects, The Society of Consumption,* and *For a Critique of the Political Economy of the Sign,* he explored the structural dynamics of consumerism.

Marx had discovered the difference between use value and exchange value, but Baudrillard "discovered" that there was a third value—a discourse value inherent in all objects. This is to say that objects or commodities communicate to us in unique ways. Every object or commodity constitutes a sign in a semiological position, in a system of communication. This communicating system idea he borrows from Levi-Strauss.

He delves into cultural anthropology to recall the potlatch of the Kula tribe who did not see their possessions as having value equivalents for the purpose of trade, but rather saw imbedded in each object a spirit—something more than the thing itself—something representing the culture. Baudrillard talks about a symbolic exchange value, and he uses Thorstein Veblen's idea of conspicuous consumption to support it.

Each commodity is imbued with meaning and the meaning is unspoken, often silent, unconscious. However, just as Lacan applied structural linguistics to psychoanalysis, Baudrillard applied semiotics, the study of signs, to map the communication of commodities. Thus, when one buys a Rolex watch, for example, one is buying much more than an accurate timepiece. One is buying into what the watch symbolizes. If one were to look at an array of commodities, they each seem to be saying things. Often they are advertised in ways that help give them meaning. They are set against other objects in an array of other signifiers, constituting a signifying chain that communicates to us more effectively than words strung together. Items placed in a department store window constitute complete narratives: adventures, romances, sexual perversion, and the like. Things tell us about their owners. They are indexes of social membership. They are fetishized representations of labor that constitutes them. They are codes with their own logic and rules. This is a structuralist idea.

By buying the watch one is buying into a system of hierarchial differentiation. Consumption, in this sense, is far from natural. It is cultural. All commodities are encoded with meaning and demand consumer conformity, or at least rational choice. According to Baudrillard, commodities communicate like any language. They have their own grammar and structure. He asserts that one can study consumption and consumerism like one can study language. Just as language defines and gives meaning to individuals, so do commodities.

In postmodern societies even the body is a sign or a set of signs: makeup, clothing, hair style, eyeware. Like other commodities it is fetishized—cut off from nature. The exterior is valorized at the expense of personal essence because there is no essence.

Ideologically, Baudrillard contends that just as we are imprisoned and controlled by our language, we are imprisoned and controlled by commodities. "The liberty to consume," he asserts, "is no more freedom than selling one's labor in the labor market." It is part of systemic coercion. Needs exist, he contends, because the system needs them to exist. They can no longer be defined as innate, instinctive, or spontaneous. They are induced. Needs are as much a part of the capitalist system as is labor. They are systematically produced, curbed, and controlled as a means of social manipulation. This assertion is very close to that of Herbert Marcuse.

Baudrillard goes on to say that "the system of needs must wring liberty and pleasure from the consumer as so many functional elements of reproduction of the system of production and the relations of power to sanction it. The individual is therefore tied up in a knot of drives, repressed by a system of ego defense functions."

Beyond Marxism

Although Marx is not rejected out of hand in Baudrillard's work, he does level heavy criticism upon him. However, Baudrillard claims that Marx's critique of capitalism did not go far enough. It was too tame. Marx placed production at the center of his work, something that Baudrillard finds problematic. Like Georg Simmel, he views consumption as central.

Baudrillard asserts that the postmodern world cannot find adequate usefulness in the aging Marxist theory that focused primarily on production and exploitation. For Baudrillard there is no more production; there is only reproduction! This is to say that in postmodern society the forces of production give way to the forces of reproduction as an organizing principle. Also, labor is no longer a factor of production in postmodern societies; it is a symbol of one position. Wages bear almost no relationship to one's output, but are determined by values placed upon individuals in a system of hierarchy.

In his later work Baudrillard drops most references to Marx and to capitalism, which has disappointed many of those on the left. Instead, he moves further into the murky realm of abstract structural symbolism that he believes constitutes postmodern reality, or to use his term—hyper-reality. All traces of humanistic sentiment disappear from his later works. The postmodern world is a retreat from reality into the joys of hyper-reality brought to us by technological innovation. Imitations or simulations become more real, more worthwhile than the original. In this world there are no subjects, only objects.

Baudrillard becomes more inventive with language, more playful in his tone. This is another sign that he has entered the realm of postmodern thought. The world (and Baudrillard) is caught up in a play of images with little relationship of one to the other. People come to understand in postmodern society that there is no meaning because there are many meanings. There is no one truth because there are many truths. Therefore, rather than seeking meaning or truth, people seek out spectacles. War has no reason so war become a spectacle, something easily made into a video game.

Simulacra

Baudrillard asserts that postmodern life is dominated by simulacra—copies of real objects or events. Plato referred to simulacrum as a false copy, overshadowing our experience of essential forms. In a set of studies on the history of simulacra in Western civilization, Baudrillard develops what he calls an Order of Simulacra, or stages in the development of simulacra over time. He sees three stages appearing in history.

The first stage is characterized by a break with the Church's monopolization of signs and idols. At one time religion maintained strict control over images. One can see such images contained in Western religious art, in the facades of churches. Sacred texts were kept in the hands of cloistered monks who alone knew the secrets of copying images and passed these skills to other monks. It was a secretive and involved process. Art, too, was strictly controlled by Church patronage. However, with the advent of capitalism the rising bourgeoisie, interested in accruing the power of signs for themselves, produced simulations. Secularization of literature, theater, art, structures of governance stood against the originals, undermining them. Simulacra of sacred imagery displaced and undermined their hold of religion on the world.

The second order began with the Industrial Revolution when machines made possible the mass duplication of objects: books, furniture, fashion, automobiles, housing, and works of art. Things are engineered so that there are precision-made duplicates. A mass production of signs fill the marketplace.

The third wave or order is what we have today. It is an order characterized by the dominance of the copy over the original—some might say the unreal over the real. Here the duplicate has even more power than the original—usurping and undermining its originality. Here, the world is made up of simulacra responding to predetermined codes of existence—codes that have been mass produced. The artificial flower is more perfect than the flower of what was once natural. Its colors are more vibrant; its fragrance is more sweet; it does not die. Here simulacra are a result of serial production. The artificial experience is believed to be superior to the so-called authentic experience. With the breaking of the DNA code, life is now modeled on visions of perfection; copies of exemplary ingredients that make up the perfect individual can be systematically pieced together, and again, mass produced.

It is Baudrillard's contention that just as there are structures for determining language, there are structures for determining what social life will be. All of social life is simulacra, guided by unwritten codes inherent in any particular society. He posits that with the advent of informational technology, fictional choices arise. All postmodern codes necessarily become binary: yes or no, *x* or *y*. However, what actually appears oppositional is complementary, just a half of the whole. One, therefore, believes that a choice exists when actually there is none. The individual is controlled and directed by prefabricated models and predetermined choices. This makes everything subject to cybernetic manipulation.

It is within his notion of hyper-reality that we find people desiring the artificial to the real, the imaginary world to the real world, the simulated experience to the real experience. The popularity of television, movies, video games, theme parks, botanical gardens, artificial seaports, and Disney worlds all attest to the dominance of simulacra. He often uses the term "death of the real" to describe the postmodern world in which we live. But he suggests that attempts to resurrect the real are doomed to failure. Can we actually keep tribal people in their villages away from television and ads for underarm deodorant? Is this not just as artificial?

For Baudrillard, we are locked into a world of simulacra with little chance for escape. Like in a fun house, we live in a hall of mirrors where the real and unreal merge. We have constructed such a world for ourselves. There is something within our nature that has led to this and that prevents our liberation.

Conclusion

Baudrillard's range of discourse appears to be limitless. We have only explored a bit of the surface of his work. He has become a postmodern celebrity in France and is a guru to many who see in his cynicism a bold truth. He has spent much of his time to discussing popular culture and art and to critiquing media.

Evident in his work, however, is a dark cynicism that has grown deeper as he has become older. His movement from a 1960s radical to a man who believes people prefer watching television to experiencing the eroticism of life is telling. Occasionally, if one looks closely enough, one can see in his work the remnants of a social idealist long ago abandoned. His world is indeed dark and bleak with no sense of self-emancipation from the prison constructed by forces beyond our control.

DONNA HARAWAY

If Baudrillard's view of the postmodern world is bleak and dehumanizing, Donna Haraway's postmodernism celebrates this dehumanization as opening up avenues for personal liberation.

Born in Denver, Colorado in 1944 Donna Haraway attended Catholic schools in her early years and majored in zoology and English at Colorado College. Upon graduating in 1966, she won a Fulbright scholarship to study philosophy and evolution in Paris and eventually received her doctorate in biology at Yale University. After teaching in the area of Women's Studies and General Science at the University of Hawaii and moving on to Johns Hopkins, she settled into a position at the University of California at Santa Cruz where she headed the Consciousness Program.

Like most postmodern feminist theorists, Haraway rejects humanism because it is based on a patriarchal ideal. She sees embedded in the term racism, sexism, and heterocentrism. Associated with it is cultural and sexual dominance, the control of nature, and colonialism. To move away from humanism, in this sense, is to be unleashed from a controlling world of patriarchal domination.

Haraway is a strict social constructionist. It is her belief that the world in which we live, both the natural and cultural world, is a human construction. Her search is not focused on language, nor on those deep structures that determine how we think and behave. She believes that human beings and the worlds in which they live are constructed by themselves. Thus, the individual is most central to her writing.

Like other postmodernists, she rejects binary polarizations established in patriarchal society as confining and views the world as flexible and free-flowing. She embraces fragmentation and chaos that she believes characterizes the postmodern world as containing the seeds for personal liberation. Yet she recognizes the need for opposing the potential onslaught of oppression and domination that exists in the world. Thus, a form of social consciousness becomes essential to her feminism.

Haraway argues that communication sciences and modern biology too often want to translate the world into a common code that can produce a common language in order to impose greater unity and control. However, she believes that this is not inevitable or even likely. Although the forces of capital have much at stake in what she terms the "informatic of domination," she believes that the liberating power inherent in the new technologies, if intelligently used, will not let this occur. Generally, she sees technology as a force of human liberation, breaking down polarization and boundaries once established by positivist science.

The Cyborg Manifesto

Although some of her earliest ideas have been modified, the perspective she developed on the relationship between humans and machines has been tremendously influential. Her seminal work, *Simians, Cyborgs and Women: The Reinvention of Nature* (1991), became one of the most important postmodernist works of the last century. In this book, Haraway not only deconstructs the white patriarchal politics behind categories of race and gender, but also calls into question the whole notion of separation of men from women, humans from animals, and people from machines. What constitutes nature is challenged by Haraway. In her view, even the human body is a social construction.

As a historian of science and student of primatology, Haraway challenges the way so-called objective science was distorted by the characteristics of those conducting primate studies in the 1960s and 1970s. Male observers of primate life constantly misinterpreted behavior by seeking descriptions in human male metaphors of aggression, hunting, violence, and the like. Female studies produced very different descriptions. For instance, frequently, dangers for apes were dealt with by cunning, not fighting, something missed in male descriptions; likewise, mother-centered kinship patterns often went unnoticed as did the fact that most tools were created and invented by females. Haraway posits that the political-scientific struggle to communicate the rules of science and the methods by which research is conducted is male dominated. Science is used as a tool of domination and patriarchal control shaping and constructing how we view the world. She posits "imagine what evolutionary theory would look like in any language other than classical capitalistic political economy."

Her book exposes the history of how race, gender, and class were constructed and made into "natural" phenomena. She also examines how these distinctions serve the interests of those who have controlled scientific discourse. As a postmodern theorist, Haraway rejects the efforts of science to assemble people into categories for the purpose of assigning identities in order to impose some form of control over them. She views these artificial boundaries as tools for division and manipulation. Still, she rejects what she sees as the antiquated efforts of the left to bring about homogeneity as unrealistic and equally oppressive. In her work she recognizes innate fluidity between these artificial boundaries seeing both nature and biology as mere extensions of the human imagination. She calls for a greater understanding of how the rigidity of so-called nature governs us.

Nevertheless, it is Haraway's belief that high-tech cultures cannot help but break down the old dualisms inherent in the language of the past. She refuses to condemn technology and rather sees in technological innovation the potential for personal expression and growth. By fusing flesh and machine, people become capable of expanding themselves.

Those of us in postmodern societies have become cyborgs—an integration of human flesh and machines. She is not horrified by this but rather celebrates it. "I'd rather be a cyborg than a goddess," she notes. Unlike some feminists who retreat from technology as a realm of patriarchal dominance, she views it as a site for liberation for all, especially women. She attacks the artificial distinctions between people and machines. She sees the distinction that one is natural as the other is not as misguided and reactionary, since each is a social construction. In fact, she proposes that embedded in the idea of "nature" is the defense of patriarchal society because nature is also a human creation. Nature stands as an end, closing all possibilities of flexibility and change.

Thus, at one time it was the nature of women to be overemotional, submissive, dependent, and incapable of abstract thought. They were intended by nature to be mothers rather than military leaders. However, if women and men are not dictated by nature, they are capable of change. They are not guided by rigid rules. They can be socially constructed or reconstructed. All assumptions come into question. Humans are not biologically determined.

According to the Cyborg Manifesto, we are all part machine. Once we have entered into the realm of being assisted by a machine, it becomes part of us. Machines can range from prostheses, such as eyeglasses, to automobiles and drugs. Sometimes it is difficult to ascertain where the body leaves off and the machine begins.

For Haraway, with the advent of new technologies we are forever reconstructing ourselves.

Conclusion

Haraway's unique approach to the postmodern condition is not a despairing one as in the case of many others. It is not filled with cynicism, but proposes avenues for the growth of personal potential and the movement away from rigid and immutable structures imposed from above. She offers a utopian vision of a world in which boundaries no longer separate people from one another, but rather connect them.

ZYGMUNT BAUMAN

A very different vision of postmodernity comes to us from Zygmunt Bauman.

Bauman was born in Paznon, Poland in 1925 to poor Jewish parents. The Nazi invasion of his country in 1939 forced his family to leave and to move to Soviet Russia where he was educated. During the World War II he fought in the Polish division of the Soviet Army and served in the Battle of Berlin. When he returned to Poland after the War, he was the youngest major in the Free Polish Army. He was twenty-eight. He joined and was active in the local Communist Party and subscribed to utopian socialist ideals.

However, growing anti-Semitism spread throughout the military as well as the party. After his father sought information on securing a visa to visit Israel, Bauman was forced out of the army and was required to resign his position in the party.

Earning a master's in sociology, he became a lecturer at the University of Warsaw in 1954. He was a visiting scholar at the London School for Economics in the late 1950s. He wrote several important books, became chairman of his department, and dedicated himself to his scholarship. However, because of his Jewish background and increasing anti-Semitism, he was stripped of his teaching post in 1968. In that year he moved to Tel Aviv where he taught until 1972. In 1972 he migrated to Great Britain and secured a teaching post as a Professor of Sociology at the University of Leeds in Yorkshire. Today, he retains the title of Emeritus Professor at both Leeds and the University of Warsaw.

Bauman's Postmodernism

As a social theorist, Bauman does not easily fit the postmodern stereotype. He avoids the jargon of postmodernese and the hip imagery of both Baudrillard and Haraway. Yet, he is one of the foremost social theorists of postmodernity. His work is seriously concerned with the failures of modernity.

Bauman's work reflects his personal transition from an idealistic communist to a disillusioned one. His hopes for revolutionary reform and a socialist utopia were dashed not only by what he saw as the growing corruption and antisemitism within the Communist Party, but in what he viewed as the paranoia that the Communist Party generated. He came to his postmodern position not through any particular intellectual influences, such as French poststructuralism, but chiefly through his disillusionment with modernity itself.

Bauman did not flee communism to embrace the ideals of capitalistic heterotopia. His views on capitalism are equally critical. His journey west brought him to the realization that the Enlightenment project, and all for which it stood, had at its base values incompatible with his own sense of fairness and social justice. In some respects, his work continues in the critical tradition of the Frankfurt school, but bridges the gap between critical theory and postmodern thought.

Much of his postmodernism is based on his critique of modernity. In fact, one might go as far as to say that he embraces postmodernism as an alternative to the essential faults he sees in modernity—its top-down imposition of one-dimensional order. For Bauman, capitalism and socialism are two sides of the same modernist coin—struggles for utopian wholism based on reason. Inherent in these systems is an emphasis on control to advance an agenda of social betterment. Likewise, he asserts that the Enlightenment project and its intentions to create a world of personal liberation based on reason has ironically produced mechanisms of oppression—what Max Weber called "iron cages."

Bauman's Modernity

History is the narrative of steady industry, directed by a privileged few, to control the majority in order to benefit from them. Although this was obvious for the Middle Ages, it has been less obvious of the modern era given the monopoly of these few over the channels of mass education and communication. The romantic narrative of modernity, as the application of reason and science to improve the well-being of all, is nothing more than a colorful fairy tale. Even though modernity espoused many noble ideals and objectives, as a force it has given the world horror and bloodshed on a massive scale—a continuation of the domination of the many by the few. It was the idealistic intent of modernity, guided by Enlightenment thought, to wrestle from religion and mysticism the control of the dominant paradigm.

Bauman sees two essential components that constitute essential underlying problem of modernity: the ambivalence it generates and the amoral efficiency associated with its administrative mechanisms.

Modernity and Ambivalence

According to Bauman, the modern world is characterized by confusion and contradiction—a result of the failure of its administrative/bureaucratic machinery to maintain total order. The messages coming at us in modern societies are often disjointed, fragmented, and ambiguous. Given this state, the individual is left to make sense of this world for his or her self. In such a world, identity does not come easily, but it is often fashioned for us by forces beyond our control.

The sense of a fully integrated self has been shattered by the forces of specialization and bureaucratization. The self cannot be pieced together again. Given the complexity and heterogeneity characteristic of the modern world and the variety of options the market seemingly offers in terms of material answers, it is too difficult to make a decision about anything. It is easier to have these decisions made for us.

Modernity frequently locks individuals into a state of dependency by denying them direct control over their own lives. It distances people from the tools they need for making decisions. At the same time, modernity disenchants the world. Although this observation was also made by Max Weber, Bauman uses this idea to mean that through undermining the mystical aspects of life modernity promotes reason as the sole criterion for decision making. The world becomes an object of willed action—given both meaning and design by a select few who are able to amass power.

Most people become objects of manipulation. As Bauman notes in *Imitation of Postmodernity* (1992), "the world was split between wilful subject and will-less object; between the privileged actor whose will counted and the rest of the world whose will did not count. . . ." Out of this division grew increased anxiety, a drive for security and a need for imposed order. A world of disenchantment was a world without God, a world liberated from the constraints of religious tradition. Like Erich Fromm, Bauman sees modernity leading to an escape from the terror of nothingness into the certainty of structure.

In his book *Modernity and Ambivalence* (1991), Bauman shows how the ambivalence associated with modernity was exemplified by Jews attempting to assimilate into modern nation-states in the nineteenth century. This was especially true for German assimilationist Jews. Even though many were committed to the social values associated with the 1848 revolution and wanted to see a truly democratic Germany, anti-Semitism prevented them from ever fully participating in German cultural life. Although many were outstanding scholars, artists, and businesspeople, they were resented and marginalized. Jews developed an ambivalence as they were torn between acceptance for their achievements and rejection for their genealogy. They, like other marginalized groups, could not be accommodated in the Teutonic drive for purity and control. Their focus on assimilation, a modernist ethic, did not help them.

Modernity and the Holocaust

It is Bauman's contention that the Holocaust was a logical and inevitable consequence of the forces of modernity—the desire to improve, to control, to impose homogeneity. The rationality associated with the German state in the 1930s and 1940s testifies to both the failure of the Enlightenment and its notion of applied universal reason to address important social problems.

For Bauman, the Holocaust was a rational response to the Jewish question. It was not a pogrom, highly charged with racist passions. It is his assertion that antisemitism was indeed present in German culture, but it was not as vehement there as it was in France. The Holocaust was a quiet and rational set of administrative plans put into the service of the state to achieve the modernist goal of homogeneity. Like Hannah Arendt, Bauman's analysis draws him closer to her banality of evil hypothesis.

Buried deep within the Holocaust is the reason for Bauman's rejection of modernity. For him, the human inclination to act as moral beings is pre-social—we are thought to be born with a natural tendency to care for others we believe are in need of our help. Modernity is seen as substituting rules and regulations for such innate moral sentiment.

Like Stanley Milgram's well-known study of obedience to authority, Bauman insists that those of us in modern societies act to satisfy organizational needs at the expense of more human ones. Like Milgram's subjects who were willing to give lethal shocks to subjects to satisfy the demands of those in control of the research project, people in Nazi Germany were conditioned by the forces of modernity to suspend their own sense of moral judgment and substitute a bureaucratic imperative. The mass murder of millions, he insists, was more a testament to technological and bureaucratic achievement than it was an indictment of human nature. The indirectness of bureaucracy and administration suffocated any sense of moral outrage.

Bauman's Postmodernity

Bauman's support for postmodernity is to a large part based on his rejection of modernity. He believes that postmodernity's path away from totalizing grand theoretical designs and rationally planned utopias, of either the capitalistic or communistic variety, offers us maximum freedom. He finds much in poststructuralism liberating—putting the individual, not the envisioned group, at the center. His embrace of postmodernity is the empowerment of the other.

Within postmodernity and its relativistic approach, he sees hope for the emergence of a new ethical code that rejects universals and absolutes and rejects coercive ethical systems aimed at uniting all.

BIBLIOGRAPHY

Baudrillard, Jean. 1981. *For a Critique of the Political Economy of the Sign.* St. Louis, MO: Telos Press.

———. 1975. *The Mirror of Production.* St. Louis, MO: Telos Press.

Bauman, Zygmunt. 1992. *Imitations of Postmodernity.* London: Routledge.

———. 1991. *Modernity and Ambivalence.* Cambridge, Polity Press.

———. 1989. *Modernity and the Holocaust.* Cambridge: Polity Press.

Haraway, Donna. 1991. *Simians, Cyborgs and Women.* New York: Routledge.

———. 1989. *Primate Visions: Gender, Race and Nature in the World of Modern Science.* New York: Routledge.

Hollinger, Robert. 1994. *Postmodernism and the Social Sciences.* Thousand Oaks, CA: Sage.

Kellner, Douglas. 1989. *Jean Baudrillard: From Marxism to Postmodernism and Beyond.* Stanford, CA: Stanford University Press.

Rosenau, Pauline Marie. 1992. *Post-Modernism and the Social Sciences.* Princeton, NJ: Princeton University Press.

Smith, Dennis. 1999. *Zygmunt Bauman: Prophet of Postmodernity.* Oxford: Polity Press.

27

Jürgen Habermas: Communicative Action

Born in Dusseldorf, Germany on June 18, 1929, Jürgen Habermas is the last in the line of renown Frankfurt school theorists. Known as a second-generation member of the *Institut für Sozialforschung,* he studied with Horkheimer and Adorno when they returned to Germany after the Second World War.

Habermas's father was a well-known industrialist, civic leader, and director of the chamber of commerce. As a child, young Jürgen was a member of the Hitler Youth. His family did not oppose the Nazis and, in fact, cooperated with them. They were dedicated Protestants. Still, according the Habermas, he was horrified in 1945 when he learned of the Nazi arocities by listening to the Nuremberg trials on the radio. He was shocked by how quickly many Nazi leaders assumed positions of legitimate power immediately after the War.

In 1949 he became a student of philosophy, history, and psychology at the University of Göttingen and moved on to the University of Bonn from which he received his doctorate in 1954. His dissertation was on the German Idealist philosopher, Friedrich Schelling. In the mid-1950s he worked as a journalist, writing for various newspapers on social issues and cultural trends. In 1956, he arrived at the postwar University of Frankfurt where he worked as an assistant to Theodor Adorno at the *Institut für Sozialforschung* where he persued his *habilitation.* However, Adorno was to reject this project, *Structural Transformation of the Public Sphere.* However, it was eventually accepted at the University of Marburg where he worked with Wolfgang Abendorf. It was later published and in 1962, Habermas moved on to the University of Heidelberg where he began teaching. In 1964, he was offered a position as a professor in philosophy and sociology at the University of Frankfurt.

THE WORK OF HABERMAS AND THE FRANKFURT SCHOOL

Jürgen Habermas is considered by many to be one of the world's leading social theorists. His scope of interests certainly make him one of the world's most expansive thinkers.

Although significantly different from his Frankfurt school teachers, many of Habermas's concerns reflect their focus on culture; their integration of philosophy, psychology, and sociology; their progressive politics; and the importance of critical thought for the purpose of communicating and understanding. Unlike them, he has moved away from aesthetics and has taken a position in defense of the Enlightenment. He has moved even further from Marxism, but has remained quite critical of capitalism.

Like Adorno and Horkheimer, he draws on classical theorists to build his own theories, but cannot be classified as a Left Hegelian in the same sense as his teachers. He is far less humanistic. He moves his sociology much closer to functionalism, integrating Parson's systems models and action theory into his own work. He has become a defender of modernity and an avowed enemy of postmodernism.

Habermas's commentaries are far less cynical than those of the early critical theorists. Unlike most critical theorists, he does not identify inequality and domination as the central problems. Nowhere does alienation become an important issue. The problems concerning him most seem to be a crisis in reason and a breakdown in communication. The essential elements of critical analysis are lost here including the critique of contemporary culture and the strong theoretical focus on aesthetics.

He takes a lead in moving social philosophy away from existential considerations and toward communicative ones. This was certainly the hallmark of social theory of the 1970s and 1980s when he was at the height of his career. Such a linguistic turn was justified through his firm belief in knowledge as the key to human liberation. Certainly, this position gained considerable popularity in the United States as the country swung further to the right in reaction to the radical movements of the early and mid-1960s.

Habermas contends that there is an objective reality and that the methods of science are capable of discovering and exploiting it. However, it is his belief that the methods of the natural sciences are not well suited to explore the human elements of society. This is because societies and their respective cultures are organized around symbols, and all symbols require interpretation. Thus, he proposes that positivism must stand alongside of hermeneutics, or interpretive study, in the quest for human liberation. To this end, Habermas identifies three knowledge systems and their respective interests: analytic or classical positivist knowledge that lends itself to technical control and has been applied to directing nature, people, and societies; humanistic knowledge that has as its object an understanding of the world and the self; and, finally, critical knowledge that is a type of knowledge directed at human emancipation. This is the type of knowledge focused on by his Frankfurt school forebears and one in which he is also keenly interested.

In line with Marx's project, Habermas wants to see the development of human potential and believes capitalism gets in the way of this. However, he asserts that by focusing primarily on labor, Marx neglected the social or subjective side of interaction that Habermas refers to as communicative action. For him, the positive-rational world of action takes on too much significance for Marx and his critical theory successors. Without a deeper understanding of this side of human action, liberation is impossible. To this end, he goes on to develop a theory of communicative action based on what he calls the "ideal of reason."

THEORY OF ACTION

Although it is the objective of positive action to achieve a particular goal or set of goals (such as the material goals of the worker), it is the aim of communicative action to acquire human understanding. Habermas sees this type of goal-oriented action as central to modern life. Therefore, any distortion of communication impedes healthy interaction, social progress, and human development. For Habermas undistorted communication is essential to social progress and should be the aim of social science.

With the aim of making all communication clear or undistorted, Habermas needs a tool. There can be no better instrument than human reason.

It must be remembered that Max Weber had seen the bureaucratization of society as a corruption of the classical notion of rationality. He refers to bureaucratic thinking as instrumental reason. By this he means reason cut off from the world and confined to a means-end schema. This was a type of reason that might have worked within a bureaucracy, but outside of it could appear irrational or misguided. It was a type of bounded rationality. This sort of rationality challenged society. Habermas lays blame for this on modern capitalism and its associated purposive-rational action. For him, it is primarily the system of capitalism that distorts reason. He proposes that capitalism has captured rationality and has converted it into its instrumental form. By controlling communication and the rules of reason, it dominates culture and subordinates all to its distorted model. He sees the real challenge to critical theory as rescuing reason from its captor and liberating it, so that it can contribute to the drive for human freedom and democracy.

For Habermas rationalization of communicative action is the solution. It requires removing restrictions on communication and liberating the concept of rationality. In doing this, he wants a new understanding of reason that goes beyond its instrumental form, and transcends its classical definition in traditional philosophy in which reason was confined to propositional statements about the objective world.

A THEORY OF COMMUNICATION

Building upon the sociological tradition, Habermas weaves together the theories of scholars ranging from Emile Durkheim to Talcott Parsons to examine the basis of rational communication. For Habermas, only through language and under the condition of rational argument does the actor coordinate action to achieve material understanding. In this sense, rationality is the removal of distortion in the communicative process. To achieve this, he relies on the notion of "ideal speech" in which all parties have an equal opportunity to engage in dialogue without one party dominating the other. It is through this process that the weight of evidence and the quality of argument determines validity.

It is Habermas's contention that truth is reached through consensus—free from distorting influences. Every consensus rests on intersubjectivity wherein there is a mutuality of openness and acceptance. There is no subject as opposed to object in such a dialogue. Both parties meet on a common ground.

His model in this sense is Hegelian and dialectical. With a free flow of dialogue he sees participants as entering into an argument, presenting reasons for their respective positions, critically examining the truth of the other argument, and accepting or rejecting positions, and if there is contention, a new argument begins until a new consensus is reached. Thus, argument confronts argument until there is consensus. Habermas does not believe this is what happens today. The state of too much current discourse is contrivance and distortion. Too much of the communicative flow is rigidly controlled. He sees open dialogue as an ideal situation.

Habermas moves on to establish conditions for rational argumentation in communicative acts and sorts through validity claims based on various criteria: normative, evaluative, and authoritative. He examines how different types of discourse develop to address these claims to validity such as moral-practical discourse, therapeutic discourse, and aesthetic discourse. One problem that makes his analysis difficult at times and hard to follow is that he often becomes bogged down in the categories and definitions: types of discourse, aspects of speech, types of action, types of discourse ethics. This is too much to present in a simple overview of his work.

Nevertheless, one of the central problems confronted by Habermas in his theory of communicative action is the asymmetry between the systems world of economy and technical knowledge characterized by instrumental reasoning and the life-world of community with its own unique social background and its subjective, taken-for-granted knowledge. For him, this notion of a life-world takes on a special significance because it represents cultural, social, and personal dynamics of the society that possesses its own knowledge orientation. This is compared to the more uniform systems world. The difference between the system arena and its respective life-world as well as the internal issues within each represent challenges to integrative rational communication. Even though he believes that the rationale of communication might be defined differently for each segment, it is necessary that there be some sort of comprehensive integrative understanding. This is basic to what Habermas refers to as communicative competance—the capacity to make oneself understood and to understand others.

Rationality becomes the basis for communicative competence. Such rationality is both a means for domination as well as a tool for emancipation. Through appropriate application of communicative competence, problems can be addressed and a plan for human development and social progress can be established.

CONCLUSION

Habermas has become the last in a long line of critical theorists with Frankfurt lineage. However, de-radicalization of his theory has been achieved through heightened abstraction. His overconceptualization makes his theory too weighty. His integration of Marx and Parsons along with sociologists such as Harold Garkinkel seem to have diminished his credibility on the left and his program in defense of modernity makes him a target of postmodern attackers.

It is his defense of the European Enlightenment, his advocacy of reason as the solution to individual and social crises, and his rejection of revolutionary action that make him one of the most prominent liberal thinkers of today.

In the 1960s, he and Adorno became targets of student radicals at the University of Frankfurt who believed that each man had sold out Marxism and its revolutionary spirit in exchange for grant money. Nevertheless, Habermas has continued to move forward, taking on his attackers from both the political left and far right.

In 1971 he was named director of the Max Planck Institute in Starnberg for research into the Conditions of Life in the Scientific-Technical World and during some of that time served as a visiting professor at the University of California at Berkeley. But in 1983 he returned to teaching philosophy and sociology at the University of Frankfurt. In 1994, he retired from teaching. He continues to write important works in social theory and can be considered central to ongoing debates relevant to modern social life.

BIBLIOGRAPHY

Bernstein, Richard. 1985. *Habermas and Modernity*. Cambridge, MA: MIT Press.

Braaten, Jane. 1991. *Habermas's Critical Theory of Society*. Albany, NY: State University of New York.

Habermas, Jürgen. 1987. *Theory and Communicative Action, Vol. II, Lifeworld and System: A Critique of Functional Reason,* trans. by T. McCarthy. Boston: Beacon Press.

———. 1984. *The Theory of Communicative Action, Vol. I, Reason and Rationalization of Society,* trans. by T. McCarthy. Boston: Beacon Press.

———. 1979. *Communication and the Evolution of Society,* trans. by T. McCarthy. Boston: Beacon Press.

White, Stephen. 1989. *The Recent Work of Jürgen Habermas*. Cambridge: Cambridge University Press.

28

Pierre Bourdieu: *Habitus*

Pierre Bourdieu was the leading sociologist in France at the end of the twentieth century. Like many French public intellectuals, he was not only associated with scholarship, but also with important social causes.

He was born in the small village of Denguin in the Béarn area of the Département des Basses-Pyrenées in the south of France on April 1, 1930. He grew up in a lower-middle-class household. His father was a postal worker, and he was the first in his family to complete a high school education.

Educated at the *lycée* in Pauard and later the *Lycée Louis-le-Grand* in Paris, he gained entry to the elite Ecole Normale Superieur where he studied philosophy with the renowned Marxist, Louis Althusser. Among his more famous classmates was Jacques Derrida. Although he excelled in his studies, he refused to write his final thesis because he objected to what he viewed as the inferior education being offered at the school as well as its authoritarian administration. He joined with others in objecting to the "Stalinist style" of control over curriculum and methods and the inability of students to have any degree of choice in their studies. Nevertheless, Bourdieu was awarded his degree and won his *agrégation,* which allowed him to teach for a year in a rural lycée. In 1956, however, he was drafted into the French army and stationed in Algeria for two years.

It was there that he developed an intense social conscience, observing the dire plight of the Algerian people, and gained an understanding of the horrors of war and the social injustice of French colonialism that characterized Algeria at the time. This experience impacted his life so dramatically that he spent two additional years in Algeria, after the completion of his military service, teaching at the University of Algiers. There he began collecting data and writing a book that was to deal with the dynamic culture of that society and the social conditions there. The book contained a wealth of empirical and ethnographic research.

In 1960, he returned to France and worked as an assistant in the Faculty of Arts of the University of Paris. During that time he attended lectures given at the *College de France* by Claude Levi-Strauss and secured a position as an assistant to the renowned sociologist, Raymond Aron. Bourdieu's interest at this time fluctuated between sociology and anthropology. He took seminars in ethnographic research at the *Musée de l'Homme.*

In 1961 he secured a teaching post at the University of Lille and married Marie-Claire Brissard. He spent the following three years teaching and writing. In 1964 he returned to Paris where he became Director of Studies at *L'Ecole Pratique des Hautes Etudes.* It was from this position that he launched his career as an important research sociologist, gathering around him not only vast financial resources, but also a cohort of scholars with whom he worked.

In 1968 he helped to create the *Centre de Sociologie Européenne* and was named its director. *Actes de la Recherche en Sciences Sociales,* an important journal he launched, became an outlet for his work as well as that of some leading social thinkers of the time. Bourdieu also worked with Raymond Aron to establish a center for education and culture at the *Ecoles des Hautes en Sciences Sociales.* When Aron retired from his distinguished position as Chair of Sociology at the *College de France,* the job was awarded to Bourdieu.

BOURDIEU'S WORK

The expansiveness of Bourdieu's thought led him into various realms of social and anthropological research. Education, consumerism, and culture were among the subjects upon which he focused. It was not so much the subject as it was the method that set him apart from other social investigators.

His book, *Distinction: A Social Critique of the Judgement of Taste,* was a comprehensive ethnographic study of contemporary French culture in which Bourdieu dissected both the material life as well as the mind of bourgeois society. What accounts for taste becomes a daunting sociological investigation in his hands.

Overall, there is a theme running through his work and that is the need to better comprehend the tools of social and cultural domination at work in the world. His studies are always assessments of power—how it is conceptualized and how it is used. He sees sociology as a means of unearthing deeply buried structures of the social world that constitute our universe.

Yet, he was careful not to push understanding into the realm of structure alone. His work reflects a keen interest in how we make sense of the world and how we act within the confines of that understanding. Even though he rejects the radicalism of social constructionism in favor of a more objectivist worldview in which reality exists beyond our awareness, he refuses to go to the extremes of the more conservative structuralists. To this end, he positions himself somewhere between existentialism on one hand, and objective structuralism on the other. Although he was a staunch defender of the underdog and decried the abuses of capitalism, his work reflects an inherent fatalism, believing that experiences and background determine outcomes. Influenced by the work of structuralists as well as poststructuralists, Bourdieu was focused on finding some theoretical midway between structure and personal agency.

Bourdieu wanted to uncover those social structures that lay hidden away and to discover how these so-called objective structures influenced subjective social construction. Not only did he conclude that such structures constrained thought, but they were also responsible for a considerable degree of action and interaction. He insisted that it was the task of sociology to invest effort into exposing these embedded structures and discovering how they reproduce themselves. Still, structures were not immutable. They could change.

HABITUS AND FIELD

Although there are many important constructs in his work, one that has gained considerable attention and illustrates his focus on structure and agency is his notion of habitus and field.

Bourdieu adopts the term habitus to represent internalized mental or cognitive structures that people use to interpret and evaluate the world. Habitus constitutes a socially acquired and conditioned system of dispositions and predispositions that are learned, unconsciously, through experiences in one's social environment and function as categories of perception and assessment as well as principles for organizing action. He indicates that these are in some ways comparable to Chomsky's notion of deep structures, but they are learned environmental products rather than neurological ones. Also, habitus is neither rigid nor rational; it is not fixed; it does not act like a computer determining behavioral and mental outcomes. One's habitus is very much a product of one's personal and social history. It is produced by the social structure and in turn represents it. Still, it has a high degree of interpretive creativity or flexibility. The personal system of habitus is transposable in that it allows the actor to invent and extemporize under comparable circumstances.

For Bourdieu habitus constitutes classification schemes and values that are simultaneously the internalized site of so-called objective reality and the externalization of subjective internality. It establishes a set of personal and social parameters of what is thinkable or unthinkable in that the constraints of one's formative environment and personal experiences are usually inscribed in the habitus. Thus, it reproduces an internalized logic. In capitalistic society it is certainly one that is supportive of capitalist social formation. Outlooks and opinions, personal deportment, and even bodily posture are derived from cultural conditioning and absorbed into the habitus. Habitus becomes an instrument in building a class society.

Bourdieu is concerned in his work with the relationship between habitus and what he refers to as field. By field, he means a structured system of social positions occupied by individuals or institutions. Each field is a network or social arena in which there is a concentrated struggle or battle over specific resources or outcomes. Each field has its own particular logic, value, and belief system, and is characterized by a hierarchy of institutions or individuals engaged in power relationships; and each has a relevance that is simultaneously a producer and product of habitus. A collective of interrelated fields constitutes a society; the more complex the division of labor or the degree of heterogeneity, the greater the number of fields.

Bourdieu perceives each field as a market with its own producers and consumers of goods and sees the struggles within and between fields as centering around four types of goods: economic capital, social capital, cultural capital, and symbolic capital. Economic capital is a most obvious form; it is constituted by wealth or one's access to it. Social capital is comprised of important social relationships and associations. Cultural capital is legitimate information and knowledge; it is frequently the sources of domination through which intellectuals produce culture. Finally, symbolic capital is the amount of honor or prestige possessed by the actor. Each field lends legitimacy to the struggle for particular types of capital and, therefore, creates a belief in its own legitimacy for those who participate in it. Occupants of positions in each field seek to enhance or safeguard their position relative to such capital. In doing so they engage in strategies often expressed through what Bourdieu calls symbolic violence.

He asserts that symbolic violence includes processes through which order and constraint are produced, indirectly, through cultural mechanisms. In his theory of symbolic violence the educational system plays an important role. It is an exemplary form of such mechanisms. Significant cultural mechanisms (such as educational systems) present us with ways of looking at the world and making sense of it. This is done through imposing the use of language and other cultural symbols by those in power on the rest of the population. Through this symbolic system, dominance is maintained over society by a relatively small group who secure legitimacy. This legitimacy helps to obscure the power relations, but it also bolsters the position of those in power. The educational system, in particular, reproduces and sustains the existing class and power relations. States are sites of struggle for a monopoly over symbolic violence. However, this violence is always maintained by the complicity of it subjects.

Positions of dominance and subordination within each field are determined by the amount of cultural capital possessed. When one's possession of cultural capital is thought to be more valuable than the capital of one's competitors that agent gains the right to impose its values on others. Conquest is the imposition of one symbolic system on a group by another through the use of symbolic violence.

THE TASTE IN CULTURE

Bourdieu made extensive use of this idea of habitus and field in his research of the cultural tastes he believes are shaped by habitus—deeply rooted dispositions toward types of art, cooking, furniture, clothing, and the like. However, he notes that dispositions constituting habitus only function in a field—a set of possible relationships or positions. In his important book, *Distinction,* published in 1979, he examined aesthetic preferences of various groups throughout society. The book is a repudiation of the Kantian and universalist transcendent notions of aesthetics.

It is Bourdieu's position that people learn to consume culture according to their social class and habitus. He discusses the differences between legitimate taste, middlebrow taste, and popular taste. Of course, the legitimation of taste is a function of class and cultural capital. Taste frequently functions to give the individual a sense of place within the culture and often helps to differentiate one group of people from another. It also becomes possible to classify and categorize people according to their cultural preferences and tastes. Thus, it becomes a way of establishing boundaries.

Although our taste isn't assigned to us, and we do have choice as to either see a play or go to a movie, our position within the structure of society determines to a large extent what we will do. Not only does class condition us, but it helps to maintain our cultural preferences and those of the existing power structure. Much like Veblen, Bourdieu proposes that taste is a function of status competition. High culture or good taste are marks of distinction, setting one apart from those with middlebrow taste. Along with education, manners, and interests, it is an expression of cultural capital, not necessarily material wealth. Legitimate taste is inculcated not only in families but in elite schools. The wealthy, who need not concern themselves with the basic necessities of economic survival, are generally unconcerned with an aesthetic that emphasizes the practical. The working class is more geared toward popular culture just because of their practical outlook. Taste for the unusual often signals one's class as does taste for the common and vulgar. Bourdieu proposes the greater the distance from economic necessity, the greater the legitimacy of taste.

He recognizes how taste remains an effective tool of domination. Good taste becomes an essential part of the struggle for the monopolization of symbolic violence, which gives the dominant class legitimacy.

CONCLUSION

By the late 1980s, Bourdieu had become one of the most important social scientists in the world. Aside from having published over thirty books and a wealth of articles, he became an outspoken advocate for social justice and human rights. He participated in rallies in support of striking railroad workers in France in 1995 and criticized his government's treatment of the homeless.

Unlike those poststructuralists who left behind their Marxism as unproductive grand theory, Bourdieu drew not only upon Marx but also borrowed from Durkheim and Weber as well. He saw no difficulty of integrating the work of Foucault and Freud with that of his own. Although he was an excellent theorist, he was also an empiricist and conducted major ethnographic and empirical research projects.

In his last remaining years, he became an outspoken critic of neoliberalism and globalization. He appeared in rallies along with such popular French celebrities as Jose Bové, who led the fight to "de-McDonaldize France." He died of cancer on January 28, 2002.

BIBLIOGRAPHY

Bourdieu, Pierre. 1998. *Acts of Resistance: Against the Tyranny of the Market.* New York: New Press.

———. 1984. *Distinction: A Social Critique of the Judgement of Taste.* Cambridge, MA: Harvard University Press.

———. 1983. *Outline of a Theory of Practice.* Cambridge: Cambridge University Press.

Jenkins, Richard. 1992. *Pierre Bourdieu.* New York: Routledge.

Ritzer, George. 2003. *Contemporary Sociological Theory and Its Classical Roots.* New York: McGraw-Hill.

29

Anthony Giddens: Structuration Theory

Anthony Giddens is one of the most prominent contemporary sociologists. Having published over forty books and more than three hundred articles in thirty different languages, he has emerged as a central figure in British intellectual and political life.

Giddens was born on January 18, 1938 in Edmonton, North London. He attended local schools, including the Minchenden School at Southgate, where he graduated with below average grades. He was the first in his family to attend college. In 1939 he was awarded a bachelor's degree in sociology and psychology from the University of Hull. His teachers there, particularly the sociologist Peter Worsley, were the first to inspire him to further study sociology, which he did at the London School of Economics. There he received a master's degree, writing his thesis on the development of sports in nineteenth-century England. Graduating with honors, he was hired as a lecturer at the University of Leicester where he served between 1961 and 1970. There he worked alongside of prominent sociologists such as Norbert Elias.

During the 1960s, he took a leave of absence to teach at Simon Fraser University in Vancouver, Canada, and the University of California at Los Angeles where he worked in 1968 and 1969. It was the experience of the turbulent 1960s that had a significant impact on his work. It was to force him to reevaluate his role as a sociologist when he returned to Great Britain. In 1970 he was named Lecturer and, later, Reader at the University of Cambridge; he was awarded a Professorship of Sociology there in 1985.

Although Giddens's interests as a sociologist cover a wide range of subjects, he is particularly known for his work in social theory. In his earlier work he sets out to be both a leading interpreter of classical sociological thought and a contributor to contemporary ideas. In the 1970s he produced several volumes in which he reexamined classical and contemporary theory in order to better define and understand the modern world. Much of his work has focused on the process of modernization and the culture of modernity. His work has often stretched the boundaries of sociological thinking. Not only has his work been an attempt to understand the larger structural changes taking place in the world, but also the connection of these changes to personal psychological development.

STRUCTURATION THEORY

Like Bourdieu, Giddens has attempted to keep clear of the controversy surrounding poststructuralist and postmodern theory. In so doing, he has embraced the need to understand society in terms of both structure and agency—the two main determinants of social outcomes.

Structure is constituted by the underlying rules (sometimes referred to as deep structures) and resources that are responsible for the production of the social outcomes and, particularly, the networks of social arrangements. Agency is human action, personal autonomy, and choice.

For many theorists, social life is thought as largely determined by social structure. Claude Levi-Strauss certainly believed this. As noted in a previous chapter, he viewed the work of Marx and Freud as advancing a structural analysis by seeking to comprehend surface reality through reference to a deeper structural level. For many structuralists, individual agency is primarily explained as the outcome of structure. In some circles, however, there is a reverse emphasis. Individuals can be seen as constructing their own worlds, giving these worlds both personal significance and a life of their own. This is based on the belief that structure can never determine as much as the individual. An alternative way of looking at structure and agency is to emphasize the complementary nature of the two processes. An example of this could be Bourdieu's notion of habitus and field.

Giddens's notion of structuration attempts to break free from the idea of a dualism of structure and agency. In his book, *The Constitution of Society*, published in 1984, he takes a mid-range position claiming that neither the experience of the individual, nor the existence of a social totality are responsible for explaining society. It is his assertion that structure creates social practices arranged over time and space; however, such practices are a product of both preexisting structural rules and individual agency. It is the dialectical interplay between the two that moves society forward, giving it life. Structure and agency cannot be thought of in opposition to one another, but are vitally intertwined.

For Giddens, all structure involves structuration, and all social action involves structure. Even though all structure is not brought into being by social actors, it is recursive, meaning that it is continually recreated by actors. People produce structure as well as consciousness through their actions. Giddens makes a distinction between discussive and practical consciousness. The first has to do with a person's ability to describe his or her own actions in words; the latter involves actions that actors take for granted without needing to be expressed in words. Actors are not only conscious of themselves but of the structural conditions of which they are a part. Thus, social actors are reflexive, meaning that they monitor their own thoughts and activities as well as the social and physical contexts in which these actions take place.

Actors tend to rationalize the world by developing routines that give them a sense of security. This helps them to engage in life. But actors are also agents of change. In his discussion about agency, Giddens proposes that actors or agents have an ability to make a difference. Although there are definite constraints on what an actor can do, his or her degree of agency is determined very much by his or her degree of power, which is a measure of agency itself.

Giddens describes structure as rules and resources that make it possible for similar social practices to exist across spans of time and space and lend them systematic form. He asserts that they are only brought into being by agents. Even though he believes structure can constrain human action, he believes that too many theorists emphasize content over agency and fail to recognize structure's enabling aspects. That is, structure not only allows action, but also encourages and enables action allowing agents to do things they would not ordinarily do. However, he warns, actors can easily lose control over structure. In some sense, one can see this at work in Weber's notion of bureaucracy in which the "iron cage" becomes not a choice but an inevitability. For Giddens, structure always becomes partial memory of human agents.

Structures are manifested in social systems, which Giddens views as reproduced relations between actors and collectivities. Although structures do not exist in a particular time and space, social systems do and tend to be products of intentional action. He sees societies as particular types of social systems with their own institutional features and structural properties. The structural properties that these social systems possess (they are not themselves structures) are the means through which social practices and actions come into being and are organized and from which emerge patterns of social relations. He refers to this as the duality of structure. Here structure is both a medium and an outcome of social action.

Although social systems consist of acting subjects, structures do not. They exist only as possibilities—perhaps predispositions for acting subjects. They are constantly being transformed.

TIME, SPACE, AND STRUCTURATION

Giddens believes that all social systems (including societies) that are constituted by social practices are "embedded in time and space." In his attempt to incorporate time and space into his theory of structuration, he draws upon Heidegger and claims that time and space relations express the nature of objects and are irreducible elements of human existence. Actors in social systems produce space in which social practices take place. They also bind action to a spatial-temporal context. An example of this might be school, which determines the space as well as the time in which actions take place. Actions of administrators, teachers, staff, and students constitute a social system that establishes a space and time for various actions.

Although the primary condition of human interaction is "face to face" in which actors are present in the same time and space, due to technology and, particularly, advancements in communication and transportation, social systems extend in time and space and, therefore, face-to-face communication might not be necessary for the system to still exist. This distanciation, or the stretching of the social system across time and space, becomes an important characteristic of structuration.

If social practices become stable over time and space, activities in which actors habitually engage become routine practices and the "taken-for-granted" character of social life. Thus, all social interaction is interaction situated in time and space and is best understood through the routinized occurrence of encounters. These routinized encounters represent institutionalized features of the social system.

Structuration, therefore, is the process in which the duality of structure evolves and is reproduced over time and space.

THE THIRD WAY

In 1997 Giddens was appointed Director of the London School of Economics. He soon became a public intellectual and an advisor to Prime Minister Tony Blair.

Giddens helped to popularize the idea of the "Third Way," which is an attempt to find midground between traditional left-right political polarization and to provide solutions to the challenges related to globalization. It is his firm belief that his ideas on structuration are relevant to the issues raised by the new global economy. Despite the tendency in social theory to move away from grand theoretical schemes, Giddens moves toward applying his ideas on a grand scale. Much of his recent work, such as *Beyond Left and Right,* published in 1994, and *The Third Way,* released in 1998, makes a shift from social theory to political strategy. It is his assertion that such a move is in keeping with the left's view that social theory cannot be philosophy; it must find its way into the application to change the state of things. Nevertheless, this is a reformist strategy, not a revolutionary program. It tinkers with the elements and does not anticipate revolutionary change. In doing this, critics have claimed that Giddens has abandoned the left in his search for solutions and compromises. However, Giddens rejects such criticism, noting that all change must come from within.

Unlike Bourdieu who opposed economic globalization, Giddens embraces it, but he does so critically. He still remains very much a self-proclaimed liberal socialist at heart, rejecting neoliberal policies. He calls for a "renewal of social democracy." Third Way politics recognizes that social structures and institutions are products of individual action and he tends to be optimistic about the transformations that can potentially emerge from new ways of looking at things.

Giddens has come up with concepts like the "radical center" to camouflage, as some have claimed, his growing conservative tendencies. For Giddens, this center contains valuable aspects of both socialism and capitalism. It is his contention that reform can only come from left-right coalitions that recognize shared concerns—human rights, environmental issues, and the like. His faith in the state is confirmed in his belief that governments can represent all people of antagonistic interests, regulate markets when they threaten the public interest, secure peace through the enforcement of its monopoly on violence and force, help provide for direct investment and monetary stability, nourish a national culture, and contribute to transnational alliances. They can also cooperate with coalitions of new and old social movements. Giddens views such successful movements, such as the environmental movement in Europe, as illustrating this idea that structure can be changed from the inside through already established means. He calls for a dialogic democracy—building consensus on open and free dialogue.

Although some see Giddens's positions as pragmatic and self-serving, others see his project as sensible.

CONCLUSION

Despite his attempts to connect all of the pieces, there appears to be discontinuity between Giddens's structuration hypothesis and his proposition of a Third Way political agenda. His "new way" appears at times to be a recapitulation of the European Enlightenment's scheme for the advancement of reason and the domination of liberal ideology in the service of plans. Inherent in his work is the adherence to the principles of democratic capitalism and a rejection of radical changes to this model.

Few sociologists have taken to heart the call to apply theory to policy. As theory grows gradually more impenetrable, Giddens remains accessible, both personally and theoretically. In his project there has been overall consistency.

BIBLIOGRAPHY

Giddens, Anthony. 2000. *Beyond Left and Right.* Cambridge: Polity Press.
———. 1998. *The Third Way.* Cambridge: Polity Press.
———. 1984. *The Constitution of Society.* Cambridge: Polity Press.
———. 1979. *Central Problems in Social Theory.* London: Macmillan.
———. 1971. *Capitalism and Modern Social Theory.* Cambridge: Cambridge University Press.
Kaspersen, Lars Bo. 2000. *Anthony Giddens: An Introduction to a Social Theorist.* Oxford: Blackwell Publishers.

Bibliography

Arendt, Hannah. 2000. *The Portable Hannah Arendt*, ed. by Peter Baehr. NewYork: Penguin Putnam.
———. 1967. *The Origins of Totalitarianism*. London: Allen and Urwin.
———. 1963. *Eichmann in Jerusalem: A Report on the Banality of Evil*. London: Faber and Faber.
Bair, Deirdre. 1990. *Simone de Beauvoir: A Biography*. New York: Summit Books.
Baudrillard, Jean. 1981. *For a Critique of the Political Economy of the Sign*. St. Louis, MO: Telos Press.
———. 1975. *The Mirror of Production*. St. Louis, MO: Telos Press.
Bauman, Zygmunt. 1992. *Imitations of Postmodernity*. London: Routledge.
———. 1991. *Modernity and Ambivalence*. Cambridge, Polity Press.
———. 1989. *Modernity and the Holocaust*. Cambridge: Polity Press.
Benhabib, Seyla, et al., eds. 1993. *On Max Horkheimer*. Cambridge: MIT Press.
Benjamin, Walter. 2002. *Arcades Project*. Cambridge, MA: Harvard University Press.
———. 1968. *Illuminations*, ed. by H. Arendt. New York: Schocken Books.
Bernstein, Richard. 1985. *Habermas and Modernity*. Cambridge, MA: MIT Press.
Bottomore, Tom; Harris, Laurence; Kiernan, V. G.; and Miliband, Ralph, eds. 1983. *A Dictionary of Marxist Thought*. Cambridge: Harvard University Press.
Bourdieu, Pierre. 1998. *Acts of Resistance: Against the Tyranny of the Market*. New York: New Press.
Braaten, Jane. 1991. *Habermas's Critical Theory of Society*. Albany, NY: State University of New York Press.
Bradshaw, Leah. 1989. *Acting and Thinking: The Political Thought of Hannah Arendt*. Toronto: University of Toronto Press.

Brodersen, Momme, and Green, Malcolm. 1997. *Walter Benjamin: A Biography,* trans. by I. Ligers. New York: Verso.

Burns, Tom. 1992. *Erving Goffman.* New York: Routledge.

Butler, Judith. 1999. *Gender Trouble: Feminism and the Subversion of Identity.* New York: Routledge.

———. 1993. *Bodies That Matter.* New York: Routledge.

Canovan, Margaret. 1992. *Hannah Arendt: A Reinterpretation of Her Political Thought.* Cambridge: The University of Cambridge Press.

Cassirer, Ernest. 1968. *Philosophy of the Enlightenment.* Princeton, NJ: Princeton University Press.

Caute, David. 1970. *Frantz Fanon.* New York: The Viking Press.

Champagne, Ronald. 1987. *Claude Levi-Strauss.* Boston: Twayne Publishers.

———. 1995. *Derrida.* New York: Maxwell McMillan.

Chodorow, Nancy. 1979. *The Reproduction of Mothering.* Berkeley, CA.

Comte, Auguste. 1853. *Positive Philosophy,* trans. and ed. by Harriet Martineau. New York: D. Appleton.

Coser, Lewis. 1977. *Masters of Sociological Thought.* New York: Harcourt Brace.

Coser, Lewis. 1977. *Masters of Sociological Thought.* New York: Harcourt Brace. University of California Press.

Cottrell, Robert D. 1976. *Simone de Beauvoir.* New York: Frederick Unger Publishing.

de Beauvoir, Simone. 1989. *The Second Sex,* trans. by H. Parshley. New York: Vintage Books.

———. 1972. *The Coming of Age,* trans. by P. O'Brian. New York: G. P. Putnam.

———. 1958. *The Human Condition.* Chicago: University of Chicago Press.

Derrida, Jacques. 1982. *Margins of Philosophy.* Chicago: University of Chicago Press.

Diggins, John Patrick. 1996. *Max Weber: Politics and the Spirit of Tragedy.* New York: HarperCollins.

———. 1976. *Of Grammatology.* Baltimore: Johns Hopkins University Press.

Du Bois, W. E. B. 1989. *The Souls of Black Folk.* New York: Bantam.

———. 1968. *Autobiography of W. E. B. Du Bois: A Soliloquy on Viewing My Life From the Last Decade of its First Century.* New York: International Publishers.

Durkheim, Emile. 1984. *The Division of Labor in Society,* trans. by W. D. Halls. New York: The Free Press.

———. 1951. *Suicide,* trans. J. Spaudling. New York: The Free Press.

———. 1915. *Elementary Forms of Religious Life,* trans. by J. Swain. New York: The Free Press.

Elias, Norbert. 1994. *The Civilizing Process,* trans. E. Jephcott. Oxford: Blackwell Publishers.

Elliot, Hugh. 1917. *Herbert Spencer.* New York: Henry Holt & Company.

Eribon, Didier. 1991. *Michel Foucault.* Cambridge: Harvard University Press.

Fanon, Frantz. 1968. *The Wretched of the Earth.* New York: Grove Press.

———. 1967. *Black Skin, White Masks.* New York: Grove Press.

Fiori, Giuseppe. 2000. *Antonio Gramsci: Life of A Revolutionary.* New York: Pluto Press.

Fletcher, Jonathan. 1997. *Violence and Civilization: An Introduction to the Work of Norbert Elias*. Cambridge: Polity Press.

Fogacs, David, ed. 2000. *The Gramsci Reader*. New York: NYU Press.

Foucault, Michel. 1977. *Discipline and Punish*. New York: Random House.

———. 1965. *Madness and Civilization*. New York: Random House.

Freud, Sigmund. 2000. *Three Essays on the Theory of Sexuality*, trans. by James Strachey. New York: Basic Books.

———. 1999. *The Interpretation of Dreams*, trans. by Joyce Crick. Originally published in German in 1900. New York: Oxford.

———. 1961. *Civilization and Its Discontents*, trans. by James Strachey. New York: W. W. Norton.

———. 1960. *The Id and the Ego*, trans. by Joan Riviere. New York: W. W. Norton.

Frisby, David. 1984. *Georg Simmel*. London: Travistock.

Gay, Peter. 1998. *Freud: A Life for Our Time*. New York: W. W. Norton.

———. 1996. *The Enlightenment: An Interpretation*. New York: W. W. Norton.

Geismar, Peter. 1971. *Fanon: A Biography*. New York: Dial Press.

Gerhandt, Unta. 2002. *Talcott Parsons: An Intellectual Biography*. Cambridge, MA: Cambridge University Press.

Giddens, Anthony. 2000. *Beyond Left and Right*. Cambridge: Polity Press.

———. 1998. *The Third Way*. Cambridge: Polity Press.

———. 1984. *The Constitution of Society*. Cambridge: Polity Press.

———. 1979. *Central Problems in Social Theory*. London: Macmillan.

———. 1971. *Capitalism and Modern Social Theory*. Cambridge: Cambridge University Press.

Goffman, Erving. 1974. *Frame Analysis: An Essay on the Organization of Experience*. Garden City, NY: Doubleday.

———. 1967. *Interaction Ritual: Esays on Face-to-Face Behavior*. Garden City, NY: Doubleday.

———. 1963. *Stigma: Notes on the Management of Spoiled Identity*. Englewood Cliffs, NJ: Prentice-Hall.

———. 1961. *Asylums: Essays on the Social Situation of Mental Institutions*. Garden City, NY: Doubleday.

———. 1959. *The Presentation of Self in Everyday Life*. Garden City, NY: Doubleday.

Gordon, Lewis R.; Sharpley-Whiting, T. Denean; and White, Renée T., eds. 1996. *Fanon: A Critical Reader*. Oxford: Blackwell Publishers.

Gramsci, Antonio, and Boothman, Derek, ed. 1995. *Further Selections from the Prison Notebooks*. Minneapolis, MN: University of Minnesota Press.

Habermas, Jürgen. 1987. *Theory and Communicative Action, Vol. II, Lifeworld and System: A Critique of Functional Reason*, trans. by T. McCarthy. Boston: Beacon Press.

———. 1984. *The Theory of Communicative Action, Vol. I, Reason and Rationalization of Society*, trans. by T. McCarthy. Boston: Beacon Press.

———. 1979. *Communication and the Evolution of Society*, trans. By T. McCarthy. Boston: Beacon Press.

Hansen, Philip. 1993. *Hannah Arendt: Politics, History and Citizenship*. Stanford, CA: Stanford University Press.

Haraway, Donna. 1991. *Simians, Cyborgs and Women*. New York: Routledge.
———. 1989. *Primate Visions: Gender, Race and Nature in the World of Modern Science*. New York: Routledge.
Hayman, Roland. 1980. *Nietzsche: A Critical Life*. New York: Oxford University Press.
Hegel, G. W. F. 1977. *Phenomenology of Spirit*, trans. by A. V. Miller. Oxford: Oxford University Press.
Hénaff, Marcel. 1998. *Claude Levi-Strauss and the Making of Structural Anthropology*, trans. by Mary Baker. Minneapolis, MN: University of Minnesota Press.
Hill, Michael R., and Hoecker-Drysdale, Susan. 2001. *Harriet Martineau: Theoretical and Methodological Perspectives*. New York: Routledge.
Hollingdale, R. J. 1973. *Nietzsche*. London: Routledge.
Hollinger, Robert. 1994. *Postmodernism and the Social Sciences*. Thousand Oaks, CA: Sage.
Hook, Sidney. 1994. *From Hegel to Marx*. New York: Columbia University Press.
hooks, bell. 1984. *Feminist Theory: From Margin to Center*. Boston: South End Press.
———. 1981. *Ain't I A Woman: Black Women and Feminism*. Boston: South End.
Horkheimer, Max, and Adorno, Theodor. 1996. *Dialectic of Enlightenment*. New York: Continuum Press.
Hudson, William Henry. 1916. *Herbert Spencer*. London: Constable and Company.
Israel, Jonathan Ivan. 2001. *Radical Enlightenment: Philosophy and the Making of Modernity*. New York: Oxford University Press.
Jay, Martin. 1996. *The Dialectical Imagination*. Berkeley, CA: University of California Press.
———. 1984. *Adorno*. Cambridge: Harvard University Press.
Jenkins, Richard. 1992. *Pierre Bourdieu*. New York: Routledge.
Jones, Ernest. 1961. *The Life and Work of Sigmund Freud*, ed. by L. Trilling and S. Marcus. New York: Basic Books.
Kaspersen, Lars Bo. 2000. *Anthony Giddens: An Introduction to a Social Theorist*. Oxford: Blackwell Publishers.
Kaufmann, Walter. 1968. *The Portable Nietzsche*. New York: Viking Press.
Kellner, Douglas. 1984. *Herbert Marcuse and the Crisis of Marxism*. Berkeley, CA: University of California Press.
———. 1989. *Jean Baudrillard: From Marxism to Postmodernism and Beyond*. Stanford, CA: Stanford University Press.
Kennedy, James. 1978. *Herbert Spencer*. Boston: Twayne Publishers.
Kramnick, Isaac, ed. 1995. *The Portable Enlightenment Reader*. New York: Penguin.
Lacan, Jacques. 1981. *Language of the Self*. Baltimore: Johns Hopkins Press.
———. 1977. *Écrits: A Selection*. New York: Norton.
Lauer, Quenten, ed. 1977. *Essays in Hegelian Dialectic*. New York: Fordham University Press.
Lefebvre, Henri. 1982. *The Sociology of Marx*, trans. by N. Gutterman. New York: Columbia University Press.
Lemert, Charles, ed. 1999. Social theory: its uses and pleasures. In *Social Theory: The Multicultural and Classical Readings*. Boulder, CO: Westview Press.
———. 1997. *Postmodernism Is Not What You Think*. Malden, MA: Blackwell.
Lenzer, Gertrud, ed. 1975. *Auguste Comte and Positivism*. New York: Harper and Row.

Levi-Strauss, Claude. 1963. *Structural Anthropology,* trans. by C. Jacobson. New York: Basic Books.

Lewis, David Levering, ed. 1995. *W. E. B. Du Bois: A Reader.* New York: Henry Holt.

———. 1993. *W. E. B. Du Bois: Biography of a Race.* New York: Henry Holt.

Loewenberg, J., ed. 1957. *Hegel Selections.* New York: Charles Scribner's Sons.

Lukács, Georg. 1976. *Young Hegel: Studies in the Relations Between Dialectics and Economics.* Cambridge, MA: M.I.T. Press.

Marcuse, Herbert. 1974. *Eros and Civilization.* Boston: Beacon Press.

———. 1964. *One-Dimensional Man.* Boston: Beacon Press.

Marini, Marcelle. 1992. *Jacques Lacan: The French Context.* New Brunswick, NJ: Rutgers University Press.

Martineau, Harriet. 1877. *Autobiography with Memorials by Maria Weston.* London: Smith, Elder and Co.

———. 1838. *How to Observe Morals and Manners.* London: Charles Knight.

———. 1837. *Society in America.* London: Saunders & Otley.

Marx, Karl. 1967. *Capital,* trans. by S. Moore and E. Aveling. New York: International Publishers.

———. 1956. *Economic and Philosophic Manuscripts of 1844,* trans. By M. Milligan. Moscow: Foreign Languages Publishing House.

———. and Engels, Friedrich. 1967. *The Communist Manifesto,* trans. By S. Moore. New York: Penguin Books.

McGowan, John. 1998. *Hannah Arendt: An Introduction.* Minneapolis, MN: University of Minnesota Press.

Mennell, Stephen. 1989. *Norbert Elias: Civilization and the Human Self-Image.* Oxford: Basil Blackwell.

Mills, C. Wright. 1977. *The Sociological Imagination.* Oxford: Oxford University Press.

Mitzman, Arthur. 1969. *The Iron Cage: An Historical Interpretation of Max Weber.* New York: Grosset and Dunlap.

Nietzsche, Friedrich. 1967. *Thus Spake Zarathustra.* New York: Heritage Press.

———. 1907. *Beyond Good and Evil.* New York: Macmillan.

Noris, Christopher. 1987. *Derrida.* Cambridge: Harvard University Press.

Parsons, Talcott. 1951. *The Social System.* New York: The Free Press.

———. 1949. *The Structure of Social Action.* New York: McGraw-Hill.

Payne, Robert. 1971. *The Unknown Karl Marx.* New York: New York University Press.

Paz, Octavio. 1970. *Claude Levi-Strauss: An Introduction,* trans. by J. S. Bernstein and M. Bernstein. Ithaca, NY: Cornell University Press.

Peel, J. D. Y. 1971. *Herbert Spencer: The Evolution of a Sociologist.* New York: Basic Books.

Pichanick, Valerie Kossew. 1980. *Harriet Martineau: The Woman and Her Work, 1802–1876.* Ann Arbor, MI: The University of Michigan Press.

Pickering, Mary. 1995. *Auguste Comte: An Intellectual Biography,* Vol. I & II. Cambridge: Cambridge University Press.

Pinkard, Terry. 2000. *Hegel: A Biography.* Cambridge: Cambridge University Press.

Pitkin, Hanna Fenichel. 1998. *The Attack of the Blob: Hannah Arendt's Concept of the Social.* Chicago: University of Chicago Press.

Porter, Roy. 2000. The *Creation of the Modern World: The British Enlightenment.* New York: W.W. Norton

Ritzer, George. 1996. *Sociological Theory*. New York: McGraw-Hill.
———. 2003. *Contemporary Sociological Theory and Its Classical Roots*. New York: McGraw-Hill.
Rocher, Guy. 1975. *Talcott Parsons and American Sociology*. New York: Barnes & Noble.
Rosenau, Pauline Marie. 1992. *Post-Modernism and the Social Sciences*. Princeton, NJ: Princeton University Press.
Roudinesco, Elisabeth. 1997. *Jacques Lacan*. New York: Columbia University Press.
Salih, Sara. 2002. *Judith Butler*. New York: Routledge.
Sarup, Madan. 1989. *Post-Structuralism and Postmodernism*. Athens, GA: University of Georgia Press.
Schumway, David. 1989. *Michel Foucault*. Boston: Twayne Publishers.
Seidel, Georg J. 1976. *Activity and Ground: Fichte, Schelling and Hegel*. New York: G. Olms.
Simmel, Georg. 1970. *The Philosophy of Money*, trans. by T. Bottomore and D. Frisby, ed. by D. Frisby. New York: Routledge.
Smith, Dennis. 1999. *Zygmunt Bauman: Prophet of Postmodernity*. Oxford: Polity Press.
Solomon, Robert. 1987. *From Hegel to Existentialism*. New York: Oxford University Press.
Spencer, Herbert. 1969. *The Principles of Sociology* [abridged edition]. Hamden, CT: Archon Books.
———. 1954. *Social Statics*. New York: The Robert Schalkenbach Foundation.
———. 1904. *Autobiography*, Vol. I & II. London: Williams Norgate.
———. 1888. *The Principles of Psychology*, Vol. I & II. New York: Appleton & Company.
———. 1884. *Principles of Biology*. New York: D. Appleton.
———. 1880. *First Principles*. New York: H. M. Caldwell.
Tar, Zoltan. 1985. *The Frankfurt School*. New York: Schocken Books.
Thomas, Gillian. 1985. *Harriet Martineau*. Boston: Twayne Publishers.
Thompson, Kenneth. 1962. *Emile Durkheim*. London: Travistock.
Turner, Jonathan. 1991. *The Structure of Social Theory*. Belmont, CA: Wadsworth.
Weber, Marianne. 1975. *Max Weber: A Biography*, trans. by H. Zohn. New York: Wiley.
Weber, Max. 1978. *Economy and Society*, trans. by Fischoff and Gerth. Berkeley, CA: University of California Press.
———. 1956. *Sociology of Religion*, trans. by E. Fischoff. Boston: Beacon.
———. 1930. *The Protestant Ethic and the Spirit of Capitalism*, trans. By T. Parsons. London: Unwin.
Wheen, Frances. 1999. *Karl Marx: A Life*. New York: W.W. Norton.
White, Stephen. 1989. *The Recent Work of Jürgen Habermas*. Cambridge: Cambridge University Press.
———. 1984. *Distinction: A Social Critique of the Judgement of Taste*. Cambridge, MA: Harvard University Press.
———. 1983. *Outline of a Theory of Practice*. Cambridge: Cambridge University Press.

Wolf, Kurt H., ed. 1950. *The Sociology of Georg Simmel,* trans. by K. Wolf. New York: Free Press.

Wolin, Richard. 2001. *Heidegger's Children: Hannah Arendt, Karl Löwith, Hans Joas, and Herbert Marcuse.* Princeton, NJ: Princeton University Press.

Wyrick, Deborah. 1998. *Fanon For Beginners.* New York: Writers and Readers Publishers.

Young-Bruehl, Elizabeth. 1982. *Hannah Arendt: For Love of the World.* New Haven: Yale University Press.

Index

About the Author

ROGER A. SALERNO is a Professor of Sociology at Pace University, where he teaches courses in social theory and the sociology of cities.